LOW INTERMEDIATE
Workbook

OXFORD
PICTURE
DICTIONARY

SECOND EDITION

OPD

Marjorie Fuchs
Margaret Bonner

OXFORD
UNIVERSITY PRESS

198 Madison Avenue
New York, NY 10016 USA

Great Clarendon Street, Oxford OX2 6DP UK

Oxford University Press is a department of the University of Oxford.
It furthers the University's objective of excellence in research, scholarship,
and education by publishing worldwide in

Oxford New York

Auckland Cape Town Dar es Salaam Hong Kong Karachi
Kuala Lumpur Madrid Melbourne Mexico City Nairobi
New Delhi Shanghai Taipei Toronto

With offices in

Argentina Austria Brazil Chile Czech Republic France Greece
Guatemala Hungary Italy Japan Poland Portugal Singapore
South Korea Switzerland Thailand Turkey Ukraine Vietnam

OXFORD and OXFORD ENGLISH are registered trademarks of
Oxford University Press.

© Oxford University Press 2009

Database right Oxford University Press (maker)

Executive Publishing Manager: Stephanie Karras
Managing Editor: Sharon Sargent
Development Editor: Katie La Storia
Design Director: Susan Sanguily
Design Managers: Maj-Britt Hagsted, Stacy Merlin
Project Manager: Allison Harm
Project Coordinator: Sarah Dentry
Cover Design: Stacy Merlin
Senior Image Editor: Justine Eun
Manufacturing Manager: Shanta Persaud
Manufacturing Controller: Eve Wong

ISBN: 978 0 19 474048-7 OPD Low Intermediate Workbook with Audio CD (Pack)
ISBN: 978 0 19 474008-1 OPD Low Intermediate Workbook
ISBN: 978 0 19 474049-4 Audio CDs (4)

Printed in China

10 9 8 7 6 5 4

This book is printed on paper from certified and well-managed sources.

Chapter icons designed by Von Glitschka/Scott Hull Associates

Art Credits:

Gary Antonetti: 201; Argosy: 194, 286, 306; Barb Bastian: 15, 156; Kenneth Batelman: 13, 46; John Batten: 3, 88-89, 285; Kathy Baxendale: 32, 108, 119, 195, 241; Annie Bisset: 12, 26, 123, 143, 159, 177; Arlene Boehm: 70, 71; Kevin Brown/Top Dog Studio: 7, 238, 302, 315; Dominic Bugatto/Three-in-a-Box: 100, 114; Carlos Castellanos: 58, 62, 245; Andrea Champlin: 25, 91, 241, 284; Dominik D'Andrea: 97; Mona Daly/Mendola Art: 90, 106; Jim Delapine: 235; Bill Dickson/Contact Jupiter: 10, 42, 269, 294; Jody Emery: 67, 131, 178, 246, 290; Jim Fanning/Ravenhill Represents: 66, 81; Mike Gardner: 142, 175; Glenn Gustafson: 76, 124, 296; Ben Hasler/NB Illustration: 148; Betsy Hayes: 139; Kevin Hopgood: 2, 43, 179, 299; Infomen/Debut Art: 51, 54, 74, 115, 150, 172, 207, 244; Emma Jacob/Lemonade: 33, 94; Janos Jantner/Beehive Illustration: 79, 171, 181, 217, 256; Ken Joudrey/Munro Campagna: 68; Mike Kasun/Munro Campagna: 74, 102, 158, 189, 291; Keithley Associates: 153, 248; Denis Luzuriaga: 34, 47; Scott MacNeill: 19, 66, 75, 112, 236, 292; Adrian Mateescu/The Studio: 28, 55, 242; Karen Minot: 116, 155, 184, 225; Paul Mirocha/The Wiley Group: 211, 216; Terry Pazcko: 47, 53, 83, 215; Pronk&Associates: 4, 5, 6, 8, 9, 11, 14, 16, 17, 18, 19, 20, 21, 27, 28, 29, 33, 35, 36, 37, 38. 40-41, 49, 50, 52, 57, 59, 65, 68, 71, 72-73, 77, 78, 82, 83, 84, 85, 92, 94, 95, 97, 101, 105, 106, 110, 113, 117, 128, 132, 142, 144-145, 152, 154, 157, 160. 161, 165, 173, 175, 179, 185, 192, 193, 198, 203, 210, 215, 219, 223, 227, 235, 239, 261, 262, 263, 265, 266, 268, 270, 277, 278, 279, 280, 296, 301, 310; Mark Reidy/Munro Campagna: 134 (stamp); Robert Roper/Wilkinson Design Studio: 23, 60, 267; Marcos Schaaf/NB Illustration: 76, 93, 281; Phil Scheuer: 167, 218, 251; Robert Schuster: 24, 34, 48, 69, 151, 227 (icons), 229; Ben Shannon/Magnet Reps: 143, 282, 303; Geoffrey Paul Smith: 180, 233, 315; Sam Tomasello: 63, 176, 208, 209; Anna Veltfort: 129, 259; Ralph Voltz/Deborah Wolfe: 154, 237, 249, 264, 296; William Waitzman: 18, 163, 174; Mark Watkinson/Illustrationweb. com: 169, 228, 234; Simon Williams/Illustrationweb.com: 45; Graeme Wilson/Graham-Cameron Illustration: 56, 62, 107, 287, 288; Tracey Wood/Reactor Art: 105, 317.

Photo Credits:

Agefotostock: Creatas, 49 (Smithfield home); Mike Kemp, 140 (woman reading newspaper); Andersen Ross, 48; Kord.com, 127 (Times Square); Uselmann Foto Design, 250 (construction worker); Alamy: ACE STOCK LIMITED, 204 (Angel Falls); Directphoto. org, 199 (I.M. Pei); Clint Farlinger, 221 (cavern); JTB Photo Communications, Inc., 221 (bear); The Print Collection, 199 (Alessandro Volta); Visual&Written SL, 221 (coral reef); Dennis Kitchen Studios: 8, 99 (nylon), 276, 313, 316; Getty Images: Christian Science Monitor, 140 (Mosque); Hulton Archive, 40; Iconica, 32; David Paul Morris, 140 (rally speaker); Scott Olsen, 140 (demonstration); Photographer's Choice, 51 (Police woman), 177; Popperfoto, 199 (Vasco da Gama); Time & Life Pictures, 199 (Rosa Parks), 243 (kiss); Zane Williams, 84; Inmagine: Corbis, 80, 115 (optometrist); Brand X Pictures, 49 (Greenville home); Blendimages, 171; Digitalvision, 250 (factory worker); fstop, 250 (farmer); GoGo Images, 108; Image100, 72; Photodisc, 133; Polkadot, 207 (African-American female); Redchopsticks, 26 (Asian teen); Somos, 207 (Hispanic male); Istockphoto: 19 (watch), 61, 66, 78, 98 (silk), 99 (lace), 110, 168, 182, 197, 213, 214 (sparrow), 231 (basketball), 313; Jupiter Unlimited: Comstock Images, 26 (Hispanic teen, Caucasian teen), 99 (denim); Pixland, 207 (Caucasian male); Jupiterimages: 98 (wool), 99 (corduroy), 184, 207 (Asian male); Foodpix, 98 (linen); Magnum Photos: Bruno Barbey, 243 (elderly Chinese men); Leonard Freed, 243 (father and son); Masterfile: 120; Michael Goldman, 127 (Trinity Church); Omni-Photo Communications: Grace Davies, 49 (Lincoln home); David Parket, 50; Rondal Partridge at www.rondalpartridge.com: 243; Punchstock: Brand X Pictures, 57; Corbis, 51 (firefighter); Image Source, 207 (Hispanic female), 250 (office worker); Moodboard, 119; PhotoAlto, 115 (depressed man); Rubberball, 136; Stockbyte, 140 (witness stand), 152; Robertstock.com: Morgan Howarth, 186; Shutterstock.com: 39, 95, 118, 141, 204 (globe); 205, 214 (peacock), 224, 226, 231 (volleyball), SuperStock: 98 (leather); Society of Friends of Music, 199 (Bach).

Cover Art: CUBE/Illustration Ltd. (hummingbird), 9 Surf Studios (lettering).

Acknowledgements

The publisher and authors would like to acknowledge the following individuals for their invaluable feedback during the development of this workbook:

Patricia S. Bell, Lake Technical County ESOL, Eustis, FL

Patricia Castro, Harvest English Institute, Newark, NJ

Druci Diaz, CARIBE Program and TBT, Tampa, FL

Jill Gluck, Hollywood Community Adult School, Los Angeles, CA.

Frances Hardenbergh, Southside Programs for Adult and Continuing Ed, Prince George, VA

Mercedes Hern, Tampa, FL

(Katie) Mary C. Hurter, North Harris College, Language and Communication, Houston, TX

Karen Kipke, Antioch Freshman Academy, Antioch, TN

Ivanna Mann-Thrower, Charlotte Mecklenburg Schools, Charlotte, NC

Holley Mayville, Charlotte Mecklenburg Schools, Charlotte, NC

Jonetta Myles, Salem High School, Conyers, GA

Kathleen Reynolds, Albany Park Community Center, Chicago, IL

Jan Salerno, Kennedy-San Fernando CAS, Grenada Hills, CA

Jenni Santamaria, ABC Adult School, Cerritos, CA

Geraldyne Scott, Truman College/ Lakeview Learning Center, Chicago, IL

Sharada Sekar, Antioch Freshman Academy, Antioch, TN

Terry Shearer, Region IV ESC, Houston, TX

Melissa Singler, Cape Fear Community College, Wilmington, NC

Cynthia Wiseman, Wiseman Language Consultants, New York, NY

Special thanks to:

Stephanie Karras and Sharon Sargent for their dedication and hard work in managing a very complex project; and Justine Eun, Maj-Britt Hagsted, and Stacy Merlin for making sure that the many graphic elements illustrated and enhanced the text; and Pronk&Associates for their commitment and skill;

Bruce Myint, who contributed to the early stages of the *Workbook* and made excellent suggestions for bringing this new edition into a new century;

Katie La Storia, who applied her sharp mind and eyes to the manuscript, always offering excellent advice. With her steadfast energy, enthusiasm, and encouragement, she was a pleasure to work with;

Kathryn O'Dell for her fine, creative contributions to the listening exercises and story pages;

Melinda Beck, who made insightful comments and queries;

Sarah Dentry, who made things flow smoothly, assuring that we always had what we needed when we needed it;

Jayme Adelson-Goldstein, who provided support and who, along with Norma Shapiro, created a rich trove of materials on which to base the exercises in the *Workbook*;

Luke Frances for always being himself. His honesty, spontaneity, and humor make creativity happen;

Rick Smith, as always, for his unswerving support and for his insightful comments on all aspects of the project. Once again, he proved himself to be equally at home in the world of numbers and the world of words.

To the Teacher

The *Low Beginning*, *High Beginning*, and *Low Intermediate Workbooks* that accompany *The Oxford Picture Dictionary* have been designed to provide meaningful and enjoyable practice of the vocabulary that students are learning. These workbooks supply high-interest contexts and real information for enrichment and self-expression.

Writing a second edition has given us the wonderful opportunity not only to update material, but also to respond to the requests of our first-edition users. As a result, this new edition of the *Low Intermediate Workbook* contains more graphs and charts, more writing and speaking activities, more occasions for critical thinking, opportunities to use the Internet, and a brand-new listening component. It still, of course, has the features that made the first edition so popular.

The *Workbooks* conveniently correspond page-for-page to the 163 topics of the *Picture Dictionary*. For example, if you are working on page 50 in the *Dictionary*, the activities for this topic, Apartments, will be found on page 50 in all three *Picture Dictionary Workbooks*.

All topics in the *Low Intermediate Workbook* follow the same easy-to-use format. Exercise 1 is always a "look in your dictionary" activity where students are asked to complete a task while looking in their *Picture Dictionary*. The tasks include judging statements true or false, correcting false statements, completing charts and forms, categorizing, odd one out, and pronoun reference activities where students replace pronouns with the vocabulary items they refer to.

Following this activity are one or more content-rich contextualized exercises, including multiple choice, quizzes and tests, describing picture differences, and the completion of forms, reports, letters, articles, and stories. These exercises often feature graphs and charts with real data for students to work with as they practice the new vocabulary. Many topics include a personalization exercise that asks "What about you?" where students can use the new vocabulary to give information about their own lives or to express their opinions.

The final exercise for each topic is a Challenge which can be assigned to students for additional work in class or as homework. Challenge activities provide higher-level speaking and writing practice, and for some topics will require students to interview classmates, conduct surveys, or find information outside of class by looking in the newspaper, for example, or online.

Each topic also has a listening activity recorded on CDs which come with the *Workbook*. The CDs give students the opportunity to hear the language of each topic in natural, real-life contexts including short conversations, news and weather reports, radio ads, store and airport announcements, instructions, directions, and interviews. The listening exercises are in the back of the *Workbook* beginning on page 261. In some cases, the target language is in the listening itself and students need to recognize it. In other cases, the target language is in the exercise text and students need to interpret the listening to choose the correct answer.

Each of the 12 units ends with Another Look, a review which allows students to practice vocabulary from all the topics of a unit in a game or puzzle-like activity, such as picture comparisons, "What's wrong with this picture?" activities, photo essays, word maps, word searches, and crossword puzzles. These activities are at the back of the *Low Intermediate Workbook* on pages 242–253.

Throughout the *Workbook*, vocabulary is carefully controlled and recycled. Students should, however, be encouraged to use their *Picture Dictionaries* to look up words they do not recall, or, if they are doing topics out of sequence, may not yet have learned.

The *Oxford Picture Dictionary Workbooks* can be used in the classroom or at home for self-study.

We hope you and your students enjoy using this *Workbook* as much as we have enjoyed writing it.

Marjorie Fuchs   Margo Bonner

Marjorie Fuchs and Margaret Bonner

To the Student

The *Oxford Picture Dictionary* has over 4,000 words. This workbook will help you use them in your everyday life.

It's easy to use! The *Workbook* pages match the pages in your Picture Dictionary. For example, to practice the words on page 23 in your *Picture Dictionary*, go to page 23 in your *Workbook*.

It has exercises you will enjoy. Some exercises show real information. A chart showing men's and women's favorite fast foods is on page 79 and a bar graph comparing how long different animals live is on page 216. Another exercise, which asks "What about you?" gives you a chance to use your own information. You will find stories, puzzles, and conversations, too.

At the end of each topic there is a Challenge, a chance to use your new vocabulary more independently. There are also listening exercises where you hear conversations, news and weather reports, and interviews. And finally, every unit has a puzzle activity or picture comparison called Another Look. This can be found at the back of the book.

Learning new words is both challenging and fun. We had a lot of fun writing this workbook. We hope you enjoy using it!

Marjorie Fuchs   Margo Bonner

Marjorie Fuchs and Margaret Bonner

Table of Contents

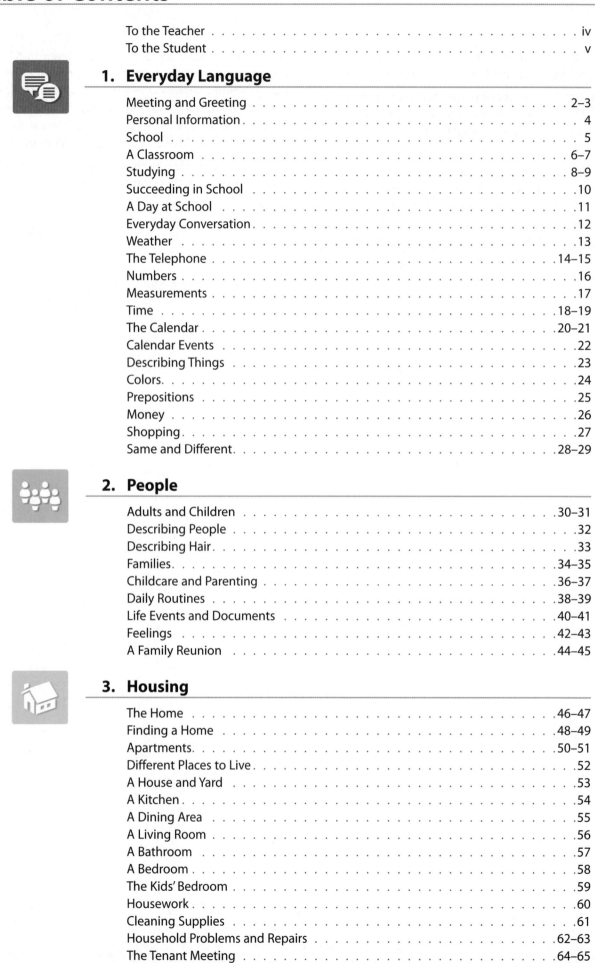

4. Food

5. Clothing

6. Health

Contents

7. Community

8. Transportation

9. Work

10. Areas of Study

11. Plants and Animals

12. Recreation

1. Look in your dictionary. How many people are . . . ? Write the number.

_4_ **a.** saying "Hello"

____ **b.** hugging

____ **c.** smiling

____ **d.** waving

____ **e.** asking "How are you?"

____ **f.** introducing themselves

____ **g.** introducing a friend

____ **h.** kissing

____ **i.** bowing

____ **j.** shaking hands

____ **k.** saying "Goodbye"

____ **l.** greeting people

2. Look at the pictures. _True_ or _False_?

a. Picture 1: Eric says "Hello" to Ana. _____false_____

b. Picture 1: Lisa and Ana smile. _____

c. Picture 1: Lisa and Ana kiss. _____

d. Picture 2: Eric introduces himself. _____

e. Picture 2: Eric smiles. _____

f. Picture 3: Ana and Eric bow. _____

g. Picture 4: Eric says "Goodbye." _____

h. Picture 4: Ana waves goodbye. _____

3. **Match. Then write what they are doing. You can use your dictionary for help.**

<u>4</u> **a.** Hi, I'm Mario.

b. Bye.

c. How are you?

d. Carlo, this is Beata.

e. Hello.

1. Fine, thanks. _____

2. Goodbye. _____

3. Hi. _____

4. Hi, I'm Olga. <u>*introducing themselves*</u>

5. Nice to meet you. _____

4. **Circle the words to complete the sentences.**

DIFFERENT GREETINGS

People from different countries (greet) / meet in different ways.
a.

In some countries, people <u>bow / kiss</u>.
b.

In some countries people

<u>wave / shake</u> hands.
c.

In other countries people <u>hug / wave</u>,
d.

and sometimes good friends <u>hug / kiss</u>.
e.

Sometimes people just

<u>smile / wave</u> and say,
f.

"Goodbye" / "Hello."
g.

a. b. c. d. e. f.

Hello.

5. **What about you? How do you greet people? Check (✓) the columns.**

	Bow	Shake Hands	Kiss	Hug	Say, "Hello."
a good friend (woman)					
a family member (man)					
a classmate (man)					

Challenge Look at Exercise 2. Write the story. Begin: *Eric and Lisa are in school. Lisa sees Ana . . .*

See page 261 for listening practice.

1. **Look in your dictionary. Match the information with its number on the School Registration Form. Write the number.**

   a. January 15, 1980   _13_

   b. *John Zakarovsky*   ____

   c. 037-22-7982   ____

   d. Zakarovsky   ____

   e. 210 Parker Road   ____

   f. 94610   ____

2. **Circle four more mistakes on Ann Brown's registration form.**

   L.A. ADULT CENTER   **REGISTRATION FORM**

   1. Name (please print): ⟨Ann⟩   ⟨Brown⟩   M.
                                            last name   first name   middle initial

   2. Sex: ☐ male ☑ female   3. Social Security number: 077 - 22 - 8765

   4. Address (please print): 92 Adams Street   3
                                          street   apt. #

      Los Angeles   CA
                city   state   ZIP code

   5. Phone number: (310) 555-3253   6. Cellular phone: 555-6434
               (area code)   (area code)

   7. Date of birth: March 1, 1981   8. Place of birth: Germany
                                                 city   country

   9. Signature: Ann M. Brown

3. **What about you? Fill out the form with your own information.**

   L.A. ADULT CENTER   **REGISTRATION FORM**

   1. Name (please print): _____
                                        last name   first name   middle initial

   2. Sex: ☐ male ☐ female   3. Social Security number: ___ ___ ___

   4. Address (please print): _____
                                        street   apt. #

      _____
                city   state   ZIP code

   5. Phone number: _____   6. Cellular phone: _____
               (area code)   (area code)

   7. Date of birth: _____   8. Place of birth: _____
                                                   city   country

   9. Signature: _____

Challenge Describe the mistakes in Exercise 2. **Example:** *In number 1, she wrote her first name first.*

1. Look in your dictionary. Complete the notes with the job titles.

Sunnydale School **NEWSLETTER**

September / October 2008

Sunnydale STAFF NOTES

a. Welcome, all. It's going to be a great year! *Maria Gomez,* _____Principal_____

b. Seniors—Let's talk about college soon. *Rita Cheng,* _____

c. If you're late, come to the office to sign in. *Miki Kato,* _____

d. Our class will visit historic places near school. *Doug Tran,* _____

e. Meet me at the track for running practice. *Sam Powell,* _____

2. Look at the list of events. Write the names of the places. Use the words in the box.

| computer lab | ~~library~~ | gym | main office | cafeteria | auditorium |

DATE	TIME	EVENT	PLACE
a. Sept. 24	2:00	Reading Club	*library*
b. Oct. 1	12:00–1:00	Pizza Lunch	
c. Oct. 15	7:00 p.m.	Concert: Sunnydale Chorus	
d. Oct. 23	2:30	Learn Internet Safety	
e. Oct. 25	all day	Registration for Senior Class Trip	
f. Oct. 30	4:30	Girls Basketball Practice	

3. Make words with the scrambled letters.

SCHOOL SCRAMBLE

a. rcakt ___t___ ___r___ ___a___ (__c__) ___k___

b. lacsmoors ___ ○ ___ ○ ___ ___ ___ ___

c. erstmoros ___ ___ ___ ___ ___ ○ ○ ___ ___

d. lalhyaw ○ ___ ___ ___ ___ ___

Make a new word with the circled letters: ___ ___ ___ ___ ___

Challenge Draw a map of your school. Label the places.

See page 261 for listening practice.   5

A Classroom

1. **Look in your dictionary. *True* or *False*? Correct the <u>underlined</u> words in the false sentences.**

   a. **Picture A:** <u>~~The teacher~~</u> is raising his hand.   *A student*   _____*false*_____

   b. **Picture B:** The teacher is listening to <u>the student</u>.   _____

   c. **Picture C:** The student is using <u>headphones</u>.   _____

   d. **Picture G:** The student is opening his <u>dictionary</u>.   _____

   e. **Picture I:** The student is picking up a <u>CD</u>.   _____

   f. **Picture J:** The student is <u>picking up</u> a pencil.   _____

2. **Circle the words to complete the instructions.**

   ## Test Instructions

   Tomorrow is our first test. Please bring a <u>pen / (pencil)</u> with an eraser.
   a.

   When you come into the classroom, please <u>sit down / stand up</u> at your
   b.

   <u>desks / LCD projectors</u>. <u>Close / Open</u> your test books, <u>pick up / put down</u>
   c.   **d.**   **e.**

   your pencils, and begin the test. If you have a question for me,

   <u>listen to a CD / raise your hand</u> and ask. Please do not talk to other
   f.

   <u>students / teachers</u> during the test. When you are finished,
   g.

   <u>pick up / put down</u> your pencils, and bring your tests to me. Good luck!
   h.

3. **Cross out the word that doesn't belong.**

a.	chalk	~~headphones~~	pen	pencil
b.	bookcase	chair	clock	desk
c.	dry erase marker	3-ring binder	workbook	spiral notebook
d.	dictionary	picture dictionary	notebook paper	textbook
e.	chalkboard	marker	screen	whiteboard

4. Look at the picture. Complete the classroom inventory.

Classroom Inventory—Room 304

	NUMBER	ITEMS		NUMBER	ITEMS
a.	2	bookcases	h.		computers
b.	0	bulletin boards	i.	19	
c.		LCD projector	j.		markers
d.	20		k.		overhead projectors
e.	1		l.	3	
f.		chalkboard erasers	m.		screen
g.		clocks			

5. What about you? Write about items that are in your classroom. Use your own paper.

Example: *There are four bookcases. There aren't any bulletin boards.*

Challenge Describe the ideal classroom. What does it have? How many of each item?

1. **Look in your dictionary. What are the students using to . . . ?**
   Check (✓) the correct box or boxes.

	Textbook	Dictionary	Notebook
a. check pronunciation	☐	✓	☐
b. copy a word	☐	☐	☐
c. draw a picture	☐	☐	☐
d. look up a word	☐	☐	☐
e. share a book	☐	☐	☐

2. **Fill in the blanks to complete the instructions for the test. Then take the test.**

Review Test

1. ___*Circle*___ the words to complete the questions.
   a. (What) / Who is your name?   b. When / Where do you live?

2. _____ the word that does not belong.
   a. coach   principal   ~~marker~~   teacher
   b. pen   chalk   computer   pencil

3. _____ the words.
   _3_ a. Check   1. a sentence.
   ___ b. Help   2. a classmate.
   ___ c. Dictate   3. the pronunciation.

4. _____ the blanks.
   Put ___*away*___ your books and _____ a piece of paper.
       a.   b.

5. _____ the words.
   a. n a t r s t a l e ___*translate*___   b. s c u d s i s _____

6. _____ the pictures.

   a. ___*pencil*___   b. _____

---

3. Circle the words to complete the article.

There are many different ways to learn. Here are just a few.

* "Word-smart"	students like to <u>dictate / read</u> books and <u>copy / cross out</u> information **a.** **b.** in their notebooks.

* "Picture-smart"	students like to <u>check / draw</u> pictures. They also find it helpful to
	            c.
	<u>ask / copy</u> new words.
	  d.

* "People-smart"	students love to <u>ask / work</u> with a partner or in a group. They like to
	          e.
	<u>brainstorm / translate</u> solutions. They often <u>help / share</u> their classmates.
	    f. **g.**

* "Feelings-smart"	students like to <u>discuss / translate</u> problems and <u>put away / share</u> their **h.** **i.** feelings with their classmates.

In which ways are **you** smart? Find your style, and make learning fun!

4. What about you? What helps you learn? For each activity, check (✓) the column that describes your learning style.

Activity	Helps me a lot	Helps me some	Helps me a little	Doesn't help me
Looking up words				
Copying words				
Translating words				
Helping classmates				
Asking questions				
Reading definitions				
Discussing problems				
Dictating sentences				
Working in groups				
Drawing pictures				
Other: _____				

Challenge Interview someone about his or her learning style. Use the ideas in the questionnaire.
Write a paragraph about what you learn.

See page 262 for listening practice.

1. **Look in your dictionary. *True* or *False*? Correct the underlined words in the false sentences.**

   a. **Picture D:** The student is studying ~~in school~~. *at home*   _____*false*_____

   b. **Picture E and Number 4:** The student's test grade (78%) is <u>C</u>. _____

   c. **Picture G and Number 4:** The student's test grade (96%) is <u>B</u>. _____

   d. **Picture J:** The student is working <u>in a group</u>. _____

2. **Match.**

   _3_ **a.** set a goal   **1.** "Oh. That's not right. The answer is 4c."

   ___ **b.** hand in a test   **2.** "Last time I got a C. This time I got a B!"

   ___ **c.** make progress   **3.** "I want to read the newspaper in English."

   ___ **d.** correct a mistake   **4.** "Here you are, Mr. Smith."

3. **Complete the paragraph. Use the words in the box.**

asked	bubbled in	checked	corrected	got	handed in
participated	~~passed~~	set	studied	took	

Carlos is a student. He _____*passed*_____ his first test, but his
                       a.

grade was only a D. Carlos _____ a goal: He wanted
                         b.

to get better grades. Before his next test, he _____
                                    c.

at home for several days, and he _____ for help in
                            d.

class when he didn't understand something. He also

_____ better notes and _____ more
       e.   **f.**

in class discussions. During the test, Carlos carefully _____ the answers with his
                                            g.

pencil. Then, before he _____ his answer sheet to the teacher,
                         h.

he _____ his answers and _____ one or two mistakes. Yesterday
    i.   **j.**

Carlos got his test back. He _____ a good grade—a B! Carlos was happy.
                              k.

Challenge Make a list of ways to succeed in school. Compare your list with a classmate's list.

1. Look in your dictionary. Answer the questions.

a. What time do the students enter the classroom?   6:55

b. Who turns on the light?   _____

c. How many students are taking a break?   _____

d. Which room number does the student deliver the books to?   _____

e. What time do the students leave class?   _____

2. Complete the student's composition. Use the correct form of the words in the box.

buy	carry	drink	have	go back
leave	~~run~~	take	turn off	walk

My Day at School

I go to school every Tuesday and Thursday after work. Sometimes I

_____run_____ to class. I don't want to come late! When I have more time,
a.

I _____. I like it better that way because I always _____
b.   **c.**

a lot of things—my textbook, a dictionary, and a 3-ring binder. Class

meets for two hours, and we always _____ a fifteen-minute
d.

break. I usually _____ a snack in the cafeteria. I also
e.

_____ a cup of coffee while I _____ a conversation with
f.   **g.**

some of my classmates. After the break, we _____ to class. At
h.

8:00 p.m., the teacher _____ the lights and we all _____
i.   **j.**

the classroom and go home.

Challenge Write about a day at your school.

See page 263 for listening practice.   11

1. Look in your dictionary. Match.

<u>4</u> **a.** start a conversation

___ **b.** explain something

___ **c.** disagree

___ **d** decline an invitation

___ **e.** check your understanding

1. "Sorry. I'm busy Friday night."

2. "You're wrong! It's not bad. It's good!"

3. "Then, sign your name here."

4. "Tell me about your class."

5. "Now?"

2. Read part of a story. Match each numbered sentence with its description below.

"Ouch!" Nikki cried, as something hard

fell on her foot. "I'm really sorry. My
                1.

science book fell out of my locker," said

Ben. He picked it up. "That's OK," said Nikki
                   2.

as she looked at the handsome face. "I'm

just glad it wasn't that big dictionary!"

"My name's Ben. Are you a new
                  3.

student here?"

"Yes, I'm Nikki. Nikki Lewis."

"Oh! I heard your piano concert last

week. You were great!"
         4.

"Oh, thanks! I'm playing again Friday
    5.

night. Would you like to come?"
            6.

"Sure! Where is it?" Ben asked.
  7.

"I'll give you the address," said Nikki.

"Thanks. I'm glad we met, Nikki."

"Me, too. See you soon, Ben!"
      8.

a. ___ Ben started a conversation.

b. ___ Ben accepted an invitation.

c. <u>1</u> Ben apologized.

d. ___ Nikki agreed with Ben.

e. ___ Nikki invited Ben.

f. ___ Nikki accepted an apology.

g. ___ Ben complimented Nikki.

h. ___ Nikki thanked Ben.

Challenge Choose an item in your dictionary (for example, *making small talk*). Make a list of ways
to do this. Compare your list with a classmate's. **Example:** *What do you think of this weather?*

1. Look in your dictionary. Label the weather symbols.

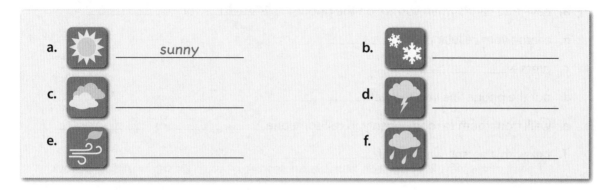

a. _sunny_

b. _____

c. _____

d. _____

e. _____

f. _____

2. Look at the weather map. Write reports for six cities. Use your own paper.

Example: *It's windy and very cold in Chicago, with temperatures in the 20s.*

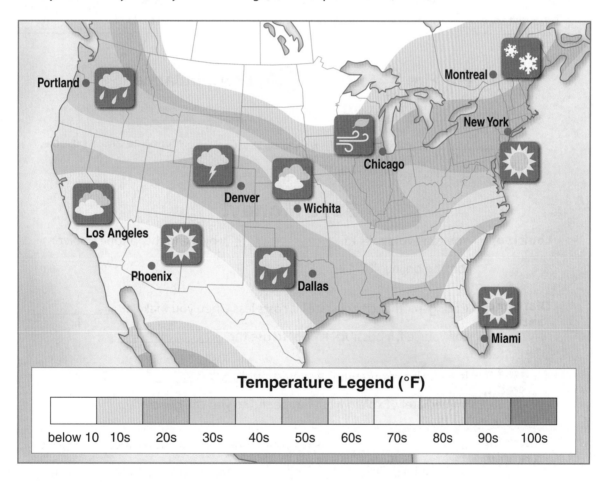

3. What about you? Write today's weather report for your city. Use Exercise 2 as an example.

Challenge Look at page 254 in this book. Follow the instructions.

1. **Look in your dictionary. What do you need to . . . ?**

   a. have free hands when you are on the phone ___*headset*___ or _____

   b. charge your cellular phone _____

   c. press * _____

   d. put the phone line into the wall _____

   e. walk from room to room when you call someone _____ or _____

   f. talk with a person who is deaf _____

2. **Complete this information from a phone book. Use the words and numbers in the box.**

country	dial	directory assistance	~~emergency~~	state
give	hang up	international	local	stay
long distance	operator	pay phone	911	0

   ## For Fire 🔥 , Police 🛡 , or Ambulance ⚕

   To make an ___*emergency*___ call, dial: _____ .
          a.   **b.**

   _____ the emergency, _____ your name, and, if possible,
     c.   **d.**

   _____ on the line. Don't _____ !
     e.   **f.**

   ## Save Money!

   Look it up!   You can avoid calls to _____ by using the phone book or
                   g.

   looking online.

   Dial direct and save.   Calling another city or state? It costs less when you make a _____
                                     h.

   call yourself. If possible, try not to use the _____ .
                                     i.

   Ask for credit.   If you call a wrong number, you should _____ "0"
                                   j.

   immediately. Explain what happened so you can get credit.

   Ask for a refund.   If a _____ takes your money but you don't speak to anyone,
                   k.

   report it by dialing _____ (operator) from another phone.
                               l.

   We'll see that the phone gets repaired and mail you a refund. To make an

   _____ call, you will need: the _____ code, the
        m.   **n.**

   city code, and the _____ number.
                o.

3. Look at Linda Lopez's phone bill. Answer the questions.

rtr

Page 1 of 2

Your Phone Company Statement
October 8-November 8, 2010

Customer ID 505-555-6090

Linda Lopez
1212 Marble Lane
Roswell, NM 88203

LOCAL CALLS

DATE	NUMBER CALLED	TIME	RATE
OCT 12	505-555-2346	2:15 p.m.	day
OCT 17	505-555-7890	7:30 p.m.	night
NOV 1	505-555-6176	7:00 a.m	day
NOV 8	505-555-7890	6:30 p.m	night

rtr

Customer ID 505-555-6090
Linda Lopez

LONG DISTANCE CALLS

DATE	NUMBER CALLED	WHERE	TIME	RATE
OCT 10	212-555-1234	New York, NY	3:00 p.m.	day
OCT 31	415-555-6874	Marin, CA	9:45 p.m.	eve

INTERNATIONAL CALLS

DATE	NUMBER CALLED	WHERE		
OCT 30	56-2-555-1394	Chile		
OCT 30	81-3-555-2086	Japan		

a. What is Linda's area code? _505_

b. How many local calls did she make in November? _____

c. How many long distance calls did she make in the United States? _____

d. What is the area code for New York, NY? _____

e. How many international calls did Linda make? _____

f. What's the country code for Japan? _____

4. What about you? How often did you use the telephone last week? Answer the questions. How many times did you . . . ?

a. make or receive an international call ___

b. call from a pay phone ___

c. make an Internet phone call ___

d. use a calling card ___

e. leave a voice message ___

f. use an automated phone system ___

g. have a weak cellular phone signal ___

h. receive a text message ___

Challenge Look at page 254 in this book. Follow the instructions.

See page 264 for listening practice.

1. **Look at the Table of Contents <u>in the beginning</u> of your dictionary. Write the numbers.**

   a. On what page does the *Table of Contents* begin?   <u>v</u>

   b. On what page does it end?   ____

   c. How many pages are in the *Table of Contents*?   ____

   d. The first unit of your dictionary is called *Everyday Language*.
      What is the name of the eleventh unit?   ____

   e. How many pages are in the eighth unit?   ____

2. **Look at the math test. Circle all the mistakes. Then give the test a percent grade (each question = five points).**

   ### Baker High School

   Grade: _____ %

   Student's Name: ____Ryan Jones____

   1. What's next?

   a. eleven, twelve, thirteen, ___fourteen___

   b. one, three, five, ___seven___

   c. two, four, six, ___(ten)___

   d. ten, twenty, thirty, ___forty___

   e. ten, one hundred, one thousand, ___ten thousand___

   2. Write the numbers.

   a. XX ___twenty___

   b. IX ___nine___

   c. LI ___fifty-one___

   d. IV ___six___

   e. C ___one hundred___

   3. Match the numbers with the words.

   _1_ a. 12   1. ordinal number

   _3_ b. DL   2. cardinal number

   _2_ c. 2nd   3. Roman numeral

   4. Write the numbers.

   a. zero ___0___

   b. one hundred ___100___

   c. one million ___1,000,000,000___

   d. ten thousand ___10,000___

   e. one hundred thousand ___100,000___

   f. one billion ___1,000,000___

   g. one thousand ___1,000___

Challenge Explain the mistakes on the test in Exercise 2. **Example:** *Question 1c—the next number is eight, not ten.*

  See page 264 for listening practice.

1. **Look in your dictionary. Cross out the number or word that doesn't belong. Write the category.**

   a. _____Percents_____   20%   70%   ~~80~~   100%

   b. _____   1/3   .5   2/4   1/2

   c. _____   .10   .333   .75   25

   d. _____   inch   height   width   depth

2. **Forty-two percent of the students at Baker High School are female. Which pie chart is correct? Circle the correct letter.**

   a.

   b.

   c.

3. **Look at the pie chart. Answer the questions.**

   Students who want to go to college in the United States take the Scholastic Assessment Test (SAT). The highest math score = 800. The lowest math score = 200.

   What percent of students scored between 400–600 points?

   a. forty   **b.** fifty   **c.** sixty

   Based on information from: The College Entrance Examination Board, 2007.

   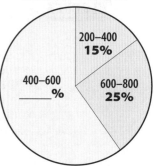

   Math SAT Scores

4. **Look at these math SAT scores. Rank the students. (first = the student with the highest score)**

Name	Rank
a. Raz	_____
b. Eva	_____
c. Ito	_____
d. Dan	_____
e. Mai	_____
f. Ali	_first_
g. Luz	_____
h. Ivy	_____

   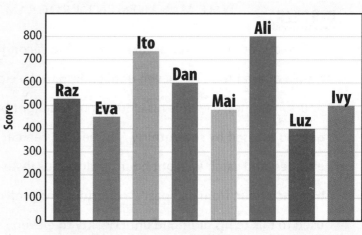

Challenge How many students are in your class? What percent are male? What percent are female? Draw a pie chart like the ones in Exercise 3.

1. Look at <u>pages 38 and 39</u> in your dictionary. Write the time of each activity in numbers and words. Use your own paper.

   a. get dressed   **b.** eat breakfast   **c.** clean the house   **d.** go to bed

   Example: *get dressed: 6:30, six-thirty*

2. Look at Ed's time management worksheet. The clocks show the time that he begins each activity. Complete his worksheet.

   a.    b.    c.    d.    e.    f.

   CLOCKER Inc.

   ### TIME MANAGEMENT WORKSHEET   *Ed Tresante*

	ACTIVITY	TIME BEGAN	TIME ENDED	TOTAL TIME
a.	get dressed	7:15 a.m.	8:00 a.m.	45 minutes
b.	brush teeth		8:01 a.m.	
c.	drive to work		9:00 a.m.	
d.	have lunch		1:15 p.m.	
e.	have class		9:15 p.m.	
f.	talk to Ana		11:40 p.m.	

3. Complete the report. Use the information in Exercise 2.

   CLOCKER Inc.

   ### TIME MANAGEMENT PROGRAM REPORT

   Before our program, Ed was taking forty-five <u>seconds / (minutes)</u> to get dressed,
                                                      a.
   from a quarter <u>to / after</u> seven until eight <u>p.m. / o'clock</u>. Now it takes him fifteen
                    b.   **c.**
   <u>hours / minutes</u>. (He puts his clothes out the night before.) Because he finishes
     d.
   getting dressed by <u>seven-thirty / -fifteen</u>, Ed can eat breakfast, brush for three
                        e.
   minutes, and catch an eight <u>hour / o'clock</u> bus instead of driving. He studies during
                            f.
   his lunch hour, from <u>half past / a quarter after</u> twelve until a quarter <u>to / after</u> one. Ed
                          g.   **h.**
   used to talk to his girlfriend until twenty to <u>eleven / twelve</u>. Now he calls her forty
                            i.
   minutes earlier, at <u>twenty to / half past</u> ten, and he gets more sleep.
                    j.

4. **Look at the time zone map in your dictionary. Ed is planning several business trips. Complete the online flight information.**

	FLIGHT NUMBER	FLIGHT	DEPARTURE TIME	ARRIVAL TIME	TOTAL TRAVEL TIME
a. **Select**	20 Q	New York, NY Los Angeles, CA	10:30 a.m. (Eastern)	*1:30 p.m.* (Pacific)	6 hours
b. **Select**	453 Q	Phoenix, AZ Anchorage, AK	8:00 p.m. (Mountain)	_____ (Alaska)	7 hours
c. **Select**	34 Q	Chicago, IL Halifax, NS	12:00 p.m. (Central)	_____ (Atlantic)	3 hours 30 minutes
d. **Select**	733 Q	Detroit, MI Dallas, TX	8:00 a.m. (Eastern)	_____ (Central)	4 hours

5. **Complete the article. Use the words in the box. (You will use two words more than once.) Use your dictionary for help.**

Atlantic	daylight saving	earlier	later	Pacific	standard	time zones

It's A Question of Time

In 1884, people in different countries agreed to have _____*standard*_____ time. They divided the
                                                                          a.
world into 24 _____ . Some large countries have more than one. The continental
                    b.
United States, for example, has four. They are Eastern, Central, Mountain, and _____ .
                                                                                              c.
Alaska and Hawaii have their own time zones. Canada has two others. They are Newfoundland and

_____ time. The time difference between one zone and the next is one hour. For
       d.
example, when it's noon Eastern time, it's 1:00 p.m. _____ time. (That's one hour
                                                                  e.
_____ .) At the same time, it's 11:00 a.m. Central time. (That's one hour
       f.
_____ .) Many countries change the clock in order to have more hours of light in the
       g.
summer. This is called _____ time. In the United States, it begins the second Sunday
                                  h.
in March and ends the first Sunday in November. The country then returns to _____
                                                                                          i.
time.

Challenge Look at page 255 in this book. Follow the instructions.

1. **Look at page 21 in your dictionary. Which month . . . ?**

    a. begins on a Sunday ___August___

    b. begins on a Tuesday and has 30 days _____

    c. begins on a Thursday and has four 7-day weeks _____

    d. begins on a weekday and ends on a weekend _____, _____,

    _____, and _____

2. **Read Eva's email.** *True* or *False*?

MYEMAIL　　　　　　　　　　　　　　　　　　　　　　　 ▬ ☐ ☒

Subject: your visit
Date: 3-19-11 11:51:11 PM EST
From: EvaL@uol.us
To: DaniaX@uol.us

Hi Dania!

It's Saturday night. I just returned to Miami yesterday. There were no classes for a week, so I flew to Chicago last Saturday to visit my parents. Classes begin again on Monday. It's a busy semester. I have English three times a week (Mondays, Wednesdays, and Fridays). I usually have language lab every Thursday, too. Next week, however, there's no language lab—I go to computer lab instead. In addition to English, I'm studying science. Science meets twice a week on the days that I don't have English. And there's science lab on Tuesdays.

Last Sunday, daylight saving time began. Do you have that in Canada? I like it a lot. The days seem much longer.

I'm glad it's the weekend. Tomorrow I'm seeing Tom. (I told you about him in my last email.) I've got to go now. On Saturdays I go to the gym to work out. We can go together when you come! I'm really looking forward to your visit. Just two weeks from today!

Oh, and bring your appetite! On Sunday there's a cake sale at the school cafeteria. See you soon.

Eva

---

a. It's March. ___true___

b. It's summer. _____

c. It's the weekend. _____

d. Eva is in Chicago this week. _____

e. Science meets three days every week. _____

f. Eva goes to the gym every day. _____

3. **Complete Eva's calendar. Use the information in Exercise 2.**

March

Sunday	Monday	Tuesday	Wednesday	Thursday	Friday	Saturday
		1	2	3	4	5
6	7	8	9	10	11	12
13	14	15	16	17	18 return to Miami	19
20	21	22	23	24	25	26
27	28	29	30	31		

4. **What about you? Complete your calendar for this month. Write the month, the year, and the dates. Then write your schedule in the calendar.**

Sunday	Monday	Tuesday	Wednesday	Thursday	Friday	Saturday

Challenge Write a letter or email to a friend. Describe your schedule for this month.

See page 265 for listening practice.

1. Look in your dictionary. Complete the chart.

Legal Holidays—U.S. 2010	
a. Christmas	12/25
b. *Columbus Day*	10/11 (2nd Mon. of the month)
c. Independence Day	
d.	9/6 (1st Mon. of the month)
e.	1/18 (3rd Mon. of the month)
f.	5/31 (last Mon. of the month)
g. New Year's Day	
h.	2/15 (3rd Mon. of the month)
i.	11/25 (4th Thurs. of the month)

2. Read the sentences. Write the events. Use the words in the box.

anniversary	appointment	~~birthday~~	religious holiday
legal holiday	parent-teacher conference	vacation	wedding

a. "I'm twenty-one today!" _____birthday_____

b. "Your son is an excellent student, Mrs. Rivera." _____

c. "Let's light candles and celebrate together!" _____

d. "The doctor will see you in a minute, Mr. Chen." _____

e. "The post office is closed today." _____

f. "I really needed this! Two weeks and no work!" _____

g. "We were married ten years ago today!" _____

h. "Jennifer looks beautiful in her white dress." _____

3. What about you? Check (✓) the events and holidays you celebrate. How do you celebrate?

☐ birthdays _____

☐ anniversaries _____

☐ New Year's Day _____

☐ Other: _____

Challenge Look at the chart on page 255. Follow the instructions.

  See page 266 for listening practice.

1. **Look in your dictionary. Write all the words that end in -y. Then write their opposites.**

   a. ___empty___ ___full___   d. _____ _____

   b. _____ _____   e. _____ _____

   c. _____ _____   or _____

2. **Look at the classrooms. Find and describe six more differences. Use your own paper.**

   Example: *The June classroom has a little clock, but the clock in the September classroom is big.*

June

WELCOME BACK!

$$\sqrt{100} = 10$$

September

3. **What about you? How does your classroom compare to the classrooms in Exercise 2? Write about the differences. Use your own paper.**

Challenge Write six sentences that describe this workbook. Use words from page 23 in your dictionary.

See page 266 for listening practice.

1. **Look at <u>page 156</u> in your dictionary. What color is the . . . ?**

   a. 4-door car ____blue____   e. hybrid _____

   b. SUV _____   f. convertible _____

   c. limousine _____   g. cargo van _____

   d. sports car _____   h. school bus _____

2. **Complete the article. Use the information in the bar graph.**

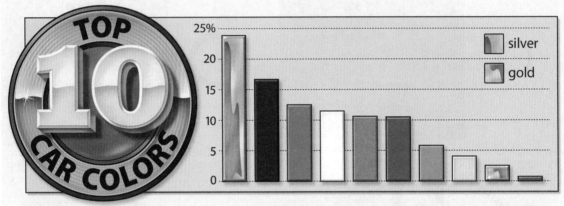

What's the most popular car color? At almost 25% of sales, silver is number 1 in the United

States. Why? Some experts say people like light colors because they don't show dirt as much.

But ____black____ (the darkest color of all) is number 2 in popularity. _____
      a.   **b.**

(the lightest color) is number 4, and _____ , another light color, only gets a little
                                                   c.

more than 4% of all sales. The number 3 color, _____ includes light and dark,
                                                            d.

and it is becoming more popular. _____ , a color like silver, is number 5 on the list,
                                        e.

and some experts say it will become more popular in the future. Sales of _____
                                                                f.

are almost the same as gray. _____ cars get about 6% of all sales, and gold cars
                                      g.

get just 2.6% of the sales. Last on the list is _____ . Now *that's* a colorful list!
                                                                    h.

Bar graph is based on information from: Dratch, Dana, Bankrate.com: Top 10 car colors for 2005, http://www.bankrate.com.

Challenge What are the three favorite car colors of your classmates? Take a survey. Are they the same as the top three colors in Exercise 2?

 See page 267 for listening practice.

1. **Look at <u>page 24</u> in your dictionary. Complete the sentences. Write the locations.**

    a. The white sweaters are ___*under*___ the black ones, on the ___*right*___.

    b. The violet sweaters are _____ the turquoise ones, in the _____.

    c. The light blue sweaters are _____ the green and the brown ones.

    d. The green sweaters are _____ the orange ones, on the _____.

2. **Look at the checklist and the picture of the school supply room. Check (✓) the items that are in the correct place.**

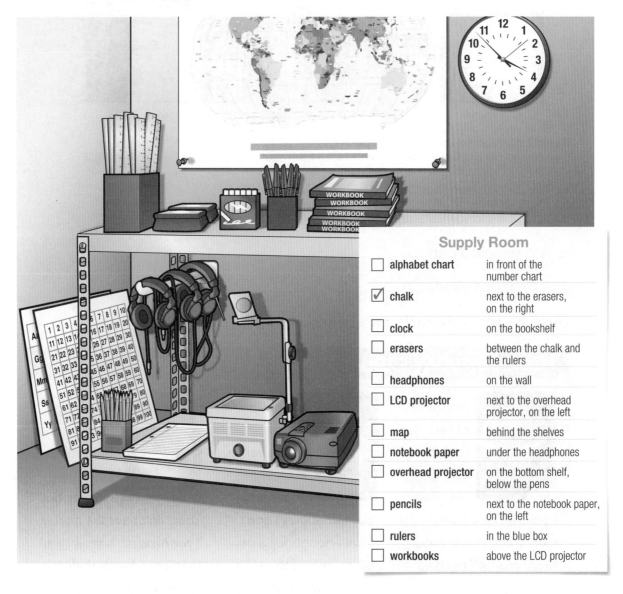

Supply Room	
☐ alphabet chart	in front of the number chart
☑ chalk	next to the erasers, on the right
☐ clock	on the bookshelf
☐ erasers	between the chalk and the rulers
☐ headphones	on the wall
☐ LCD projector	next to the overhead projector, on the left
☐ map	behind the shelves
☐ notebook paper	under the headphones
☐ overhead projector	on the bottom shelf, below the pens
☐ pencils	next to the notebook paper, on the left
☐ rulers	in the blue box
☐ workbooks	above the LCD projector

3. **Look at Exercise 2. Write about the items that are in the wrong place. Use your own paper.**

    Example: *The alphabet chart is behind the number chart. It isn't in front of it.*

Challenge Write ten sentences about items in your classroom.

1. **Look in your dictionary. On your own paper, write the fewest coins and bills you can use to make . . .**

   a. $7.05　　　　**b.** $.64　　　　**c.** $1.37　　　　**d.** $380

   Example: *$7.05: a five-dollar bill, two one-dollar bills or coins, and . . . .*

2. **Look at the chart. Complete the sentences.**

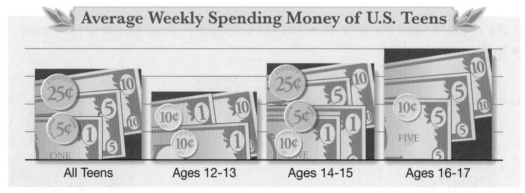

Average Weekly Spending Money of U.S. Teens

All Teens　　Ages 12-13　　Ages 14-15　　Ages 16-17

Based on information from: Magazine Publishers of America, www.magazine.org/content/files/teenprofile04.pdf citing Mediamark Research Inc, 2003.

   a. The average teen spends ___$16.30___ a week.

   b. A 13-year-old spends _____.

   c. A 15-year-old spends _____.

   d. A 17-year-old spends _____. That's _____ more than a 13-year-old.

3. **Circle the words to complete the sentences.**

How do today's teens feel about money?

 At the end of each day, I put all my bills / (coins) in a glass bottle. It's how I save money, and I never need to get change / pay back when I go to the soda machine!

 I get a weekly allowance from my parents, but sometimes I don't have enough for a new CD or video game. I hate to borrow / lend money from my friends, but…

 My best friend wanted to buy a new sweater, but she didn't have the money. I was happy to borrow / lend it to her. I know she'll borrow / pay back the money as soon as she can.

Challenge Write at least ten combinations of bills and coins that equal $2.10.

 See page 268 for listening practice.

1. **Look in your dictionary. *True* or *False*? Correct the <u>underlined</u> words in the false sentences.**

   One shopper . . .

   a. used a National First Bank ~~<u>credit card</u>~~. *debit card*   _____false_____

   b. used a $15 <u>gift card</u>.   _____

   c. wrote a <u>traveler's check</u> to pay for a lamp.   _____

   d. paid $27.06 <u>cash</u>.   _____

2. **Circle the words to complete the shopper's advice column.**

Ask Sam the Smart Shopper!

Q: Recently I bought a lamp at the (regular) / sale price. A week later I saw it at the
   a.
   same store for 20% less. Is there anything I can do?

A: When that happens, some stores will give you the cheaper price if you show your

   <u>sales tax / receipt</u>.   That's why you should always keep it.
        b.

Q: I gave my nephew a sweater for his birthday. He wants to <u>buy / return</u> it and use the
                                                              c.
   money for some CDs. When I <u>cashed / bought</u> the sweater, it was $29.99, but now
                              d.
   it's on sale for only $19.99. How much will they give him?

A: Give him the <u>receipt / gift card</u> and <u>SKU number / price tag</u> to bring to the store.
                   e.   f.
   He should get $29.99.

Q: I bought three pairs of jeans. The <u>sales tax / price tag</u> showed $14.99 each, but the
                                         g.
   cash register showed only $26.97. The clerk said the jeans just went on sale. How

   did the cash register know?

A: The new <u>price / total</u> was in the store computer. When the computer "read" the
             h.
   <u>receipt / bar code</u> (those black lines), the cash register showed the correct <u>tax / total</u>.
        i.   j.
   What a nice surprise!

Challenge Write a question for the shopper's advice column. Give it to a classmate. Try to answer your
classmate's question.

1. **Look in your dictionary. *True* or *False*? Correct the underlined words in the false sentences.**

   a. There was a ~~shoe~~ *sweater* sale on October 22nd.   _____*false*_____

   b. Manda and Anya have <u>the same</u> birthday.   _____

   c. Mrs. Kumar bought two matching <u>red</u> sweaters.   _____

   d. She paid <u>$19.99</u> for each sweater before tax.   _____

   e. She bought the sweaters on <u>October 20th</u>.   _____

   f. Manda <u>kept</u> her sweater.   _____

   g. Anya was <u>happy</u> with hers.   _____

   h. She exchanged her green sweater for a <u>white</u> sweater.   _____

2. **Look at the pictures. Complete the email with the words in the box.**

sweaters	twins	~~matching~~	return	disappointed	the same
matching	happy	shop	different	matching	keep

From: TwinsMom   _ □ X

Re: Matching clothes—Yes or *No*?

Sometimes *Yes* and sometimes *No*. When my boys were babies,

I always dressed them in ___*matching*___ clothes. They are
                              a.

_____, so in those clothes, they looked exactly
        b.

_____. I thought that was really cute, and I loved going to
        c.

the store to _____ for them. They looked adorable in their
                    d.

navy blue _____ and red pants. As kids, they were great
              e.

friends and they did everything together, especially baseball, their

favorite sport. Then, in their teens, Mike wanted to play

_____ sports. And he definitely didn't want to wear
        f.

_____ clothes. Leo was really _____ . Now
        g.   **h.**

they're grown up, and they're best friends. This year, I gave both of

them _____ baseball hats, and Mike didn't
            i.

_____ his. He decided to _____ it! I was so
        j.   **k.**

_____ .
        l.

3. **Look in your dictionary. Match.**

_5_ **a.** Mrs. Kumar likes to shop because

____ **b.** The store had a sale, so

____ **c.** Mrs. Kumar got matching sweaters because

____ **d.** Anya didn't want a matching sweater because

____ **e.** Manda kept her green sweater, but

____ **f.** Navy blue is Anya's favorite color, so

____ **g.** Now both twins have sweaters they like, and

1. she bought sweaters.

2. she exchanged it for a navy blue one.

3. she didn't want to look the same.

4. they're warm and happy.

5. she loves to buy things for her twins.

6. it was hard to choose two colors.

7. Anya returned hers.

4. **Circle the words to complete the sentences.**

My cousins Bena and Myra are twins. They (have) / don't have the same birthday,
                                                          a.
but they don't look or act the same / different. Bena was a noisy / quiet
                                      b.   **c.**
child, and you always knew when she was in the room. She was a good / bad
                                                                        d.
student because she just wasn't happy at school. Today, Bena is a big / small
                                                                              e.
woman, more than six feet tall. She's never in a hurry about anything—
especially shopping. She only buys things on sale, and she doesn't pay the
regular price / sales price for anything. She's never happy / disappointed
            f.   **g.**
with her purchases. I love to shop with her.

5. **Now complete the sentences about Myra. Use words from Exercise 4.**

Myra ___was a quiet child___, and you never knew she was in the room. She
            a.
_____ because she liked school. Today, Myra _____,
            b.   **c.**
less than five feet tall. She's always in a hurry—especially in stores. She buys the first thing

she sees, and I don't think she _____ for anything. She's often
                                              d.
_____ her purchases. When Myra says, "Let's go shopping," I usually say,
            e.
"Sorry, I'm busy today."

6. **What about you? Should parents dress twins the same? Why or why not? Discuss your answers with a classmate.**

Challenge Write a paragraph. Compare two people you know. Use Exercises 4 and 5 as a model.

1. Look in your dictionary. *True* or *False*? **Correct the <u>underlined</u> words in the false sentences.**

    seven

   a. There are ~~six~~ men and women at the round table.   _____*false*_____

   b. A <u>man</u> is holding an infant.   _____

   c. The <u>toddler</u> wants to sit in a chair.   _____

   d. The <u>six-year-old boy</u> is having a bad time.   _____

   e. The <u>senior citizen</u> is talking to a man.   _____

   f. The <u>baby</u> is sleeping.   _____

2. Put the words in the box in the correct category.

~~baby~~	boy	girl	infant	man
senior citizen	teen	toddler	woman	

Males	Females	Males or Females

_____	_____	_____*baby*_____
_____	_____	_____
		_____
		_____
		_____
		_____

3. Look in your dictionary. *Male* or *Female*? **Check (✓) the answers.**

	Male	Female			Male	Female
a. baby	✓	☐	**c.** senior citizen		☐	☐
b. teenager	☐	☐	**d.** toddler		☐	☐

4. What about you? Look in your dictionary. Imagine you are at the dinner. Who would you like to sit next to? Why?

Example: *I'd like to sit next to the baby. I love babies.*

5. **Look in your dictionary. Guess their ages. Then match.**

_5_ **a.** man   **1.** one year old

___ **b.** senior citizen   **2.** fourteen years old

___ **c.** toddler   **3.** ten years old

___ **d.** teen   **4.** six years old

___ **e.** boy   **5.** forty years old

___ **f.** infant   **6.** sixty-eight years old

___ **g.** baby   **7.** thirty-eight years old

___ **h.** woman   **8.** two months old

___ **i.** girl   **9.** three years old

6. **Look at the pie chart. Circle the words to complete the sentences.**

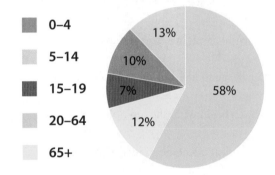

U.S. Population by Age

- 0–4
- 5–14
- 15–19
- 20–64
- 65+

13%
10%
7%
58%
12%

a. Seven percent of the U.S. population are <u>senior citizens</u> / <u>(teenagers.)</u>

b. <u>Men and women</u> / Boys and girls are 58% of the population.

c. Babies, infants, and <u>teens / toddlers</u> are in the 10% group.

d. A <u>ten-year-old girl / fifty-year-old woman</u> is in the 58% group.

e. There are more senior citizens than <u>boys and girls / teens</u>.

f. The biggest percent of the population are <u>babies, infants, and toddlers / men and women</u>.

7. **What about you? Look at the chart in Exercise 6. Which percentage group are you in?**

Challenge What's a good gift for a baby girl? A baby boy?
A teenage girl? A teenage boy? Discuss your answers with a partner.

See page 269 for listening practice.

1. **Look in your dictionary. Cross out the word that doesn't belong. Write the category.**

   a. _Weight_   heavy   thin   ~~physically challenged~~   average weight

   b. _____ tattoo   mole   pierced ear   elderly

   c. _____ elderly   pregnant   middle-aged   young

   d. _____ sight impaired   deaf   middle-aged   physically challenged

   e. _____ short   cute   average height   tall

2. **Circle the words to complete the article.**

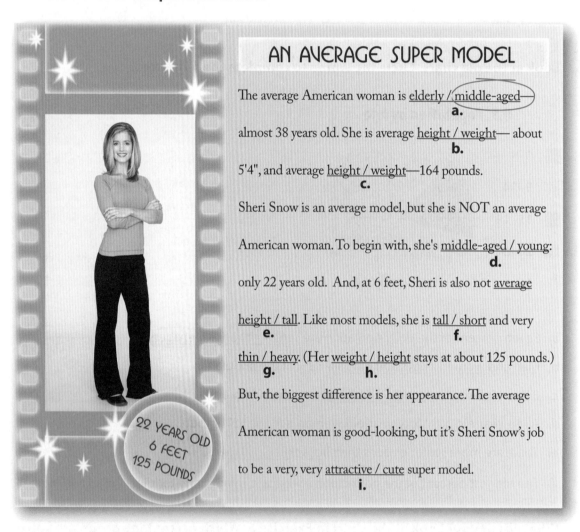

AN AVERAGE SUPER MODEL

The average American woman is elderly /(middle-aged—
                                     a.

almost 38 years old. She is average height / weight— about
                                            b.

5'4", and average height / weight—164 pounds.
                     c.

Sheri Snow is an average model, but she is NOT an average

American woman. To begin with, she's middle-aged / young:
                                        d.

only 22 years old. And, at 6 feet, Sheri is also not average

height / tall. Like most models, she is tall / short and very
    e.   **f.**

thin / heavy. (Her weight / height stays at about 125 pounds.)
  g.   **h.**

But, the biggest difference is her appearance. The average

American woman is good-looking, but it's Sheri Snow's job

to be a very, very attractive / cute super model.
                         i.

22 YEARS OLD
6 FEET
125 POUNDS

3. **What about you? Write a paragraph about a person you know. Describe the person's age, height, weight, and appearance.**

   Example: _My Uncle Tony is middle-aged. He is tall and . . ._

Challenge Compare yourself or someone you know to the average American man or woman.

1. **Look in your dictionary. *True* or *False*? Correct the underlined words in the false sentences.**

    blow dryer
    a. The bald hair stylist has a ~~brush~~ in his hand.   ___false___

    b. The woman in his chair has <u>brown</u> hair.   _____

    c. The hair stylist with red hair is using <u>scissors</u>.   _____

    d. The hair stylist with blond hair is <u>setting</u> hair.   _____

2. **Complete the advice column with the words in the box.**

beard	blond	blow dryer	color
dye	~~gray~~	mustache	perm	wavy

    ## Ask Harry

    Q: I'm only twenty, but I've got a lot of

    _____*gray*_____ hair.
    a.

    A: Why not _____ it? You can
    b.
    _____ it black, brown, red, or
    c.
    _____ . Ask your hairdresser
    d.
    about the shade.

    Q: I want _____ hair, but I hate rollers.
    e.
    A: _____ it. You'll have the style
    f.
    you want with no work.

    Q: I always use a _____ after I
    g.
    wash my hair. Is hot air bad for my hair?

    A: Yes. Use a towel some of the time.

    Q: My husband says he spends too much time

    shaving.

    A: Tell him to grow a _____ and a
    h.
    _____ . He'll have to shave
    i.
    less!

3. **Find and correct four more mistakes in this ad.**

    long
    Erica has ~~shoulder-length~~, wavy, brown hair.
    Bob has long, curly, black hair.
    Ann has beautiful shoulder-length, straight, blond hair with bangs.

    They all have great haircuts from Kindest Cuts.
    Still only $20.   *KINDEST* **CUT**

    Challenge Look in a magazine, newspaper, or your dictionary. Find a hair style you like.
    Describe what a stylist did to create the style.

1. **Look at the children on page 34 in your dictionary. Who said . . . ?**

   a. "I play softball with my two brothers."   _____Lily_____

   b. "My baby brother just started to walk."   _____

   c. "I don't have any brothers or sisters."   _____

   d. "Aunt Ana made a pretty dress for me."   _____

2. **Complete the family tree. Show the people's relationship to Danica.**

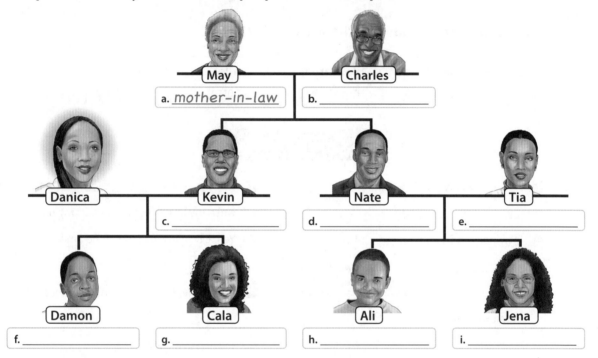

May Charles

a. _mother-in-law_   b. _____

Danica   Kevin   Nate   Tia

c. _____   d. _____   e. _____

Damon   Cala   Ali   Jena

f. _____   g. _____   h. _____   i. _____

3. **Look at Danica's niece Jena in Exercise 2. Use information from the family tree to complete Jena's blog post.**

> **Jena's Blog:** Posted on May 6 at 3:45 PM
>
> This week my ___cousin___ Cala turned sixteen, so my _____ Kevin and
>   **a.**   **b.**
>
> my _____ Danica gave her a big party. My _____ Ali and I played with
>   **c.**   **d.**
>
> the other kids, and my _____ were very busy too—Mom served the
>   **e.**
>
> food, and Dad took pictures of Cala, their only _____. Suddenly
>   **f.**
>
> someone shouted, "May is on the phone." It was our _____
>   **g.**
>
> calling from San Francisco!

4. **What about you? Draw your family tree. Use your own paper.**

5. **Look at page 35 in your dictionary.** *True* or *False*?

   a. David's father is Lisa's stepfather. _____true_____

   b. Kim's mother is married to Lisa's father. _____

   c. Mary is Kim's stepsister. _____

   d. Carol is divorced from Bill's stepfather. _____

6. **Complete the entries from Lisa's diary. Use the words in the box.**

~~divorced~~	half sister	married	remarried	single father
stepfather	stepsister	stepmother	wife	

   3/15/08—Dad moved away this week. He and Mom got __divorced__. That means
   a.
   they're not _____ anymore. I feel bad, but Mom says I didn't do anything wrong.
   b.

   4/1/08—Dad's new apartment is cool. He says he'll always be my father, but now
   he's a _____, not a married one.
   c.

   10/4/10—Mom says she wants to get _____ someday. That man Rick
   d.
   seems nice. Maybe she'll be his _____ someday.
   e.

   12/10/10—Mom and Rick got married! Rick's my _____ now.
   f.
   I wonder—can I still visit Dad?

   12/12/10—I had a great time at Dad's this weekend. Bill and Kim were there. When
   Dad and Sue get married, I'll be Bill and Kim's _____. Dad will be their
   g.
   stepfather, and Sue will be my _____.
   h.

   11/14/11—We have a new baby! Her name is Mary. I'm her _____. Mom says I
   i.
   can help take care of her.

   Challenge Look at page 256 in this book. Follow the instructions.

1. **Look in your dictionary. Read the sentences. Write the activities.**

   a. "Mmm. This looks good. Now open your mouth!"   _feed the baby_

   b. "Next you're going to have a nice bath." _____

   c. "Don't cry, sweetie. You're going to be fine." _____

   d. "Great! That's right. The spoon goes there. Next to the plate." _____

   e. "Good. Now we can drive to Grandma's!" _____

   f. "Once upon a time, there was a little boy who had a big dog." _____

   g. "Goodnight, honey. Sleep well and sweet dreams." _____

   h. "Don't touch it! It's hot!" _____

2. **Circle the words to complete the instructions to the babysitter.**

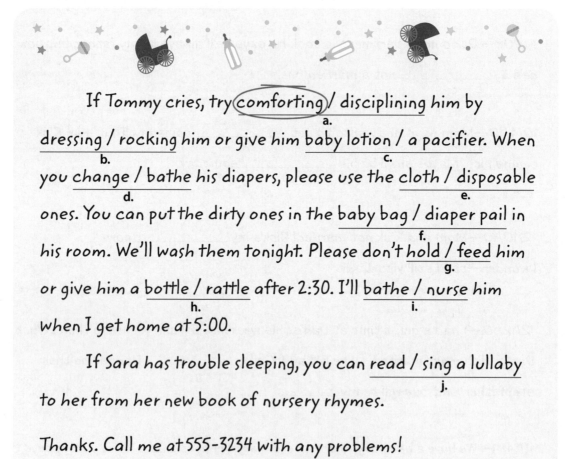

If Tommy cries, try (comforting) / disciplining him by
a.
dressing / rocking him or give him baby lotion / a pacifier. When
b.   c.
you change / bathe his diapers, please use the cloth / disposable
d.   e.
ones. You can put the dirty ones in the baby bag / diaper pail in
f.
his room. We'll wash them tonight. Please don't hold / feed him
g.
or give him a bottle / rattle after 2:30. I'll bathe / nurse him
h.   i.
when I get home at 5:00.

If Sara has trouble sleeping, you can read / sing a lullaby
j.
to her from her new book of nursery rhymes.

Thanks. Call me at 555-3234 with any problems!

Monica

3. Cross out the word that doesn't belong. Give a reason.

a. high chair ~~baby bag~~ car safety seat

   Babies don't sit in a baby bag.

b. nipple training pants diaper

   _____

c. formula baby food teething ring

   _____

d. safety pins rattle teddy bear

   _____

e. carriage stroller night light

   _____

4. Complete these thank-you notes. Use the words in the box.

| bib car safety seat carriage ~~high chair~~ nursery rhymes teddy bear |

a.
THANK YOU

Dear Elisa,

Thanks for the ___high chair___!
Now Johnny can sit and eat with us
at the table. The _____
is great, too. It's pretty.
Melissa

b.
THANK YOU

Dear Aunt Alice,

Thank you for the
_____ . Now when we
drive to visit Grandma, Julie will be
happy and safe!

Love, Angela and Scott

c.
THANK YOU

Dear Lili and Quon,
We all love the _____ !
We read them to Louisa every day. The
_____ is great, too.
Louisa loves playing with him and
can't sleep without him!
Love, Jason

d.
THANK YOU

Dear Bill,
The _____ is great!
I put Tommy in it yesterday when
I went to the market. He slept
happily and I didn't have to carry
him. Thanks so much!
Love, Amanda

Challenge Look in your dictionary. Imagine someone gave you a baby gift.
Choose an item and write a thank-you note for it.

1. **Look in your dictionary. Who does what in the Lim family? Check (✓) the correct box or boxes.**

TO DO

	Mom	Dad	Tess	Marc
a. make lunch	✓	☐	☐	☐
b. take the children to school	☐	☐	☐	☐
c. drive to work	☐	☐	☐	☐
d. go to class	☐	☐	☐	☐
e. go to the grocery store	☐	☐	☐	☐
f. pick up the kids	☐	☐	☐	☐
g. clean the house	☐	☐	☐	☐
h. exercise	☐	☐	☐	☐
i. do homework	☐	☐	☐	☐
j. read the paper	☐	☐	☐	☐
k. check email	☐	☐	☐	☐

2. **Read this article about the family in your dictionary. <u>Underline</u> six more mistakes.**

The Fast Track Family

David and Mai Lim want a lot from life, and their daily routine shows it. They both get up early in the morning. At 6:30 David <u>takes a shower</u>. Then Mai makes breakfast while David eats with the kids. At 7:30 David takes the kids to school. Then David goes to work, and Mai drives to school. At 4:30 Mai picks up the children. Then she cleans the house with the kids and cooks dinner. At 5:00 David leaves work and goes home. The family has dinner together. After dinner the children always do homework. At 8:00 Mai reads the paper and David checks email. Then David watches TV. They go to sleep at 10:30. It's a busy schedule, but the Lims enjoy it.

3. **Correct the mistakes in Exercise 2. Write the correct activity.**

a. _At 6:30 David doesn't take a shower. He gets dressed._

b. _____

c. _____

d. _____

e. _____

f. _____

g. _____

4. Make questions from the scrambled words.

a. time What you up do get _____What time do you get up?_____

b. eat breakfast When you do _____

c. you leave When the house do _____

d. home come you do time What _____

e. to bed go do When you _____

5. What about you? Complete the first PDA with information about your daily routine. Then interview another person. Use questions like the ones in Exercise 4.

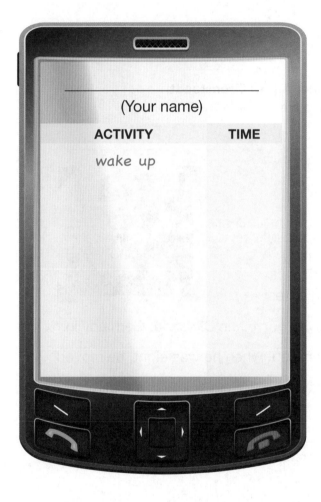

(Your name)	
ACTIVITY	**TIME**
wake up	

(Your partner's name)	
ACTIVITY	**TIME**

Challenge Compare the routines in Exercise 5. Write six sentences. **Example:** *I get up at 6:00, but Kyung gets up at 7:00. We both leave for class at 8:00.*

See page 270 for listening practice.

1. **Look in your dictionary. How old was Martin Perez when he . . . ?**

    a. learned to drive   <u>18 years old</u>

    b. graduated   _____

    c. became a citizen   _____

    d. got married   _____

    e. had a baby   _____

    f. bought his first home   _____

    g. became a grandparent   _____

    h. died   _____

2. **Complete this biography about photographer Alfred Eisenstaedt.
    Use the past tense form of the words in the boxes.**

BIOGRAPHY

Alfred Eisenstaedt
Photographer

| ~~be born~~   get   start |

Alfred Eisenstaedt was one of the greatest

photographers in the world. He ___<u>was born</u>___ in Dirschau, Germany in
                                                    a.

1898. He _____ school there, but when he was eight, he moved
                 b.

to Berlin with his family. Six years later, he _____ his first
                                                 c.

camera.

| become   buy   get   go   travel |

Eisenstaedt _____ to college in Berlin, but times were difficult.
                  d.

Soon he left school and _____ a job selling clothes. When he
                                 e.

was 24, he saved money and _____ his first Leica (a small, fast
                                        f.

camera). Five years later, he _____ a professional photographer.
                                                        g.

He _____ to France, Switzerland, Italy, and Ethiopia taking
                h.

pictures. People were his favorite subject.

| die | get | get married | immigrate | retire |

In 1935, Eisenstaedt left Germany and _____ to the United
States. A year later, he _____ a job at *Life* magazine. He worked
i.   j.
there for 36 years. After he _____ , he and his wife Alma (the
k.
two _____ in 1949) lived in their house on Martha's Vineyard. He
l.
_____ there in 1995, at the age of 96.
m.

3. **Read the sentences about Alfred Eisenstaedt. *True* or *False*? Put a question mark (?) if the information isn't in the reading in Exercise 2.**

a. Alfred Eisenstaedt was born in the United States. _____*false*_____

b. He went to college in Dirschau. _____

c. He became a citizen of the United States. _____

d. Eisenstaedt got married before he immigrated to the U.S. _____

e. He and his wife had a baby in 1951. _____

f. He lived in the United States for 60 years. _____

4. **Check (✓) the documents Alfred Eisenstaedt probably had. Use the information in Exercise 2.**

✓ high school diploma ☐ deed ☐ college degree

☐ marriage license ☐ passport ☐ birth certificate

5. **Complete the time line for Alfred Eisenstaedt. Use the information in Exercise 2.**

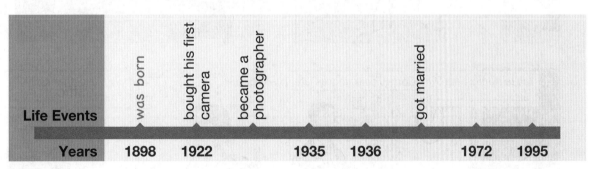

Life Events	was born	bought his first camera	became a photographer		got married		
Years	1898	1922	1935	1936	1972	1995

6. **What about you? Draw a time line with your own information. Then write a short autobiography. Use your own paper.**

Challenge Think of a famous person and look up biographical information about him or her in an
encyclopedia or online. Draw a time line and write a paragraph about the person's life.

See page 271 for listening practice.

Feelings

1. **Look in your dictionary. Find and write the opposite of these words.**

   a. worried   _relieved_

   b. hot   _____

   c. nervous   _____

   d. sick   _____

   e. happy   _____

   f. full   _____

2. **Complete the sentences. Use the words in the box.**

disgusted	full	~~homesick~~	in pain	relieved

a. What's wrong?

I'm really _homesick_.

b. Ow!

What's wrong? Are you _____?

c. Yuck! What IS that!?

You look _____!

d. You're home! I am SO _____!

Sorry. The train was late.

e. More turkey?

No, thanks. I'm _____.

3. Circle the words to complete the story.

Minh Ho had so many feelings his first day of school. When he left home, he felt (scared) / excited.
a.

His mother looked <u>nervous / calm</u>, but his little brother just looked <u>sad / sleepy</u>. When he got to
b.   c.

school, he walked into the wrong class. The teacher looked <u>bored / surprised</u>, and Minh Ho was
d.

very <u>embarrassed / thirsty</u>. He felt much better in math class. He was <u>proud / frustrated</u> when he
e.   f.

did a problem correctly. His teacher looked <u>upset / happy</u>. At lunchtime, he looked at his food
g.

and was <u>confused / relieved</u>. "What is this?" He wasn't <u>angry / hungry</u> at all. As he sat in the
h.   i.

cafeteria, Minh Ho was feeling very <u>full / sad</u> and <u>tired / lonely</u>. Then someone said, "Can I sit here?"
j.   k.

Suddenly his feelings changed. He felt <u>happy / homesick</u>. Was he <u>in love / in pain</u>?
l.   m.

4. What about you? How did you feel on your first day of school? Write sentences on your own paper.

Challenge Look at the picture on page 256. Follow the instructions.

Go to page 243 for Another Look (Unit 2). | **See page 271 for listening practice.**

1. **Look in your dictionary.** *True* or *False*? **Rewrite the false sentences. Make them true.**

   a. Ben has a <u>small</u> family.   _____false_____

       Ben has a big family.

   b. <u>Every year</u>, his family has a reunion.   _____

   _____

   c. The reunion is at <u>his aunt's</u> house.   _____

   _____

   d. This year he decorated with <u>balloons and a banner</u>.   _____

   _____

   e. His grandfather and his aunt are talking about <u>the baseball game</u>.   _____

   _____

   f. Some <u>adults</u> are misbehaving.   _____

   _____

   g. Ben's relatives are laughing and Ben is having a <u>good</u> time.   _____

   _____

   h. There are <u>two</u> new babies at the reunion this year.   _____

   _____

   i. Ben's mother-in-law is talking about <u>families</u>.   _____

   _____

   j. Ben is <u>sorry</u> the reunion is only once a year.   _____

   _____

2. **Look in your dictionary. Who is saying . . . ? Match.**

   _6_ **a.** "The Mets are terrible this year!"   **1.** Ben's grandmother

   ___ **b.** "Let's stop talking and watch the game."   **2.** Ben's aunt

   ___ **c.** "In my opinion, you should have two more children."   **3.** Ben's sister

   ___ **d.** "The babies are laughing. I guess they're having a good time!" **4.** Ben

   ___ **e.** "May, stop misbehaving! Take your hand off the cake."   **5.** Ben's mother-in-law

   ___ **f.** "Aunt Terry! I'm so glad you came."   **6.** Ben's grandfather

3. **What about you? Imagine you are at Ben's reunion. What are you doing? Write three sentences.**

Example: *I'm drinking soda.*

a. _____

b. _____

c. _____

What aren't you doing? Write three sentences.

Example: *I'm not eating cake.*

d. _____

e. _____

f. _____

4. **Complete Ben's aunt's email. Use the words in the box.**

baby	baseball game	father	glad	nephew
good time	big	opinions	relatives	~~reunion~~

My Email ▬ ☐ ☒

Every year I go to a family _____*reunion*_____ at my _____'s
                             a.   **b.**

house. All of my _____ are there. I'm always
                             c.

_____ to see them. We have a _____ family,
       d.   **e.**

and next year it will be even larger. Ben and his wife are going to have a new

_____ ! This year,
     f.

my _____ and I watched
        g.

a _____ . We had very different
     h.

_____ about it, but we also
     i.

had a _____ !
        j.

Challenge Imagine you are one of the people at the Lu Family Reunion. Write about the reunion. Use the email in Exercise 4 as an example.

1. **Look in your dictionary. *True* or *False*? Correct the underlined words in the false statements.**

   a. This home has two ~~bathrooms~~ and a baby's room.　　_____false_____

      bedrooms

   b. The <u>bedroom</u> door is open.　　_____

   c. The <u>kitchen</u> has three windows.　　_____

   d. Mr. Marino is in the <u>attic</u>.　　_____

   e. Mrs. Marino is in the <u>dining area</u>.　　_____

   f. One daughter is in the <u>basement</u>.　　_____

2. **Look in your dictionary. Label the floor plans.**

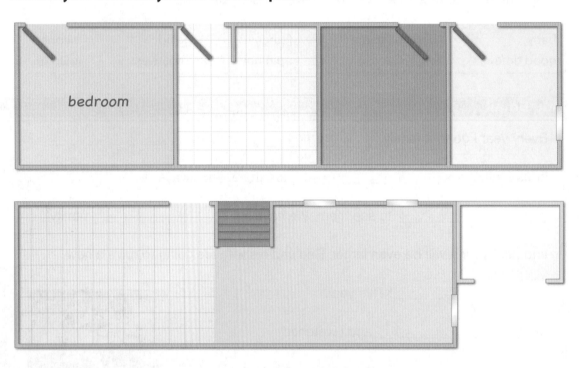

bedroom

3. **What about you? Draw a floor plan of your home. Label the rooms.**

My Home

4. **Look in your dictionary. Where are these items?**

a. <u>in the bedroom</u>

b. _____

c. _____

d. _____

e. _____

f. _____

5. **Look in your dictionary. Circle the words to complete the ad.**

Great for a Family!

Two-<u>bathroom</u> / <u>(bedroom)</u> house with baby's room. One <u>bathroom</u> / <u>bedroom</u>. Large
        a.   **b.**

<u>attic</u> / <u>kitchen</u> with dining <u>area</u> / <u>window</u>. <u>Basement</u> / <u>Living room</u> with a lot of light
      c.   **d.**   **e.**

(three <u>doors</u> / <u>windows</u>). <u>Floor</u> / <u>Basement</u> and attic. One-car <u>attic</u> / <u>garage</u>.
             f.   **g.**   **h.**

Call 555-2468 for more information

6. **What about you? Describe your "dream" home.**

a. How many bedrooms does it have? _____

b. How many bathrooms? _____

c. Does it have a dining area or a separate
   dining room? _____

d. Does it have a garage? _____
   If *yes*, how many cars can go in the garage? _____

e. Does it have a basement? _____
   If *yes*, what is in the basement? _____

f. How many windows are there? _____
   Which rooms have windows? _____

g. What color is the living room? _____

Challenge Write an ad for your "dream" house. Use the ad in Exercise 5 as an example.

See page 272 for listening practice.

1. Look at the ads on page 48 in your dictionary. Which apartment . . . ?
   Check (✓) the correct column.

	Internet Listing	Classified Ad
a. is in the city		✓
b. has one bedroom		
c. has two bathrooms		
d. is more expensive		
e. includes utilities		

2. Circle the words to complete the article.

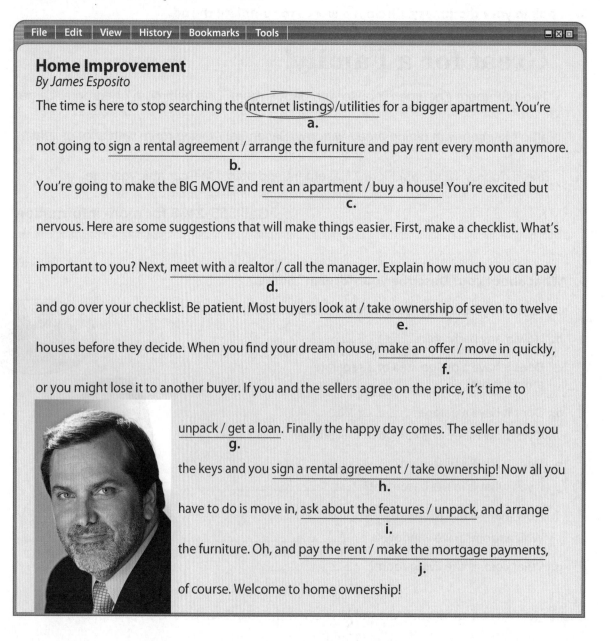

File   Edit   View   History   Bookmarks   Tools

Home Improvement
By James Esposito

The time is here to stop searching the (Internet listings) / utilities for a bigger apartment. You're
a.

not going to sign a rental agreement / arrange the furniture and pay rent every month anymore.
b.

You're going to make the BIG MOVE and rent an apartment / buy a house! You're excited but
c.

nervous. Here are some suggestions that will make things easier. First, make a checklist. What's

important to you? Next, meet with a realtor / call the manager. Explain how much you can pay
d.

and go over your checklist. Be patient. Most buyers look at / take ownership of seven to twelve
e.

houses before they decide. When you find your dream house, make an offer / move in quickly,
f.

or you might lose it to another buyer. If you and the sellers agree on the price, it's time to

unpack / get a loan. Finally the happy day comes. The seller hands you
g.

the keys and you sign a rental agreement / take ownership! Now all you
h.

have to do is move in, ask about the features / unpack, and arrange
i.

the furniture. Oh, and pay the rent / make the mortgage payments,
j.

of course. Welcome to home ownership!

3. **Look in your dictionary. What are they doing?**

a. "I think we need some more boxes!" _____ *packing* _____

b. "How about $125,000?" _____

c. "Let's put the table there, in front of the loveseat." _____

d. "The keys to our new house! Thank you." _____

e. "Thank you. Now we have the money for the house!" _____

4. **Look at the classified ads. Answer the questions.**

Smithfield New 2bdrm 2ba house large front yd near schools and shopping $300,000

Greenville 3bdrm 2ba house large sunny kit close to transportation. Move-in condition! $258,000

Lincoln Small 2bdrm, 1ba for sale or rent. Just painted! $185,000

a. Which house is the biggest? _____ *the house in Greenville* _____

   How many bedrooms does it have? _____

b. What is the price? _____

c. Which house is the smallest? _____

   How many bathrooms does it have? _____

d. Which house is the least expensive? _____

   What is the price? _____

e. Which house is best for a family with _____

   one child? Why? _____

f. Which house has a large kitchen? _____

5. **What about you? Check (✓) all the items that are important to you.**

Type	☐ Apartment	☐ House	☐ Other: _____
Location	☐ City	☐ Suburbs	☐ Country
Near	☐ School	☐ Shopping	☐ Work
Space	☐ Number of rooms	☐ Size of rooms	
Cost	☐ Rent	☐ Mortgage	

CITY **REALTY**

Challenge Write a paragraph about a time you looked for and found a new home.

1. Look in your dictionary. Where can you hear . . . ?

a. "Bye. I'm going up now."   *the elevator*

b. "The water looks great! I'll go in after this chapter."   _____

c. "All I ever get are bills and ads."   _____

d. "I watch this program every Monday night."   _____

e. "Just sign here, and the apartment is yours!"   _____

f. "Oh, good. My clothes are all dry."   _____

2. Circle the words to complete the ad.

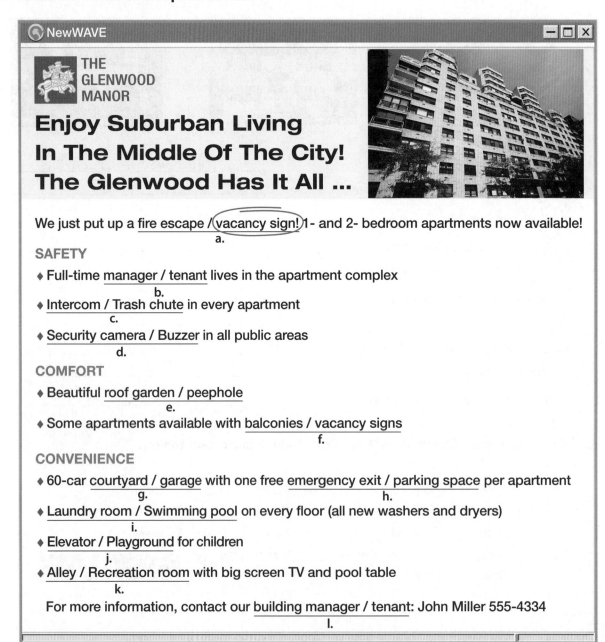

NewWAVE

THE GLENWOOD MANOR

Enjoy Suburban Living In The Middle Of The City! The Glenwood Has It All ...

We just put up a fire escape / (vacancy sign!) 1- and 2- bedroom apartments now available!
a.

SAFETY

♦ Full-time manager / tenant lives in the apartment complex
b.
♦ Intercom / Trash chute in every apartment
c.
♦ Security camera / Buzzer in all public areas
d.

COMFORT

♦ Beautiful roof garden / peephole
e.
♦ Some apartments available with balconies / vacancy signs
f.

CONVENIENCE

♦ 60-car courtyard / garage with one free emergency exit / parking space per apartment
g.   **h.**
♦ Laundry room / Swimming pool on every floor (all new washers and dryers)
i.
♦ Elevator / Playground for children
j.
♦ Alley / Recreation room with big screen TV and pool table
k.

For more information, contact our building manager / tenant: John Miller 555-4334
l.

3. Complete the safety pamphlet. Use the words in the box.

buzzer	dead-bolt lock	door chain	elevator	fire escape
~~intercom~~	smoke detector	peephole	key	stairs

Better Safe Than Sorry

▶ Don't allow strangers into the building. Always use your ___*intercom*___ to ask
a.
"Who's there?" <u>before</u> you use your

_____.
b.

▶ Look out your _____ before
c.
you open your apartment door. When you're at home, keep your _____ on.
d.

▶ Install a _____. It's the
e.
strongest lock.

▶ Give a copy of your _____
f.
to the building manager. In case of an emergency, it will be easier to enter your apartment.

▶ Keep a _____ on the wall or
g.
ceiling between your bedroom and your apartment door. Check it every month!

▶ In case of fire, do not use the

_____ (The heat can cause it
h.
to stop between floors.) Use the

_____ instead.
i.

▶ Feel the door of your apartment. If it's hot, the fire may be out in the hall. Use the

_____ to leave your apartment.
j.

For serious emergencies dial 911. All other times call your local police or fire department.

4. What about you? How safe is your home? Check (✓) the things your home has.

☐ dead-bolt lock   ☐ door chain   ☐ emergency exit   ☐ fire escape

☐ intercom   ☐ peephole   ☐ security camera   ☐ security gate

☐ smoke detector   ☐ Other: _____

Challenge Describe your ideal apartment building.

See page 272 for listening practice.

1. Look in your dictionary. Where can you hear . . . ?

a. "My roommate is studying chemistry." *a college dormitory*

b. "I became homeless after I lost my job." _____

c. "We raise horses." _____

d. "All four houses look the same." _____

2. Complete the letter. Use the words in the box.

city	condo	country	~~farm~~	mobile home
nursing home	senior housing	suburbs	townhouse	

> Dear Fran,
>
> You asked me to tell you about the places I've lived. I grew up on a potato
>
> _____ **farm** _____ . After your grandfather and I got married, we bought a small
>   **a.**
>
> _____ in a very large building. I didn't like living in a big
>   **b.**
>
> _____ like Boston. I really prefer living in the _____ , where
>   **c.**   **d.**
>
> I grew up. I was happy when we bought a _____ in the
>   **e.**
>
> _____ , only fifteen miles from the city. When your grandfather retired,
>   **f.**
>
> we wanted to travel. We bought a _____ and for a while, we moved our
>   **g.**
>
> little home every few years! After your grandfather died, I wanted to be around more
>
> people my age, so I moved to _____ . Then I got sick and needed more
>   **h.**
>
> help, so I moved here to this _____ . When you were younger, you used
>   **i.**
>
> to think all the elderly people here were your grandparents, too! We're all looking
>
> forward to your next visit.
>
> Love,
> Grandma

3. What about you? Where have you lived? Make a chart like the one below.

Name of Place	City, Suburbs, or Country	Type of Home	Year You Moved There	How Long You Lived There
New York	city	apartment	2004	6 years

Challenge Write a paragraph about the places you've lived. Use information from Exercise 3.

1. **Look in your dictionary. What can you use to . . . ?**

   a. eat outside _patio furniture_

   b. cook outside _____

   c. take a nap _____

   d. water the lawn _____ and _____

   e. grow your own tomatoes _____

2. **Look at the houses. Find and describe 8 more differences. Use your own paper.**

   Example: *House A's mailbox is red, but House B's is blue.*

3. **What about you? Plan your ideal yard. Check (✓) the items you would like.**

   ☐ a patio   ☐ flower beds   ☐ a hammock   ☐ Other: _____

   Challenge Draw your ideal yard and write a paragraph describing it.

See page 273 for listening practice.

1. Look in your dictionary. Complete the sentences.

a. The _____teakettle_____ is on the right back burner of the stove next to the pot.

b. The _____ is on the counter, to the right of the sink.

c. The _____ are on the wall, under the cabinet and above the dish rack.

d. The _____ is below the oven.

2. Look at the chart. *True* or *False*? Correct the underlined words in the false statements.

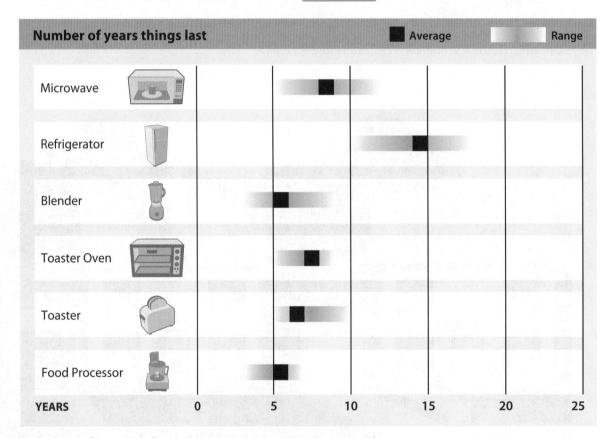

Number of years things last ■ Average ▢ Range

Microwave	
Refrigerator	
Blender	
Toaster Oven	
Toaster	
Food Processor	

YEARS 0 5 10 15 20 25

Based on information from: *Consumer Reports 2000 Buying Guide.*

a. A refrigerator lasts an average of about ~~ten~~ *fifteen* years.   *false*

b. A microwave lasts an average of about <u>nine</u> years.   _____

c. On average, a food processor lasts as long as a <u>blender</u>.   _____

d. The average life of a toaster oven is <u>shorter</u> than the life of a toaster.   _____

e. A toaster lasts from about <u>five to ten</u> years.   _____

Challenge Which five kitchen appliances do you think are the most important. Why?

1. **Look in your dictionary. List the items on the dining room table and on the tray. Use your own paper.**

   Example: *4 placemats*

2. **Complete the conversations. Use the words in the box.**

| fan | hutch | platter | serving bowl | ~~tablecloth~~ | tray | vase |

a. **Alek:** I'm setting the table. Are we going to use placemats?

   Ella: No. Put on the white _____*tablecloth*_____ instead.

b. **Alek:** Are we going to serve each guest a piece of fish?

   Ella: No. I'll put the fish on a big _____ in the middle of the table.

c. **Alek:** Where are the good plates?

   Ella: They're in the _____. The _____ for the
   vegetables is there, too.

d. **Alek:** Where should I put the coffee mugs?

   Ella: I'll carry them out on a _____ after we finish eating.

e. **Alek:** Is it hot in here?

   Ella: Yes. Why don't you turn on the _____?

f. **Alek:** The flowers are beautiful!

   Ella: I'll get a _____ for them.

3. **What about you? Draw a picture of the table at a dinner you had. Label the items.**

Challenge Find a picture of a dining area in a newspaper or magazine. Describe it to a classmate.
Your classmate will draw a picture of it.

See page 274 for listening practice.
 55

1. **Look in your dictionary. *True* or *False*? Correct the underlined words in the false sentences.**

   entertainment center

   a. There's a painting on the wall over the ~~mantle~~.   _____false_____

   b. The DVD player is to the left of the <u>stereo system</u>.   _____

   c. The magazine holder is next to the <u>fire screen</u>.   _____

   d. There are throw pillows on the <u>armchair</u>.   _____

   e. There's a candle holder and candle on the <u>coffee table</u>.   _____

2. **Look at the pictures. Circle the words to complete the sentences.**

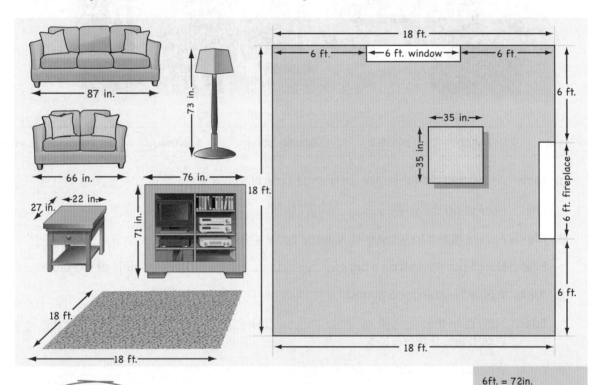

   a. The (coffee table) / end table is already in the living room.

   b. The <u>entertainment center / love seat</u> can go to the left of the window.

   c. The <u>love seat / sofa</u> won't fit to the right of the fireplace.

   d. The carpet is <u>bigger than / the same size as</u> the living room.

   e. The floor lamp is <u>shorter / taller</u> than the entertainment center.

3. **What about you? Draw a floor plan of your living room. Label the items.**

   Challenge How would you decorate the living room in Exercise 2? Write sentences. **Example:** *I'd put the sofa in the middle of the living room, across from the window . . . .*

1. Look in your dictionary. Which item is each person talking about?

a. "<u>It</u>'s in the toothbrush holder."   _____toothbrush_____

b. "Can I put my dirty jeans in <u>here</u>?"   _____

c. "I'm going to hang your bath towel and washcloth <u>here</u>."   _____

d. "There's hair in <u>it</u>. The water isn't going down."   _____

2. Complete the article. Use the words in the box.

| medicine cabinet | hot water | grab bar | soap dish | sink | showerhead |
| shower curtain | wastebasket | faucets | bath mat | ~~bathtub~~ | rubber mat | toilet |

Keep bath time safe and happy by following these safety rules:

1 Never leave a young child alone in the _____*bathtub*_____.
a.
Even small amounts of water can be dangerous.

2 Avoid burns from _____. Turn the temperature on your water heater down to
b.
100°F. Fix all dripping _____ and don't forget the _____
c.   **d.**
—hot drops from above can hurt, too.

3 Prevent falls. Keep a _____ in the bathtub and a nonslip _____
e.   **f.**
on the floor. And don't forget to put that slippery soap back in the _____ after
g.
you wash. Never hold onto the _____ when you get out of the bathtub. Install a
h.
_____ on the bathtub wall. Provide a stool so that children can reach the
i.
_____ safely to wash their hands and brush their teeth.
j.

4 Keep medicines locked in the _____. Never throw old medicines away in a
k.
_____ where children can get them. Flush them down the _____.
l.   **m.**

3. What about you? What do you do to prevent injuries and accidents in the bathroom? Write sentences on your own paper.

Example: *We put a rubber mat in the bathtub.*

Challenge Draw a picture of your bathroom. Label the items.

See page 274 for listening practice.   **57**

1. **Look in your dictionary. *True* or *False*? Correct the underlined words in the false sentences.**

    on the wood floor
    a. The cat is ~~under the bed.~~   _____*false*_____

    b. There is a full-length mirror in the closet.   _____

    c. The alarm clock is on the dresser.   _____

    d. The light switch and the outlet are on the same wall.   _____

    e. The woman is lifting the mattress and the dust ruffle.   _____

2. **Read the letter and look at the picture. Complete Tran's list. Use your own paper.**

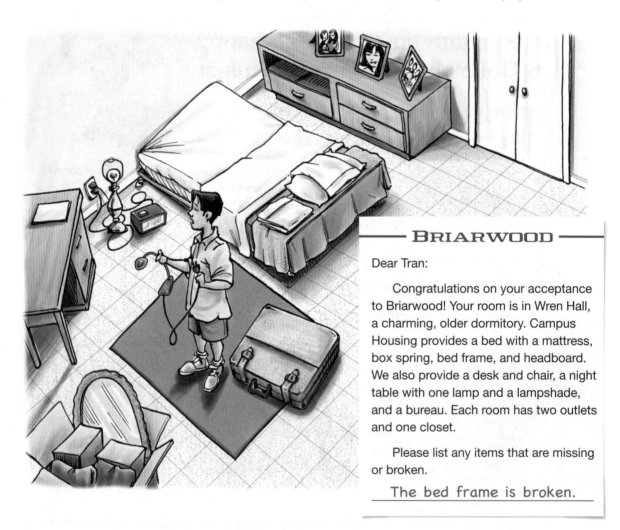

BRIARWOOD

Dear Tran:

Congratulations on your acceptance to Briarwood! Your room is in Wren Hall, a charming, older dormitory. Campus Housing provides a bed with a mattress, box spring, bed frame, and headboard. We also provide a desk and chair, a night table with one lamp and a lampshade, and a bureau. Each room has two outlets and one closet.

Please list any items that are missing or broken.

The bed frame is broken.

3. **Look at Exercise 2. What did Tran bring? Make a list.**

    Example: *sheets*

Challenge Write a paragraph about your ideal bedroom.

1. Look in your dictionary. Cross out the word that doesn't belong.

   a. For sleeping   crib   ~~puzzle~~   bunk bed   cradle

   b. For safety   baby monitor   safety rail   bumper pad   blocks

   c. For playing   ball   changing pad   doll   crayons

   d. Furniture   changing table   chest of drawers   toy chest   coloring book

2. Complete the article. Use the words in the box.

mobile	changing table	wallpaper	stuffed animals
~~crib~~	bedspread	chest of drawers	

Expecting a new family member?

HERE'S WHAT YOU'LL NEED TO MAKE YOUR BABY'S ROOM A SAFE AND HAPPY PLACE.

The biggest item is the _____*crib*_____. The mattress
                    a.

must fit tightly, with no spaces that a baby's head can fit

through. A pretty _____ will help keep baby
             b.

warm, but it should fit loosely on top of the mattress. You can change your

baby on a bed, but a _____ is better for your back. Finally,
                 c.

you will need a _____ for baby's clothing.
            d.

For decoration, hang a _____ where baby can watch it (some
                   e.

of them play music, too). Paint the room or put up colorful

_____. And don't forget some soft, cuddly _____
     f.   **g.**

for baby to play with.

3. What about you? Describe your favorite toy or game as a child.

   Example: *I loved my teddy bear. It was . . .*

Challenge   Look at page 257 in this book. Follow the instructions.

1. Look in your dictionary. Correct the underlined words.

    recycling
  a. The man in B is ~~putting away~~ newspapers.

  b. The man in D is <u>sweeping</u> the floor.

  c. The girl in N is <u>washing</u> the dishes.

  d. The woman in O is <u>dusting</u> the counter.

2. Look at the room. Circle the words to complete the note.

Hi! I wasn't quite able to do everything.

I polished the (desk) / dresser, but I didn't
             a.
dust the <u>desk / dresser</u>. I <u>swept /</u>
       b.   **c.**
<u>vacuumed</u> the floor, and I washed the

<u>dishes / windows</u>. I also washed the
        d.
<u>sheets / glasses</u>, but didn't make
        e.
<u>lunch / the bed</u>. Sorry! Could you
      f.
<u>take out / empty</u> the garbage and
        g.
put away the <u>dishes / books</u>? *Viktor*
             h.

3. What about you? Which would you prefer to do? Tell a classmate. Do you agree?

Example: *I'd prefer to dry the dishes.*

  a. wash the dishes / dry the dishes

  b. dust the furniture / polish the furniture

  c. sweep the floor / vacuum the carpet

  d. make the bed / change the sheets

Challenge Take a survey. Ask five people about their favorite and least favorite kinds of housework. Write their answers.

  See page 275 for listening practice.

1. Look in your dictionary. Add a word to complete the list of cleaning supplies.

a. glass ___*cleaner*___   d. rubber _____   g. trash _____

b. oven _____   e. recycling _____   h. scrub _____

c. vacuum _____   f. furniture _____   i. sponge _____

2. Complete the conversations. Use the words in Exercise 1.

a. **Paulo:** Do you have any ___*trash bags*___?
   I want to empty the wastebasket.

   Sara: Sorry. I used the last one.

b. **Ben:** The mirror has a lot of finger prints on it.

   Ann: Use some _____.

c. **Ada:** The _____ doesn't seem to
   be working well.

   Mario: Maybe the bag is full. Have you checked it?

d. **Taro:** What should we do with the empty bottles?

   Rika: Don't throw them away. Put them in the _____ in the alley.

e. **Amber:** I dusted the desk, but it still doesn't look clean.

   Chet: Try some _____ on it.

f. **Luis:** You're doing a great job on that stove, but that _____
   isn't good for your hands.

   Vera: You're right. Do we have any _____?

g. **Layla:** The kitchen floor is really dirty. The _____ isn't getting it clean.

   Zaki: I know. You have to get down and use the _____ on it.

3. Cross out the word that doesn't belong. Give a reason.

a. dustpan   broom   ~~disinfectant wipes~~   sponge mop

   ___*You don't use them to clean the floor.*___

b. steel-wool soap pads   dishwashing liquid   dish towel   bucket

   _____

c. scrub brush   sponge   feather duster   sponge mop

   _____

Challenge Imagine you have just moved into a new home. You need to dust the furniture, clean the
oven, wash the windows, and mop the kitchen floor. Make a shopping list.

1. **Look in your dictionary. Who should they call?**

a.

_____roofer_____

b.

_____

c.

_____

d.

_____

2. **Look at Tracy and Kung's cabin. Complete the telephone conversations. Describe the problem or problems for each repair service.**

a. **Repair person:** Bob Derby Carpentry. Can I help you?

   Tracy: _The door on our kitchen cabinet is broken._____

b. **Repair person:** Plumbing Specialists, Ron here.

   Kyung: _____,

   _____, and _____

c. **Repair person:** Chestertown Electricians. This is Pat.

   Kyung: _____

d. **Repair person:** Nature's Way Exterminators. What's the problem?

   Tracy: _____

3. **Look at the chart.** *True* **or** *False***? Write a question mark (?) if the information isn't in the chart.**

Pests	Where They Live	How to Prevent Them	How to Get Rid of Them
	on pets, carpets, and furniture	Keep pets either inside or outside all the time.	Vacuum often. Comb pets daily. Wash them with water and lemon juice.
	behind walls, under roofs and floors	Repair cracks and holes in roofs and walls. Keep garbage in tightly closed garbage cans.	Poison is dangerous to humans. Put traps along walls. Put a piece of cheese in the trap.
	in wood, especially wet or damaged places	Repair cracks and holes. Repair leaks in pipes. Check every 1–2 years.	Call the exterminator. You need a professional to get rid of these pests, which destroy your house by eating the wood.
	gardens and lawns	Repair wall cracks. Clean floors and shelves often. Wipe spilled honey or jam immediately.	Find where they enter the house and repair that hole. Put mint leaves in food cupboards.
	behind walls, in electric appliances	Clean carefully. Keep food in closed containers. Repair all cracks and holes.	Make a trap by putting a piece of banana in a wide-mouthed jar. Put petroleum jelly around the inside of the jar to keep trapped bugs inside. Place in corners or under sinks. Call an exterminator.
	in sheets, blankets, mattresses, and cracks in the bed; in cracks on the wall	Don't buy used sheets, blankets, or mattresses. Clean up around the outside of the house. Don't allow birds or squirrels to build nests on or in the house.	Wash sheets and blankets in hot water; vacuum the bed and mattress. A professional exterminator is often necessary.

a. To prevent most pests, you must repair household problems.   *true*

b. You have to use poison to get rid of mice.   _____

c. Sometimes cockroaches get into the toaster oven.   _____

d. Fleas like sweet food.   _____

e. You have to buy cockroach traps.   _____

f. Ants carry diseases.   _____

g. Mint leaves help get rid of termites.   _____

h. Mice eat people's food.   _____

i. You should put a piece of fruit in a mouse trap.   _____

j. Bedbugs live only in beds.   _____

Challenge Write some other ways of dealing with household pests.

See page 276 for listening practice.   **63**

1. **Look in your dictionary.** *True* or *False*? **Rewrite the false sentences. Make them true.**

   a. Tina and Sally are <u>sisters</u>.   *false*

   Tina and Sally are roommates.

   b. They had a <u>DJ</u> for their party.   _____

   _____

   c. The neighbors were <u>irritated</u> about the music at the first party.   _____

   _____

   d. There was a big mess in the <u>rec room</u> after the first party.   _____

   _____

   e. The tenants made two <u>rules</u> at the tenant meeting.   _____

   _____

   f. Sally and Tina were <u>happy</u> at the tenant meeting.   _____

   _____

   g. Now it's against the rules to have loud music on <u>weekends</u>.   _____

   _____

   h. Their neighbors got invitations to the <u>second</u> party.   _____

   _____

2. **Circle the words to complete the conversations.**

   Ms. Sanders: Look at this (mess)/ noise! What happened?

a.

   Mr. Clarke: There was a big <u>meeting / party</u> in 2B last night. All the <u>tenants / roommates</u> are

b. c.

   <u>irritated / happy</u>.

d.

   Mr. Dean: We need to make some <u>rules / invitations</u> about parties. Any suggestions?

e.

   Mr. Clarke: No loud <u>mess / music</u>!

f.

   Tina: Ms. Sanders, we're very <u>sorry / irritated</u> about our party.

g.

   Ms. Sanders: Thanks, girls. I know it won't happen again.

   Sally: Did you get our invitation to the <u>rec room / hallway</u> party?

h.

   Mr. Clarke: Yes, I did! Thanks. I'll be there.

3. **What about you? Do you have some rules where you are living now? Are they good rules? Why or why not? What are some good rules for people in an apartment or a dormitory room?**

4. **Look in your dictionary. When did Tina and Sally . . . ? Put the sentences in order (1–8).**

____ a. clean the mess in the hallway

____ b. dance with their neighbors in the rec room

_1_ c. clean the apartment for the first party

____ d. make Mr. Clark in 2A very irritated

____ e. make some rules at the tenant meeting

____ f. give out the invitations to the neighbors

____ g. have a party in 2B

____ h. get an invitation to the tenant meeting

5. **Complete Sally and Tina's sign with the words in the box.**

mess	noise	dance	rec room	rules
sorry	~~neighbors~~	irritated	apartment	tenants

To Our ____Neighbors____
a.

We made a lot of _____ at our party last night, and we
b.

_____ our neighbors. We're very _____ about the
c. **d.**

loud music and the _____ in the hallway. We agree with the
e.

new _____ , and it won't happen again. We've given all the
f.

_____ in the building invitations to our party on
g.

Saturday, December 13th. We'll have great food and music, so please

come and _____ with your neighbors in the _____.
h. **i.**

Tina and Sally, _____ 2B
j.

Challenge Plan a party. Work with a group. When is your party? What do you have to do and when?
Use the ideas in the word box or your own.

choose the place	choose the music	send out invitations
plan the food	clean up after the party	

See page 276 for listening practice.

1. **Look in your dictionary. Which food comes from a . . . ?**

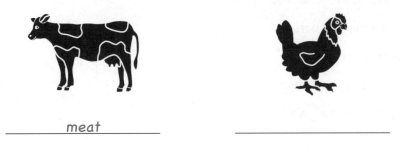

_____meat_____   _____

_____   _____

2. **Marisol is going to make these meals. Write the foods she needs.**

_____eggs_____

_____

_____

_____

_____

_____

_____

_____

3. **Look at Marisol's shopping list in Exercise 2. Check (✓) the coupons she can use.**

4. **Complete the conversations. Use the words in the box.**

coupons	fruit	grocery bag	meat	~~milk~~	shopping list	vegetables

Ana: What would you like to drink?

Luis: _____*Milk*_____, please.
a.

Liza: Would you like a hamburger?

Elek: No, thanks. I don't eat _____.
b.

Hoa: Do you like bananas?

Lan: I love bananas. They're my favorite _____.
c.

Dan: I'm going to the market. Do we need more milk?

Eva: Yes, I wrote it on the _____.
d.

Dan: What about carrots or peas?

Eva: No. We have enough _____.
e.

Eva: Oh. Don't forget to take these _____.
f.

Dan: Great. We'll save a lot of money with them!

Mike: Can I have another _____?
g.

Cashier: Sure. Paper or plastic?

5. **What about you? Do you eat . . . ? If *yes*, what types? Use pages 68–71 and page 76 in your dictionary for help.**

	Yes	No	Examples
vegetables	☐	☐	_____
fruit	☐	☐	_____
cheese	☐	☐	_____
meat	☐	☐	_____
fish	☐	☐	_____
eggs	☐	☐	_____
bread	☐	☐	_____

Challenge Work with a classmate. Plan a meal together. Use the food on pages 66 and 67 in your dictionary.

1. Look in your dictionary. Complete the sentences.

  a. A ___bunch of bananas___ costs 50¢.

  b. The _____ are between the prunes and dates.

  c. The _____ are tall and have green leaves on top.

  d. The _____ are above the blueberries.

2. Look at the pictures. Complete the chart.

Fruit		Best during	Buy ones that are
	a. ___watermelons___	June, July, August	cut open, dark red inside
	b. _____	June and July	dark red and big
	c. _____	July and August	bright orange, with soft skins
	d. _____	December to June	heavy
	e. _____	April to July	dry and dark red, size not important
	f. _____	July and August	dark green

3. Look at Exercise 2. Circle the words to complete the sentences.

  a. The best (grapefruits) / mangoes are heavy.

  b. Don't buy a watermelon / kiwi unless it is cut open.

  c. Plums / Strawberries are good in April.

  d. Grapefruits / Peaches are good in the winter.

  e. When you buy cherries / strawberries, size is important.

  f. Summer is a good time to buy lemons / limes.

  g. Apples / Peaches should have soft skins.

4. What about you? List your favorite types of fruit. When do you buy them?

‡ **Challenge** Make a chart like the one in Exercise 2 for your favorite fruit.

    See page 277 for listening practice.

1. **Look in your dictionary. Put these vegetables in the correct category.**

~~artichokes~~	~~beets~~	~~bell peppers~~	bok choy	cabbage
chili peppers	corn	cucumbers	eggplants	carrots
peas	radishes	spinach	string beans	lettuce
sweet potatoes	tomatoes	turnips	zucchini	squash

Root Vegetables	Leaf Vegetables	Vegetables with Seeds	
beets	artichokes	bell peppers	

2. **Complete the recipe with the amounts and names of the vegetables in the picture.**

Healthy Vegetable Stew

Put three cups of water on the stove to boil. While it is heating, use a sharp knife to slice

_____four_____ ____potatoes____ , _____ _____ ,
    a.   b.   c.   d.

_____ _____ , and _____ _____ .
    e.   f.   g.   h.

Cut _____ _____ into quarters and crush four cloves of _____
    i.   j.   k.

with the back of a spoon. Add these ingredients to the boiling water and cook over low for

20 minutes. Add _____ cups of _____ and cook for three more minutes.
              l.   m.

3. **What about you? Which vegetables do you like in a stew? Make a list.**

Challenge Write the recipe for a vegetable dish. Look online, in a recipe book, or ask a friend.

See page 277 for listening practice.

1. **Look in your dictionary. Cross out the word that doesn't belong. Write the category.**

a. _Poultry_   chicken   duck   ~~lamb~~   turkey

b. _____   chops   ham   sausage   tripe

c. _____   chops   leg   shank   wing

d. _____   drumsticks   ribs   steak   veal cutlets

2. **Complete the article with information from the charts.**

FAT FACTS

A 3 1/2 ounce serving of _____sausage_____ has 31 grams of fat.
                   a.

A serving of _____ and a serving of _____ have the same
               b.   **c.**

amount of fat.

_____ has the highest amount of fat.
       d.

_____ has the lowest amount of fat.
       e.

A chicken _____ with skin on it has two times as much fat as a skinless one.
                f.

With 18 grams of fat, _____ has 13 more grams than _____
                     g.   **h.**

from the same animal.

Fat Grams per 3 1/2 Ounce Serving of Cooked Meat

10 grams   5 grams   2 grams   18 grams

8 grams   4 grams   20 grams   13 grams

49 grams   31 grams

10 grams   8 grams

Challenge Keep a record of the meat you (or another person) ate last week. Figure out the fat content.
Use the information in Exercise 2.

  See page 278 for listening practice.

1. **Look in your dictionary. *True* or *False*? Correct the underlined words in the false sentences.**

   a. The swordfish is ~~frozen~~ *fresh*.   _____*false*_____

   b. The cod is next to the <u>tuna</u>.   _____

   c. The <u>scallops</u> are to the right of the mussels.   _____

   d. Salami and pastrami are in the <u>deli</u> section.   _____

   e. The <u>wheat bread</u> is between the white bread and the rye bread.   _____

   f. The woman is reaching for the <u>mozzarella</u> cheese.   _____

   g. The Swiss cheese is between the cheddar and the <u>American</u> cheese.   _____

   h. There's a special price for the <u>whole salmon</u>.   _____

2. **Look at the seafood prices and the recipe cards. How much will the seafood for each recipe cost? (You can use page 75 in your dictionary for information about weights and measures.)**

   Note: doz. = dozen = 12 pieces   1 lb. = 1 pound, 2 lbs. = 2 pounds

a. **Linguine with clams** 36 fresh raw clams ____$23.97____	b. **New Orleans shrimp** 1 1/2 lbs. of medium shrimp _____	c. **Steamed mussels with orange** 6 lbs. of mussels _____
d. **Southern style crab cakes** 1 lb. fresh or frozen crab meat _____	e. **Trout with mushrooms** 2 lbs. whole trout _____	f. **Grilled salmon with corn** 4 salmon steaks 8 oz. each _____

3. **What about you? Work with a classmate. Order lunch from the deli.**

   Example: *I'll have a smoked turkey sandwich on wheat bread with mozzarella cheese. What about you?*

Challenge What other seafood and deli food do you know? Make a list.

See page 278 for listening practice.

1. **Look in your dictionary. Cross out the item that doesn't belong. Write the section of the store.**

   a. _Canned foods_ beans ~~frozen dinner~~ soup tuna

   b. _____ bagels bananas oranges tomatoes

   c. _____ ice cream margarine sour cream yogurt

   d. _____ apple juice coffee soda oil

   e. _____ bagels cake cookies nuts

   f. _____ candy bars nuts pop potato chips

   g. _____ flour oil pet food sugar

2. **Complete this article. Use the words in the box.**

aisles	basket	beans	bottle return	cart	cashier
cash register	checkstands	coffee	~~cookies~~	customer	line
manager	margarine	produce	scale	self-checkout	vegetables

SAVE TIME and MONEY
at the supermarket

■ Never shop when you're hungry. Those chocolate ___cookies___ will
   a.
be hard to resist on an empty stomach. You should also stay away
from _____ with snack foods!
  b.

■ Do you really need a large shopping _____ or is a smaller
       c.
shopping _____ enough? Having too much room may
    d.
encourage you to buy more than you need.

■ Be a smart _____. Shop with a list. That makes it easier to
     e.
buy only what you need.

- Keep a price book of items that you buy frequently. *Example*: If you drink a lot of _____, compare prices at different stores.
  f.

- Always check the unit price. *Example*: It may be cheaper to buy a large can of black _____ than a small can. Check: How much does it cost per pound?
  g.

- Do you need a pound of potatoes? Don't guess. Use the _____ and buy the exact amount.
  h.

- Watch for sales. Buy a lot of the items you need.

- Buy the store brand. *Example*: The supermarket brand of butter or _____ will probably cost less than the famous brands.
  i.

- If the _____ doesn't look fresh, buy frozen _____.
  j.   k.
  They'll look and taste better.

- Avoid standing in _____. Try to shop when the store is
  l.
  less crowded. If all of the _____ aren't open, speak to the
  m.
  store _____. Remember: Sometimes the _____
  n.   o.
  is faster.

- Always watch the _____ when the _____ is
  p.   q.
  ringing up your order. Is the price right? Mistakes can happen!

- Don't throw away those empty soda bottles! In some states, you can get a refund. Take them to the _____.
  r.

3. **What about you? Which of the shopping tips in Exercise 2 do you use? What other ways do you save money when you go food shopping? Write about them.**

Challenge Look at page 257 in this book. Follow the instructions.

See page 278 for listening practice.   73

1.   **Look in your dictionary. Complete the flyer.**

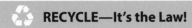 **RECYCLE—It's the Law!**

The packaging for many items on your grocery list belongs in your recycling bin, not your garbage can. Follow the recycling guidelines as you use these items.

YES

a. ✔ plastic or glass ___*bottles*___ (water)

b. ✔ plastic or glass _____ (jam)

c. ✔ metal _____ (soup)

d. ✔ cardboard _____ (cereal)

e. ✔ cardboard _____ (paper towels)

NO

f. ✖ plastic _____ (bread)

g. ✖ plastic _____ (yogurt)

h. ✖ cardboard _____ (milk)

i. ✖ plastic _____ (cookies)

j. ✖ plastic _____ (toothpaste)

Note: Recycling guidelines are different in different places.

2.   **Look at the groceries that Mee-Yon bought this week. Which items have packaging that she can recycle? Which items don't? Use information from Exercise 1. Make two lists. Use you own paper.**

Example: *She can recycle the packaging for the bottle of oil. She can't recycle the two loaves of bread.*

3.   **What about you? What can and can't you recycle in your community? Make two lists.**

Challenge Look in your dictionary. Write six sentences about other items that come in the same containers and packaging. **Example:** *Juice and vegetable oil also come in bottles.*

     See page 279 for listening practice.

1. Look at the charts in your dictionary. Circle the larger amount.

a. 3 teaspoons / (3 tablespoons)   d. 2 pints / 1 liter

b. 100 ml / 2 fluid ounces   e. 2 pounds / 36 ounces

c. 8 pints / 6 quarts   f. 5 quarts / 2 gallons

2. Look at the nutrition facts. Answer the questions. Use your dictionary for help.

Nutrition Facts
Kidney Beans – Serving Size 1/2 cup

Amount Per Serving	
Calories 110	Calories from Fat 0
Protein	8g
Carbohydrate	22g
	% Daily Value
Calcium	6%
Iron	10%

Nutrition Facts
Skim Milk – Serving Size 1 cup

Amount Per Serving	
Calories 90	Calories from Fat 0
Protein	8g
	% Daily Value
Calcium	30%
Vitamin D	25%

Nutrition Facts
Rice – Serving Size 1/4 cup raw (about 1 cup cooked)

Amount Per Serving	
Calories 170	Calories from Fat 0
Protein	4g
Carbohydrate	38g
	% Daily Value
Calcium	2%
Iron	8%

Nutrition Facts
Chocolate Candy – Serving Size 1 piece (1/2 oz.)

Amount Per Serving	
Calories 90	Calories from Fat 30
Total Fat	4g
Protein	1g

Note: % Daily Value = % of the total amount you should have in one day

a. Which has more protein, a cup of beans or a cup of milk? _____*a cup of beans*_____

b. How many pieces of chocolate candy are there in one pound? _____

c. How many pints of milk give 100% of the daily value of Vitamin D? _____

d. How much fat is there in three ounces of chocolate candy? _____

e. How many cups of milk do you need for 90% of the daily value of calcium? _____

f. What percent of the daily value of calcium do you get from a pint of milk and two servings of rice? _____

g. A serving of rice and beans contains a quarter cup of beans and a half cup of cooked rice. How much carbohydrate is there in a serving? _____

h. What percent of the daily value of iron is there in a serving of rice and beans? _____

Challenge Look at page 257 in this book. Follow the instructions.

See page 279 for listening practice.

1. **Look at page 76 in your dictionary. Then look at the pictures here. What does Laura do right? What does she do wrong? Check (✓) the correct box. Write sentences.**

	Right	Wrong	
a.	✓		She cleans the counters.
b.		✓	She doesn't
c.			
d.			
e.			

2. **Look at the chart. Complete the sentences.**

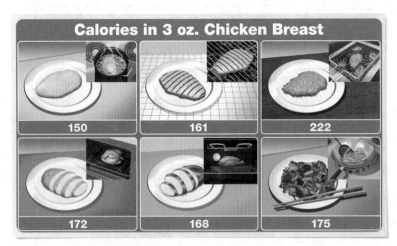

a. ___Roasted___ chicken has 172 calories.

b. _____ chicken has 11 more calories than boiled chicken.

c. _____ chicken has the most calories.

d. _____ chicken has the lowest number of calories.

e. With 168 calories, _____ chicken has 7 more calories than grilled chicken.

f. _____ chicken has 175 calories, but fewer calories than fried chicken.

3. Look in your dictionary. Circle the words to complete the cookbook definitions.

a. **beat** / stir: Make mixture smooth by quick motion with a spoon, fork, or whisk.

b. **boil** / saute: Cook in very hot liquid (212°F for water).

c. **peel** / **chop:** Cut into pieces with a knife.

d. **slice** / **dice:** Cut into very small pieces with a knife (smaller than chopping).

e. **grate** / **grease:** Cut into small pieces using small holes of a grater.

f. **mix** / **spoon:** Combine ingredients, usually with a spoon.

g. **grate** / **peel:** Take off the outer skin.

h. **saute** / **steam:** Cook in a small amount of hot butter or oil.

i. **boil** / **simmer:** Cook slowly in liquid just below the boiling point.

j. **preheat** / **steam:** Cook over boiling water, not in it.

4. Look at Paulo's recipe. It got wet, and now he can't read parts of it. Complete the recipe. Use the words in the box.

| add | bake | grease | microwave | mix | ~~preheat~~ | slice | spoon |

FISH

Baked cod in sour cream

1/2 pound cod   1/4 c. mayonnaise

1 TBS. butter   1 c. sour cream

salt and pepper   10 oz. mushrooms

    Preheat   the oven to 350°F. _____ a baking dish with a
       a.   b.

little butter. Place the fish in the dish, top with the rest of the butter.

_____ salt and pepper. _____ the mayonnaise and
   c.   d.

sour cream together and _____ it over the fish. _____
                    e.   f.

the mushrooms, and add them to the dish. _____ in the oven for
                                g.

45 minutes or _____ on high for about 7 minutes.
                h.

Servings: 2

Challenge Write one of your favorite recipes.

See page 279 for listening practice.

1. **Look in your dictionary. *True* or *False*? Change the underlined words to correct the false sentences.**

   cake
   a. There are two ~~pie~~ pans above the cookie sheets.   _false_

   b. There's a lid on the underlined casserole dish.   _____

   c. There's a roasting rack in the mixing bowl.   _____

   d. There's butter in the sauce pan.   _____

   e. There's a garlic press between the wooden spoon and the casserole dish.   _____

   f. One of the cooks is using the can opener.   _____

   g. One of the cooks is using the vegetable peeler.   _____

2. **Circle the words to complete the cookbook information.**

Some utensils you need in your kitchen

   a. **Grater / (Whisk):** to beat eggs, cream, etc.

   b. **Steamer / Colander:** to remove water from cooked pasta, vegetables, etc.

   c. **Ladle / Spatula:** to spoon soup, sauces, etc. out of a pot

   d. **Paring / Carving knife:** to cut up small fruits and vegetables

   e. **Lid / Tongs:** to cover pots and pans

   f. **Plastic storage container / Strainer:** to keep food fresh

   g. **Pot / Pot holders:** to handle hot utensils

   h. **Eggbeater / Wooden spoon:** to stir soups, sauces, etc.

   i. **Double boiler / Roasting rack:** to cook food slowly on top of the stove

   j. **Cake and pie pans / pots:** to bake desserts

Challenge Think of a recipe. Make a list of all the utensils you need for the recipe. What do you need each one for? **Example:** *I need a whisk to beat the eggs.*

 See page 280 for listening practice.

1. **Look in your dictionary. Cross out the word that doesn't belong.**

   a. cheeseburger ~~chicken sandwich~~ hamburger hot dog

   b. burrito ice-cream cone nachos taco

   c. iced tea milkshake soda mustard

   d. muffin onion rings ice-cream cone donut

2. **Look at the chart. *True* or *False*? Put a question mark (?) if the information isn't in the chart.**

Based on information from: Horovitz, B, "Restaurant sales climb with bad-for-you food," *USA Today*, May 12, 2005, http://www.usatoday.com/money/industries/food/2005-05-12-bad-food-cover_x.htm.

   a. Women order chicken sandwiches more than men.   _____true_____

   b. French fries are more popular among women than men.   _____

   c. Pizza is the third most popular food for both men and women.   _____

   d. Tacos are the fifth most popular food for men.   _____

   e. Women probably go to the salad bar more often than men.   _____

   f. Men eat more donuts than women.   _____

   g. Hot dogs are the most popular fast food for men and women.   _____

   h. Soda is more popular than iced tea for men and women.   _____

Challenge Take a survey of your classmates' top five fast foods.

See page 280 for listening practice.

1. **Look in your dictionary. What comes with . . . ?**

   a. sour cream and butter _____*baked potato*_____

   b. mashed potatoes _____

   c. rice _____

   d. raisins, milk, and brown sugar _____

   e. honey _____

   f. two slices of tomato _____

   g. a baked potato _____

   h. a pickle _____

   i. butter and syrup _____ and/or _____

   j. garlic bread _____ and _____

   k. lemon _____ and _____

   l. milk or cream _____ and _____

2. **Complete the conversation.**

   Anton: I'll have the steak and _____*potatoes*_____.

a.

   Server: Baked or mashed? Or maybe potato salad?

   Anton: Baked potato, please. And the steamed

   _____.

b.

   Server: Ok. Anything to start?

   Anton: I think I'd like a cup of

   _____ to begin with.

c.

   Server: We only have chicken noodle today. OK?

   Anton: Er, no. I'll have a small dinner _____ instead.

d.

   Oh, and bring me some garlic bread, please.

   Server: Very good. Would you like something for dessert?

   Anton: Do you have apple _____?

e.

   Server: Sorry, we don't.

   Anton: Well, then, I'll have the layer _____ and a cup of decaf

f.

   _____. Thank you.

g.

3. **Look at Exercise 2. Write the order.**

CARL'S Coffee Shop
──── ORDER FORM ────

steak

_____   _____

_____   _____

_____   _____

4. **Read the order in Exercise 3. Look at the food the server brought Anton. The server made six mistakes. Describe the mistakes.**

a. ___*The server gave him rolls, but he asked for garlic bread.*___

b. _____

c. _____

d. _____

e. _____

f. _____

5. **What about you? Look at the menu in your dictionary. What would you like? Write your order.**

CARL'S Coffee Shop
──── ORDER FORM ────

_____   _____

_____   _____

_____   _____

_____   _____

Challenge Imagine you own a coffee shop. Write your own dinner menu.

1. Look at the top picture on pages 82 and 83 in your dictionary. Who says . . . ?

a. "Your table is ready, Mr. and Mrs. Smith." ___hostess___

b. "Would you like asparagus or zucchini with that?" _____

c. "Here. Have some bread." _____

d. "We also have chocolate, coconut, and mango ice cream." _____

e. "The dishes are clean now." _____

f. "I'm coming through with some more dirty dishes!" _____

g. "I need to beat this a little more." _____

2. Circle the words to complete this restaurant review.

A.J. Clarke's 290 Park Place 555-3454

At Clarke's, you'll relax in the comfortable, green (dining room) / kitchen that can serve about
a.

50 chefs / diners. The hostess seated / served my guest and me in a quiet booth / high chair, and we got a
b.　　　　　　　　　**c.**　　　　　　　　　　　　　　　　**d.**

bread basket / soup bowl filled with fresh rolls. The service was great. The patron / server continued to
e.　　　　　　　　　　　　　　　　　　　　　　　　　　　　　　　　**f.**

pour / clear water throughout the meal.
g.

And what a meal it was! The check / menu had something for everyone. Our busser / server, Todd,
h.　　　　　　　　　　　　　　　　**i.**

recommended the fish of the day, tuna. My friend ordered / served the chicken l'orange. After Todd
j.

carried / took our orders, he brought us two salad plates / saucers with the freshest lettuce I've ever eaten. This was
k.　　　　　　　　　　　　　　　　　　**l.**

followed by two large bowls / plates of onion soup. Our main dishes did not disappoint us. The tuna was so tender
m.

that you could cut it without a steak knife / teaspoon. The chicken, too, was wonderful.
n.

When we were finished, the busser cleared the dishes / set the table. Time for dessert! Todd
o.

carried / left out the dessert fork / tray filled with cakes and pies—all baked in the restaurant's
p.　　　　　　　　**q.**

kitchen / dish room. Raspberry pie and a cup / saucer of delicious hot coffee ended our perfect meal. We
r.　　　　　　　　　　　　　　　　　　**s.**

happily paid / poured the check and left / took Todd a nice tip. My tip to you: Eat at A.J. Clarke's.
t.　　　　　　　　　　　**u.**

And don't forget to ask for a napkin / to-go box to take home the food you can't finish!
v.

Reservations recommended.

3. **Look at the picture. Complete the article.**

A Formal _Place Setting_
a.

A _____ is in the center, usually with
b.

the _____ on top of it. The utensils
c.

are on both sides. To the left of the plate are

(from closest to farthest) a _____ and a _____.
d.   e.

To the right of the plate are a _____, a _____, and
f.   g.

sometimes a shellfish _____. Above the plate is a water
h.

_____ and to the right are two _____. There is also a
i.   j.

small _____ above and to the left of the dinner plate. The butter
k.

_____ is on top of it.
l.

4. **What about you? Most people's table settings do not look like the formal one in Exercise 3. Draw your table setting. How is it the same as the table setting in Exercise 3? How is it different? Write sentences.**

Example: _We put the napkin under the fork._

_____

_____

_____

_____

_____

_____

_____

_____

Challenge Write a description of a meal you had at a restaurant or at someone's home.

Go to page 245 for Another Look (Unit 4). | **See page 281 for listening practice.**

1. **Look in your dictionary. *True* or *False*?**

   a. Two men are playing <u>football</u>.   *false*

   b. Cara's sells <u>organic vegetables</u>.   _____

   c. The <u>watermelons</u> are three for $3.00.   _____

   d. The herb vendor sells <u>flowers</u>, too.   _____

   e. A market worker is <u>weighing</u> eight avocados.   _____

   f. The children are tasting the <u>samples</u>.   _____

   g. Mr. Novak's father is drinking some <u>tea</u>.   _____

   h. The lemonade stand is across from the <u>hot food vendor</u>.   _____

2. **Write the letter of the false sentences in Exercise 1. Make them true.**

   a.   *Two men are playing live music.* _____

   ___   _____

   ___   _____

   ___   _____

   ___   _____

3. **Circle the words to complete the blog post.**

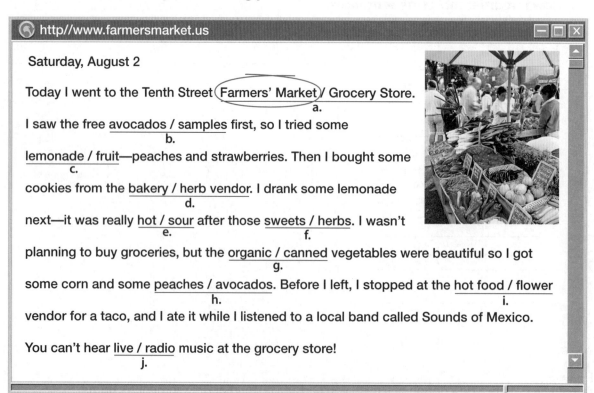

http//www.farmersmarket.us

Saturday, August 2

Today I went to the Tenth Street (Farmers' Market) / Grocery Store.
         a.

I saw the free <u>avocados / samples</u> first, so I tried some
         b.

<u>lemonade / fruit</u>—peaches and strawberries. Then I bought some
     c.

cookies from the <u>bakery / herb vendor</u>. I drank some lemonade
        d.

next—it was really <u>hot / sour</u> after those <u>sweets / herbs</u>. I wasn't
      e.   **f.**

planning to buy groceries, but the <u>organic / canned</u> vegetables were beautiful so I got
           g.

some corn and some <u>peaches / avocados</u>. Before I left, I stopped at the <u>hot food / flower</u>
        h.   **i.**

vendor for a taco, and I ate it while I listened to a local band called Sounds of Mexico.

You can't hear <u>live / radio</u> music at the grocery store!
     j.

4. **Look in your dictionary. What's at the farmers' market? Check (✓) the items.**

- ✓ live music
- ☐ frozen foods
- ☐ baked goods
- ☐ flowers
- ☐ vendors

- ☐ fruit
- ☐ pet food
- ☐ herbs
- ☐ bottle return
- ☐ samples

- ☐ organic vegetables
- ☐ soup
- ☐ beverages
- ☐ canned foods
- ☐ hot food

5. **Complete the flyer. Use words from the box.**

dill	samples	cucumbers	hot food	~~farmers' market~~	fruit
basil	lemonade	organic	live music	vegetables	sweets

Tenth Street <u>Farmers' Market</u>
a.

> _____—Sounds of Mexico and Fruity Tunes will play this week.
> b.
> Free _____—taste before you buy
> c.
> _____ food—chemical-free, grown nature's way
> d.
> _____—peaches and watermelons are here!
> e.
> _____—local corn and _____ , much fresher than the supermarket
> f.   g.
> Herbs—parsley, _____ , and _____
> h.   i.
> _____—tacos, falafel, burgers, and barbecue
> j.
> _____—fresh-baked cookies and cakes
> k.
> Beverages—herbal teas, _____ , and vegetable juices
> l.

JOIN US THIS WEEKEND

6. **What about you? Look in your dictionary. What do you like about the farmers' market? What do you like about a grocery store? Make a list for each.**

Farmers' market

_____fresh vegetables_____

_____

_____

_____

Grocery store

_____open all week and all year_____

_____

_____

_____

Challenge Work with a classmate. Make a flyer for a farmers' market. Use Exercise 5 as a model.

See page 281 for listening practice.

1. Look in your dictionary. Complete the diagram.

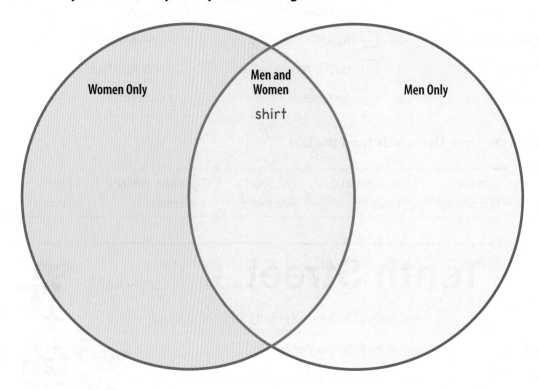

Women Only

Men and
Women

shirt

Men Only

2. Look in your dictionary. What can people wear . . . ?

a. under a sweater ____*shirt*____ _____ _____ _____

b. with a skirt _____ _____ _____ _____

c. on their feet _____ _____ _____

d. on their heads _____

3. What about you? Check (✓) the clothes you have. Where do you wear them?

Where?

☐ jeans ____*at home,*_____

☐ athletic shoes _____

☐ T-shirt _____

☐ suit _____

☐ sweater _____

☐ baseball cap _____

4. Look in your dictionary. Circle the words to complete the sentences.

    a. The man in the blue shirt is wearing (jeans) / slacks.

    b. The woman in the blue blouse has a handbag / sweater.

    c. The man at the ticket window is wearing a blue shirt / T-shirt.

    d. The woman in the yellow dress / white skirt is putting on a sweater.

    e. The girl with the handbag / baseball cap is tying her shoe.

    f. The girl in the athletic shoes / shoes is wearing socks.

    g. The man in jeans / the suit is looking at his watch.

5. Look in your dictionary. Complete the phrase *a pair of . . .*

    a. _____ *jeans* _____

    b. _____

    c. _____

    d. _____

    e. _____

6. What about you? What will you wear? Imagine you are going to . . . .
You can use your dictionary for help.

    a. a jazz concert   _____

    b. a job interview   _____

    c. the park   _____

    d. school   _____

    e. a Friday night party with your classmates   _____

    f. a family reunion   _____

    g. the grocery store   _____

Challenge Look at Exercise 1. Name two more pieces of clothes for . . .
You can use pages 86–91 in your dictionary for help.

Only Women   _____   _____

Women and Men   _____   _____

Only Men   _____   _____

See page 281 for listening practice.

1. Look in your dictionary. Who is . . . ?

a. wearing sandals   *the woman in capris*

b. carrying a briefcase _____

c. wearing a bow tie _____

d. talking to the man in the tank top _____

e. wearing a pullover sweater _____

f. wearing high heels _____

g. talking on the phone _____

h. helping a woman with her luggage _____

i. sitting on the couch _____

j. sitting on the floor _____

2. Circle the words to complete the advice column.

Clothes Encounters

Q I'm looking for a job as an office manager.

What should I wear on interviews?

A You can't go wrong with a dark blue
~~business suit~~ / tuxedo. Wear it with
      a.
a white shirt and <u>bow tie / tie</u>. Then
        b.
just grab your <u>briefcase / clutch bag</u>
        c.
and you're good to go! After you get

the job, you can change to a

<u>sports jacket / vest</u>. Wear it with
      d.
<u>shorts / a sports shirt</u> or a
     e.
<u>cardigan / pullover</u> sweater for a neat look.
    f.

Q I'm going on a business trip to Florida. Can you suggest something casual to wear between meetings? I don't want to wear jeans, but I want to feel comfortable.

A After work, relax in a pair of
<u>capris /sweatpants</u>, a T-shirt, and
     g.
<u>high heels / sandals</u>. You'll feel very
     h.
comfortable and look great. If it gets

cool, put on a <u>knit top / tank top</u>.
              i.

Q My husband and I got invited to a wedding. The invitation says "Black tie."

What does that mean?

A For men, "black tie" means a <u>tuxedo / uniform</u>, and usually a <u>bow tie / tank top</u>.
                        j.   k.
Many men don't own these items, but they can rent them! For women, black tie

can mean either <u>a cocktail dress / sweatpants</u> or <u>an evening gown / overalls</u>.
                 l.   m.
Complete the outfit with <u>high heels / sandals</u> and have fun!
                       n.

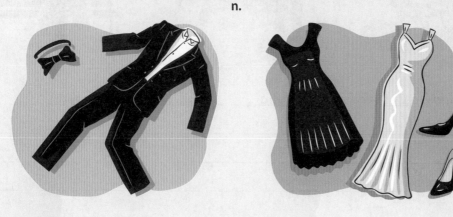

3. **What about you? What do you think are the most important items of clothing to have? Where do you wear these clothes?**

Example: *a sports shirt—I wear it at work, at school, and at home.*

Challenge Choose five people from your dictionary. Describe their clothes.

Example: *On page 73 the woman near the snacks is wearing a black skirt, a purple pullover sweater, and black high heels.*

See page 282 for listening practice.

1. **Look in your dictionary. Cross out the word that doesn't belong.**
Write the weather condition.

a. _Windy_	overcoat	~~cover-up~~	winter scarf	jacket
b. _____	poncho	rain boots	umbrella	ski hat
c. _____	straw hat	swimsuit	parka	sunglasses
d. _____	down jacket	leggings	ski mask	windbreaker

2. **Correct the ad.**

It's windy out there, but Jillian is dressed for the weather in a warm, brown
                  jacket
leather ~~parka~~, bright red earmuffs, and a red and yellow headband.

That straw hat protects her from the autumn wind.

Jillian

3. **Write ads for Abdulla, Polly, and Julio's clothing. Use Exercise 2 as an example.**

Abdulla   Polly   Julio

a. _It's sunny out there, but Abdulla_ _____

_____

b. _____

_____

_____

c. _____

_____

_____

Challenge What do you like to wear in different weather conditions? Write short paragraphs like the
ones in Exercise 3.

            See page 282 for listening practice.

1. **Look in your dictionary. Find the words that complete *a pair of*...**

   long underwear _____ _____ _____

   _____ _____ _____ _____

   _____ _____ _____ _____

   _____ _____ _____ _____

2. **Put the items in the correct list.**

Mom	Dad	Amy	Brian
bikini panties			

Challenge You're going on a trip next weekend. List the underwear and sleepwear you'll take.

See page 282 for listening practice. 91

1. **Look in your dictionary. What is it?**

   a. It protects his clothes when he cooks.   *chef's jacket*

   b. It has her name on it.   _____

   c. He keeps his hammer in it.   _____

   d. He wears it with his blazer.   _____

   e. It's blue and he wears his badge on it.   _____

   f. It helps him breathe.   _____

2. **Circle the words to complete the article.**

Dressing for Safety

Part of a job is wearing the right clothes. A manager wants to look good in

a (blazer) / work shirt and smock / tie. But many workers need to dress for safety, too.
　　a.　　　　　　　　　b.
Here are some examples—from head to toe.

★ **Protect your head.** Construction workers need hairnets / hard hats to protect
　　　　　　　　　　　　　　　　　　　　　　　　　　　c.
themselves from falling objects.

★ **Protect your face.** A medical technician needs a surgical gown / face mask to
　　　　　　　　　　　　　　　　　　　　　　　　　　　d.
avoid breathing in dangerous substances.

★ **Protect your eyes.** You only have two. That's the reason why many jobs

require special safety glasses / ventilation masks.
　　　　　　　　　　　　e.

★ **Protect your body.** Working on the road? Cars need to see you. That's why

road workers need to wear Hi-Visibility waist aprons / safety vests.
　　　　　　　　　　　　　　　　　　　　　　f.

★ **Protect your feet.** Things can fall on your feet, too. That's why road workers,

construction workers, and other workers wear coveralls / steel toe boots.
　　　　　　　　　　　　　　　　　　　　　　g.

Many workers need to protect *other* people, too. A surgeon, for example, needs a

helmet / scrub cap and a surgical mask / smock to protect patients from germs.
　　h.　　　　　　　　　　i.

*Wearing the right clothes at the right time can help make the workplace a
safe place.*

3. **Look in your dictionary. Cross out the word that doesn't belong. Give a reason.**

a. cowboy hat   bump cap   bandana   ~~badge~~

     You don't wear a badge on your head.

b. safety glasses   ventilation mask   blazer   surgical mask

_____

c. work pants   jeans   lab coat   security pants

_____

d. polo shirt   smock   apron   waist apron

_____

4. **Look at the pictures. What are the problems? Write sentences.**

a.

     He isn't wearing a hard hat.

     He isn't wearing steel toe boots.

b.

_____

_____

c.

_____

_____

d.

_____

_____

5. **What about you? Look in your dictionary. What workplace clothing do you have? When do you wear this clothing?**
   Example: *I wear an apron when I cook.*

Challenge Look at pages 166–169 in your dictionary. Find three jobs. What work clothing do people wear? **Example:** *A dental assistant wears a face mask and latex gloves.*

1. Look in your dictionary. Read the sentences. What are the people talking about?

a. "I always keep my coins in <u>one</u>—separate from my bills."   *change purse*

b. "According to this <u>one</u>, it's 3:00."   _____

c. "Wow! <u>This</u> has even more room than the backpack!"   _____

d. "Ow, my finger! <u>This</u> is pretty, but it's sharp!"   _____

e. "John gave <u>one</u> to me. I put his photo in it."   _____

f. "Oh, no. I forgot to put my credit card back in <u>it</u>."   _____

g. "<u>It</u>'s a little too big for my finger."   _____

2. Look at the ad. Complete the sentences.

Black ____*belt*____ ,
a.
silver _____ , and
b.
black leather _____
c.

White _____
d.

ER
JEWELERS

Gold _____ ,
e.
pierced _____ ,
f.
and _____ for her hand
g.

The Bag House

Red _____
h.

YOUR ONE STOP FOR
FALL FASHIONS

3. Look at the shopping list. Where can you buy these items? Use the stores from Exercise 2.

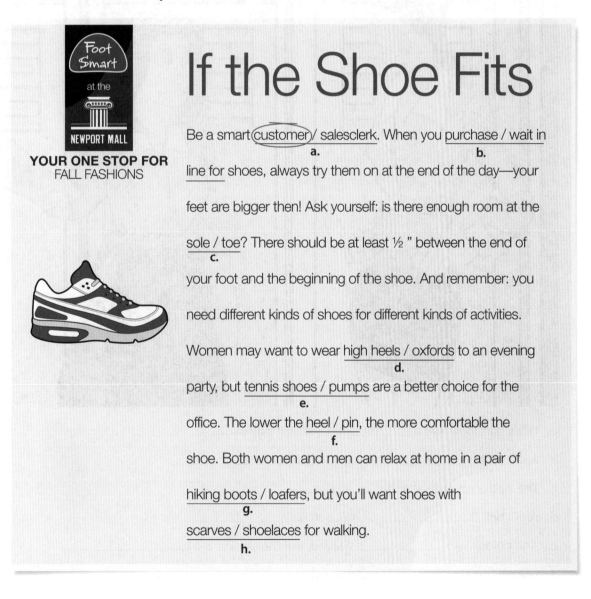

YOUR ONE STOP FOR
FALL FASHIONS

brown purse _____ The Bag House _____

gold bracelet _____

backpack _____

string of pearls _____

black flats _____

4. Circle the words to complete the information from a shoe store.

Foot Smart at the

NEWPORT MALL

YOUR ONE STOP FOR
FALL FASHIONS

If the Shoe Fits

Be a smart (customer) / salesclerk. When you purchase / wait in
   a.   **b.**

line for shoes, always try them on at the end of the day—your

feet are bigger then! Ask yourself: is there enough room at the

sole / toe? There should be at least ½ " between the end of
  c.

your foot and the beginning of the shoe. And remember: you

need different kinds of shoes for different kinds of activities.

Women may want to wear high heels / oxfords to an evening
                                    d.

party, but tennis shoes / pumps are a better choice for the
                  e.

office. The lower the heel / pin, the more comfortable the
                       f.

shoe. Both women and men can relax at home in a pair of

hiking boots / loafers, but you'll want shoes with
      g.

scarves / shoelaces for walking.
      h.

Challenge Which accessories make good gifts? Explain who you would buy them for and why.
Example: *I'd buy a backpack for my girlfriend because she loves to hike.*

1. **Look in your dictionary. Cross out the word that doesn't belong. Write the category.**

a. _Sweater styles_   V-neck   crewneck   ~~wide~~   turtleneck

b. _____   light   print   paisley   floral

c. _____   large   medium   small   too small

d. _____   ripped   sleeveless   unraveling   too big

2. **Look at the pictures. Complete the sentences.**

Lisa   Ana

a. Lisa's skirt looks like a _____ _mini_ _____ -skirt. It's also too _____ .

b. Ana's skirt is _____-length. It's too _____ .

c. The zipper on Ana's skirt is _____ .

d. Ana's belt is _____ . Lisa's belt is _____ .

e. Ana's blouse is _____-sleeved, but the sleeves are too _____ .

f. Lisa's blouse is _____-sleeved too, but the sleeves are too _____ .

g. Lisa's blouse is _____ .

h. Both women are unhappy with the clothes. And at $500, they are much too _____ !

3. Look at the pictures. Circle the words to complete the article.

Suitable Dressing

1500s

1700s

after 1789

end of 1800s

Men's formal business suits never seem to change very much these days. However, it took a long time for men to get to this basic piece of clothing.

During the 1500s in Europe, fashionable men wanted to look fat. Their pants were short / long and baggy / tight. They wore short / long, light / heavy jackets that were
a.   b.   c.   d.
sleeveless / long-sleeved, and they even stuffed their clothes to look bigger!
e.

In the 1700s, men preferred to look thinner and taller. The rich and stylish wore their pants shorter / longer and very tight / baggy, and they wore shoes with low / high heels.
f.   g.   h.
Jackets became longer / shorter and looser / tighter, and men wore fancy / plain shirts
i.   j.   k.
under them. After the French Revolution in 1789, it became dangerous to dress like the rich. Instead, many men dressed like workers in long / short pants and loose jackets.
l.
This outfit was a lot like the modern suit, but the parts did not match. The man in the picture, for example, is wearing striped / checked brown pants with a fancy
m.
polka-dotted / paisley vest and a solid / plaid green jacket.
n.   o.

Finally, at the end of the 1800s, it became stylish to match the pants, jacket, and vest.

As you can see, today's business suit has not changed much since then.

Challenge Describe traditional clothing for men or women from a culture you know well.
Example: *In Oman, women wear long, baggy pants. The weather is very hot, so clothing is usually light.*

See page 284 for listening practice.

Making Clothes

1. Look in your dictionary. Cross out the word that doesn't belong. Write the category.

a. <u>Parts of a sewing machine</u>   needle   bobbin   ~~velvet~~   feed dog

b. _____   wool   pattern   leather   linen

c. _____   fringe   zipper   snap   hook and eye

d. _____   beads   sequins   appliqué   buckle

2. Write the name of the material.

a.    b.    c.    d.

a. <u>linen</u> This was the first woven material. Ancient people learned how to make thread from the blue-flowered flax plant and weave it into cloth. Today it is often used to make light jackets and suits.

c. _____ This material is made from the hair of sheep and some other animals. It is soft, warm, and even waterproof! It is often used to make coats, sweaters, mittens, and scarves.

b. _____ Very early, people learned how to make animal skins into this strong material. They rubbed the skins with fat to make them soft. Today it is often used to make shoes, boots, jackets, coats, belts, purses, and briefcases.

d. _____ For thousands of years only the Chinese knew how to make clothing from this beautiful material. The thread is made from the eggs of worms. The fabric is often used to make underwear, blouses, and ties.

3. Circle the words to complete the conversation in a fabric store.

Isabel: I'm making a blouse for my daughter.

Kim: What type of material are you thinking of?

Isabel: (Lace) / Thread or maybe <u>cotton</u> / ribbon. I'm not sure yet.
    a.   **b.**

Kim: OK. What kind of <u>fabric</u> / closure are you going to use?
    c.

Isabel: <u>Buttons</u> / Beads.
    d.

Kim: Do you need a <u>rack</u> / pattern?
    e.

Isabel: No. I always like to design clothes myself.

Kim: Really? That's great. Do you use a <u>sewing machine</u> / bobbin?
    f.

Isabel: No. I don't have one. I sew by <u>hand</u> / machine. All I need is a needle and <u>thread</u> / feed dog!
    g.   **h.**

98

4. **Look in your dictionary. *True* or *False*? Correct the underlined words in the false sentences.**

   a. The sewing machine operators are sewing by ~~hand~~. _machine_   _false_

   b. There are seven <u>bolts of fabric</u> in the garment factory.   _____

   c. The shirts on the <u>rack</u> in the garment factory are purple, green, and blue.   _____

   d. The <u>bobbin</u> is above the presser foot.   _____

   e. The women in the fabric store are looking at <u>hook and loop fasteners</u>.   _____

5. **Write the name of the material.**

   a.    b. 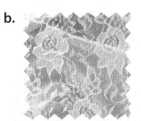   c. 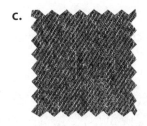   d.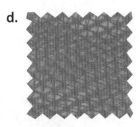

   a. ___corduroy___ This material is made from cotton. It can have a wide or narrow pattern of raised ridges (vertical lines). It is often used to make jackets and pants.

   c. _____ This strong material is usually made from cotton. In the 1800s, clothing maker Levi Strauss used it to make the first pair of blue jeans. Today this very popular material is worn all over the world, especially by young people.

   b. _____ This material is usually made from linen thread. It has a beautiful open design, often of flowers or leaves. It is often sewn by hand, but it can also be made by machine. It is used for blouses, dresses, curtains, and tablecloths.

   d. _____ This material comes from the chemistry laboratory, not from a plant or animal. It is very strong, and it is used to make stockings, panty hose, windbreakers, and many other items of clothing.

6. **What about you? What are you wearing today? Complete the chart.**

Clothing Item	Material	Type of Closure	Type of Trim

Challenge Design a piece of clothing. Draw it and write a description.

See page 284 for listening practice.

1. Look in your dictionary. What can you use to . . . ?

a. repair a rip when you don't have needle and thread   *safety pin*

b. cut material   _____

c. hold pins and needles   _____

d. remove threads from a hem   _____

e. measure a sleeve or waistband   _____

f. protect your finger when you sew   _____

g. put clothes on while you make alterations   _____

2. Circle the words to complete the instructions to the tailor.

> **TAILOR MADE**
>
> Please make these alterations:
>
> Take in the collar / (waistband).
>   **a.**
>
> Shorten / Lengthen the sleeves.
>   **b.**
>
> The right cuff / pocket is
>   **c.**
> missing—please sew it on.
>
> Let out / Take in the skirt
>   **d.**
> and lengthen / shorten it
>   **e.**
> so it's right at the knee.

Challenge Look at the sewing supplies in your dictionary. Choose five and write their functions.
         Example: *A thimble protects your finger.*

  See page 284 for listening practice.

1. **Look in your dictionary. What do you need to . . . ?**

a. make clothes softer _____fabric softener_____

b. iron the clothes _____ and _____

c. sort the laundry _____

d. make clothes whiter _____

e. dry wet clothes without a dryer _____ and _____

f. dry wet clothes quickly _____

g. hang up clean clothes in your closet _____

2. **Circle the words to complete the laundry room instructions.**

CLEANMACH   **QUICK WASH**

WASHING INSTRUCTIONS	**DRYING INSTRUCTIONS**

WASHING INSTRUCTIONS

1. Pour (laundry detergent)/ spray starch
   a.
   into the washer / dryer.
   b.

2. Load / Sort the machine. DO NOT
   c.
   OVERLOAD.

3. Choose the correct temperature.

4. Close door. Hanger / Washer will not
   d.
   operate with door open.

5. Insert coins or payment card into slot.

6. To add bleach / dryer sheets: wait until
   e.
   laundry basket / washer has filled.
   f.

7. When the rinse light goes on, add
   fabric softener / laundry detergent if
   g.
   you want.

DRYING INSTRUCTIONS

1. Clean the iron / lint trap before
   h.
   using the dryer.

2. Load / Unload the machine. DO NOT
   i.
   OVERLOAD. Overloading causes
   dirty / wrinkled clothes.
   j.

3. Add dryer sheets / clothespins
   k.
   if you want.

4. Close door. Dryer / Washer will not
   l.
   operate with door open.

5. Choose the correct temperature.

6. Insert coins or payment card into slot.
   Push *start* button.

For service, call (800) 000-WASH

Challenge Look at some of your clothing labels. Write the laundry instructions.

See page 285 for listening practice.

A Garage Sale

1. **Look in your dictionary. *True* or *False*? Correct the underlined words in the false sentences.**

   a. There's a flyer on the ~~folding card table~~. _____false_____
      tree

   b. A woman is browsing near the garage. _____

   c. A blue sticker means the price is $2.00. _____

   d. They have new clothing for sale. _____

   e. A woman is bargaining for a VCR. _____

2. **Complete the chart of items for sale at a garage sale.** ▪ = $10.00, ▪ = $5.00, ▪ = $2.00,

Type of Item	Item	Price
Electronics	VCR	$10.00
Furniture		$5.00
	jacket	
Accessories	hat	
		$2.00

3. **Circle the words to complete the conversations. Use information from Exercise 2.**

   Donna: Hi. How much is this blue jacket / (sweatshirt)?
                                                  a.

   Eddy: It's $2.00 / $5.00.
               b.

   Donna: But look, it's stained / torn.
                         c.

   Alya: Do you need a folding chair / table? This one's only $5.00.
                                   d.

   Chen: Why don't you bargain / browse a little? They might take $2.00 for it.
                             e.

   Paz: What does the green sticker / flyer mean?
                             f.

   Lia: It means the price is $10.00 / $5.00.
                           g.

   Paz: That seems expensive for a clock radio / VCR. Most people use DVD players now.
                                     h.

4. **What about you? Work with a partner. Imagine you are at a garage sale. Bargain for some of the items. Talk about the items in Exercise 2 or in your dictionary.**

5. **Look in your dictionary. Write the total for each group.**

They bought . . .

They paid . . . .

a. an ironing board and a pair of cowboy boots $10.00

b. a pair of black shoes, two purses, and a pair of jeans   _____

c. an iron, a gray coat, and a sports jacket   _____

d. a pair of athletic shoes, a pink robe, and a purse   _____

e. a hard hat, a pair of brown shoes, a blue T-shirt, and a cassette player _____

6. **Complete the article. Use the words in the box.**

browse	clock radio	folding chair	used clothing	~~garage sale~~
bargain	stickers	flyers	folding card table	VCR

TIPS FOR A SUCCESSFUL ___Garage Sale___
a.

1 Find things to sell. You have a new alarm clock, so you don't need that old

_____ anymore. You watch DVDs, so why keep that old
b.

_____?
c.

2 Show the date, time, and address on your _____ .
d.

3 Give information about sizes of _____ —for example, size
e.

10 women's dresses.

4 Set up your _____ and _____ early. People will arrive
f.   g.

before the sale starts.

5 Use colored _____ for prices. It's easier than price tags.
h.

6 Let people just look around and _____ , but also ask them what they
i.

are looking for.

7 People love to _____ , so don't insist on the full price. You want the
j.

money more than that old pair of shoes—that's why you're having the garage

sale, right?

Challenge Work with a group. Plan a garage sale for your class. Look at pages 53–56 and 86–87 in your dictionary. Choose items to sell and decide on the prices. How will you use the money?

See page 285 for listening practice. **103**

1. Look in your dictionary. Complete the definitions.

a. We use them to touch, to pick things up, and to type. _____fingers_____

b. We use them to hear. _____

c. We use them to see. _____

d. We use it to breathe and to smell. _____

e. It connects our head to our shoulders. _____

f. They are at the end of our feet. They help us walk. _____

g. It's the front part of our body, below the neck. _____

h. We use it to eat and to speak. _____

i. We have more than 100,000 of them on our head! They help keep our bodies warm. _____

2. Complete. Read these as: "Hand is to finger as foot is to toe."

a. hand : finger = foot : _____toe_____

b. leg : foot = arm : _____

c. hear : ears = see : _____

d. taste : tongue = smell : _____

e. pants : legs = shoes : _____

3. What about you? What clothes or accessories do you use for these parts of your body?
Example: *scarf, . . .*

a. neck _____

b. head _____

c. eyes _____

d. ears _____

e. hands _____

f. legs _____

g. back _____

h. feet _____

4. Look in your dictionary. *True* or *False*?

a. The man sitting on the park bench has his left leg crossed over his right leg. _____true_____

b. The man with the book is holding binoculars in his right hand. _____

c. The woman running has red hair. _____

d. The boy's arms are in front of him. _____

e. The boy isn't wearing anything on his feet. _____

5. Circle the words to complete the article.

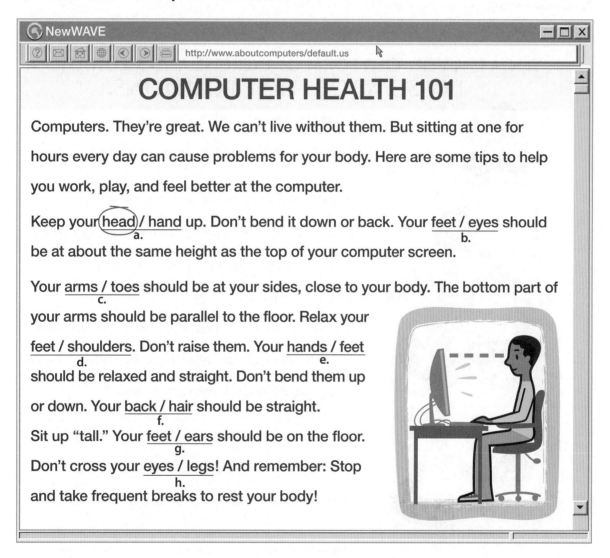

COMPUTER HEALTH 101

Computers. They're great. We can't live without them. But sitting at one for hours every day can cause problems for your body. Here are some tips to help you work, play, and feel better at the computer.

Keep your (head) / hand up. Don't bend it down or back. Your feet / eyes should
   a.   b.
be at about the same height as the top of your computer screen.

Your arms / toes should be at your sides, close to your body. The bottom part of
   c.
your arms should be parallel to the floor. Relax your feet / shoulders. Don't raise them. Your hands / feet
   d.   e.
should be relaxed and straight. Don't bend them up or down. Your back / hair should be straight.
   f.
Sit up "tall." Your feet / ears should be on the floor.
   g.
Don't cross your eyes / legs! And remember: Stop
   h.
and take frequent breaks to rest your body!

Challenge Which type of doctor should you see for problems with your . . . ?

feet _____

eyes _____

ears _____

Look online or ask someone you know.

See page 285 for listening practice.

1. Look in your dictionary. Cross out the word that doesn't belong. Write the category.

a. _The Arm, Hand, and Fingers_   elbow   ~~shin~~   wrist

b. _____   ankle   heel   knuckle

c. _____   finger   see   hear

d. _____   gums   teeth   forehead

2. Circle the words to complete the instructions.

YOGA IS A VERY OLD FORM OF EXERCISE AND MEDITATION.
TRY SOME OF THESE POSITIONS.

PALMING Rub your (palms) / gums together until your
a.
hands feel warm. Then hold them over your mouth / eyes.
  b.

BEE BREATH Place your hands / legs gently on your
  c.
knees / face: thumbs / teeth on your ears, first finger / knuckle
d.   **e.**   **f.**
on your eyelashes / eyebrows of your closed eyes, second on
  g.
your nose, third and fourth on your top and bottom

lips / eyelids. When you breathe out, gently close your ears
h.
with your thumbs and put your tongue / bone against the top
  i.
of your throat / mouth to make a "zzzz" sound.
  j.

THE BOW Lie on your abdomen / artery. Reach back and
  k.
hold your shins / ankles. Pull your thighs / elbows and
  l.   **m.**
chest / buttocks off the floor. Your lip / pelvis is on the floor.
n.   **o.**

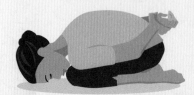

THE MOON Kneel with your buttocks / rib cage on your
  p.
arms / heels. Put your hands / feet against your
q.   **r.**
breast / lower back and hold your right wrist / vein. Bend
s.   **t.**
forward until your chin / forehead touches the floor.
  u.

3. Read the article. Label the foot with the matching parts of the body.

Some people use reflexology to stay healthy. They believe that by pressing certain parts of the foot, you can help certain parts of the body. For example, if you have a headache, you should press the top of your big toe.

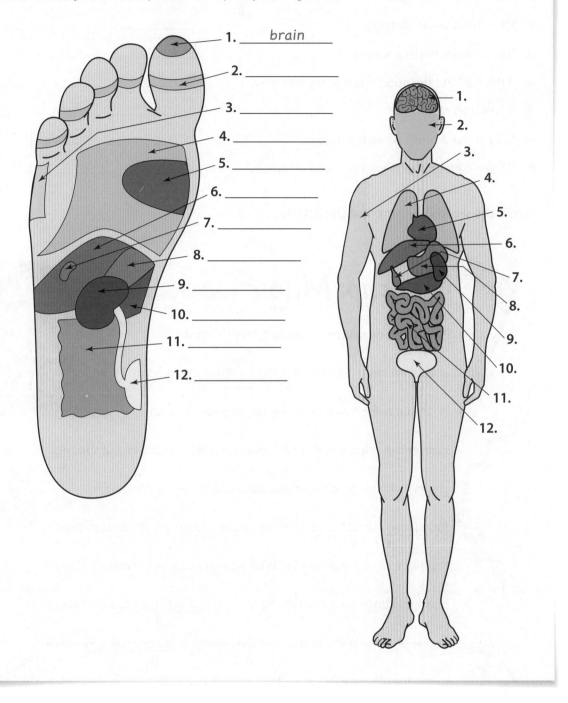

1. ___brain___
2. _____
3. _____
4. _____
5. _____
6. _____
7. _____
8. _____
9. _____
10. _____
11. _____
12. _____

4. What about you? What do you do to relax and stay healthy? What parts of the body are these activities good for? Write at least five sentences.

Challenge Write instructions for your favorite exercise.

See page 286 for listening practice.

1. **Look in your dictionary. What is each person doing?**

   a. "This air is really hot."   _drying her hair_

   b. "This cap really keeps my hair dry!"   _____

   c. "This mouthwash tastes great."   _____

   d. "I don't want to get a sunburn."   _____

   e. "I think all the shampoo is out of my hair now."   _____

   f. "I prefer a razor."   _____

   g. "I don't use a brush when it's still wet."   _____

   h. "I'll use pink on my nails after I get the red off."   _____

2. **Circle the words to complete the article.**

Makeup Magic By Magali Silveira

Putting on makeup takes time, but it's worth it for a

special evening. Here's how: Use (hair clips) / shampoo to
              a.

hold your hair off your face. Then wash your face with a

gentle soap / deodorant. While your skin is still a little wet, put shaving
      b.   **c.**

cream / moisturizer on your face and neck. When it's dry, put on

foundation / conditioner. Next, apply aftershave / eye shadow, starting at
      d.   **e.**

the inside corner of the eyelid. With a comb / an eyeliner make a smooth
                                 f.

line right above the eyelashes. Next, apply hair gel / mascara to make
                                  g.

your eyelashes look long and thick, and eyebrow pencil / hair spray to fill
                                  h.

in the line of your eyebrows. Outline your lips and then fill in the lines

with lipstick / toothpaste. Finish off with a dusting of bath / face powder,
     i.   **j.**

and you're ready to face the world!

3. **Complete the crossword puzzle. Each clue is two words.**

(crossword grid with filled letters: 1 Down spelling S-h-a-v-e-r vertically; 12 Across spelling E-l-e-c-t-r-i-c)

Clues

12 Across + 1 Down	You don't need water when you shave with it.
2 Down + 19 Down	It holds your hair in place.
3 Across + 10 Down	Use it after every meal.
5 Down + 6 Across	Be careful when you shave with them—they're sharp.
8 Across + 18 Across	Color your fingernails and toenails with it.
9 Across + 4 Down	It will make your eyes look bigger.
11 Across + 7 Down	Put it on your skin when you're finished shaving.
10 Across + 13 Down	It makes your skin feel smooth and soft.
14 Down + 21 Across	Style your hair with it.
16 Across and 20 Across	Use it outside to protect your skin from a burn.
17 Across + 15 Down	Remove food from between your teeth with it.

Now use the circled letters to answer this question:

What can you take to relax? ___ ___ ___ ___ ___ ___ ___ ___

4. **What about you? What is your personal hygiene routine in the morning? List the steps.**

Example: *First, I . . .*

Challenge Write detailed instructions for one of the following tasks:

Washing and styling your hair   Flossing and brushing your teeth
Shaving   Doing your nails

See page 286 for listening practice.

1. Look in your dictionary. Which symptom or injury are they talking about?

a. "This one in the back hurts." _____toothache_____

b. "The thermometer says 101." _____

c. "I ate too much ice cream." _____

d. "Next time I'll wear gloves to rake the leaves." _____

e. "Press on it to stop the bleeding." _____

2. Circle the words to complete the article.

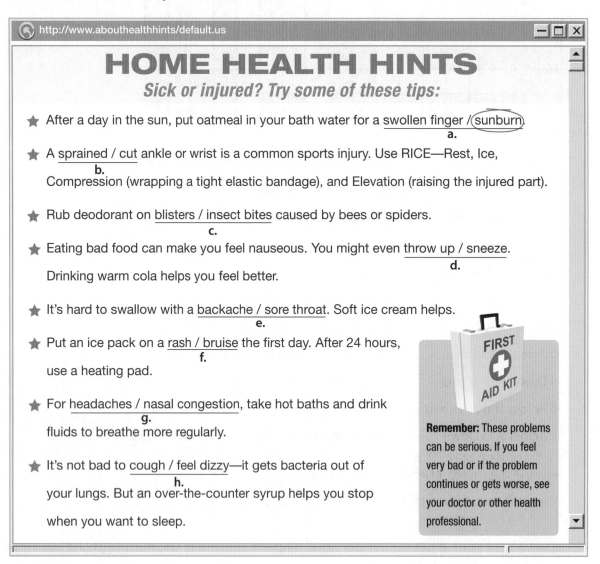

http://www.abouthealthhints/default.us

HOME HEALTH HINTS
Sick or injured? Try some of these tips:

★ After a day in the sun, put oatmeal in your bath water for a swollen finger / (sunburn).
a.

★ A sprained / cut ankle or wrist is a common sports injury. Use RICE—Rest, Ice,
b.
Compression (wrapping a tight elastic bandage), and Elevation (raising the injured part).

★ Rub deodorant on blisters / insect bites caused by bees or spiders.
c.

★ Eating bad food can make you feel nauseous. You might even throw up / sneeze.
d.
Drinking warm cola helps you feel better.

★ It's hard to swallow with a backache / sore throat. Soft ice cream helps.
e.

★ Put an ice pack on a rash / bruise the first day. After 24 hours,
f.
use a heating pad.

★ For headaches / nasal congestion, take hot baths and drink
g.
fluids to breathe more regularly.

★ It's not bad to cough / feel dizzy—it gets bacteria out of
h.
your lungs. But an over-the-counter syrup helps you stop
when you want to sleep.

FIRST AID KIT

Remember: These problems can be serious. If you feel very bad or if the problem continues or gets worse, see your doctor or other health professional.

3. What about you? What do you do when you have a stomachache? an earache? a rash?
Example: *When I have a stomachache, I drink tea.*

Challenge Find out about blisters. What are they? Write about how to prevent and treat them.

  See page 286 for listening practice.

1. **Look in your dictionary. Complete the chart.**

Illness or Condition	What is it?	Contagious?	What are some symptoms?
a. arthritis	A disease of the joints	No	painful, swollen, stiff joints, often in hands, feet, shoulders, and hips
b.	A medical condition	No	tight feeling or pain in chest, difficulty breathing, wheezing, coughing
c.	A common childhood disease	Yes	red, itchy rash on face, body, and inside throat that turns into blisters; fever
d.	A very common infection of the nose, throat, etc.	Yes	runny or stuffy nose, itchy or sore throat, cough, sneezing, low fever, tiredness, watery eyes
e.	A disease of the brain, more common in older people	No	confusion, problems with memory, language, and thinking; personality changes
f.	A condition caused by the pancreas not making enough insulin	No	tiredness, thirst, increased hunger, weight loss, blurred vision
g.	an infection most common in infants and children	No	nervousness, earache, "full" feeling in the ear, fever, difficulty hearing
h.	a condition often caused by hard and narrow arteries	No	(Often no symptoms in beginning) Later: chest pains, heart attack
i.	the virus that causes AIDS	Yes	(In the beginning) swollen glands, sore throat, fever, skin rash
j.	a common childhood disease	Yes	fever, dry cough, runny nose, red eyes, tiny spots inside mouth, red rash on forehead and around ears, and, later, whole body
k.	a childhood disease	Yes	painful, swollen glands (between ear and jaw) on one or both sides of face, fever, tiredness

Based on information from: Mayoclinic.com (1998–2007 Mayo Foundation for Medical Education and Research).

2. **What about you? Check (✓) the illnesses or medical conditions you had as a child.**

☐ measles   ☐ mumps   ☐ chicken pox   ☐ ear infection   ☐ allergy

Challenge Find out about high blood pressure. What is it? Is it contagious? What are some symptoms?

1. **Look in your dictionary. What should the people buy at the pharmacy? Circle the answers.**

   a. "I need to keep my arm still."   Buy a cast /(a sling.)

   b. "I have a backache."   Try a heating pad / a humidifier.

   c. "I have a sore throat."   Get an antacid / throat lozenges.

   d. "My nose is stuffed."   Try an inhaler / nasal spray.

   e. "I'm coughing and sneezing a lot."   Buy cold tablets / eye drops.

   f. "I have a bad headache."   Get an air purifier / a pain reliever.

2. **Read the prescription labels. Write the type of medicine after each sentence. Use the words in the box.**

capsules	cough syrup	ointment

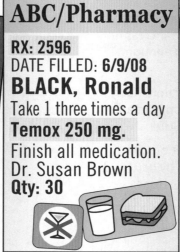

   Indications: Use on insect bites and rashes caused by poison ivy or poison oak.

   Directions: Apply a small amount of Corticurall 1 to 3 times a day.

   WARNING: FOR EXTERNAL USE ONLY

   CORTICURALL

   ABC/Pharmacy
   RX: 2596
   DATE FILLED: 6/9/08
   BLACK, Ronald
   Take 1 three times a day
   Temox 250 mg.
   Finish all medication.
   Dr. Susan Brown
   Qty: 30

   BCD Pharmacy
   RX: 789
   Date filled: 1/2/06
   Charnov, Rudy
   Take 2 tsp. by mouth
   Polyriscine CS
   every 4 hours

   Dr. Paul Rime
   Exp. 12/31/07
   Amount: 120 ml.

   a. You can use this three times a day. ___*ointment*___

   b. It's a liquid. _____

   c. The dosage is one, three times a day. _____

   d. This is an over-the-counter medication. _____

   e. Take this for ten days. _____

   f. The expiration date has already passed. _____

   g. Don't take this by mouth. _____

   h. Don't take this on an empty stomach. _____

   i. Don't drive or operate heavy machinery when taking this medicine. _____

3. **Circle the words to complete the diary entries.**

Feb 11—Woke up in the hospital with crutches / (casts) on both my
a.
legs! I can't remember anything about the accident. Jim's OK,
thank goodness. He has a sling / walker on his arm, but that's all.
b.
Here comes the nurse . . .

Feb 14—Jim visited me today and pushed me around the hospital in
a wheelchair / humidifier.
c.

March 24—They took off the casts / canes. Now I can hold my
d.
air purifier / walker in front of me and move around on my own.
e.
After a couple of weeks, I'll be ready for a pair of crutches / capsules.
f.

April 8—I can stand, but I have to learn to use my legs again. The
exercises hurt a lot. I put an antacid / a heating pad on my painful
g.
muscles after therapy. At first I used pain relievers / throat lozenges,
h.
but I don't like to take medicine.

April 28—Tomorrow I go home! It's been more than two months!
I still need to use a cane / an inhaler to get around, but it won't be
i.
long now until I can walk without any help.

4. **What about you? What over-the-counter medicine do you have at home?**
   Look at the labels and make a chart like the one below.

Type	Dosage	Indications	Warnings
tablets	1–2 tablets every 4–6 hours	to prevent nausea	Do not take if you have a breathing problem.

Challenge Write about an accident or illness that you or someone you know has recovered from. What
were the treatments and medications? What were the steps to recovery?

1. **Look in your dictionary. What are the people doing?**

    a. "This book is good."   *getting bed rest*

    b. "I have to take one capsule two times a day."   _____

    c. "This is hard exercise!"   _____

    d. "I need to see a doctor. My back really hurts."   _____

    e. "I'd like some more salad."   _____

    f. "That's OK, Doctor. It only hurt for a second!"   _____

2. **Read the doctor's notes and look at the picture. Is the patient following medical advice? What is he doing? What is he NOT doing?**

From the Desk of Dr. Wise

a. Get bed rest.

b. Drink fluids.

c. Take medicine.

d. Eat a healthy diet.

e. Don't smoke!!!

    a. *He isn't getting bed rest.* _____

    b. _____

    c. _____

    d. _____

    e. _____

3. Look in your dictionary. What's the problem?

a. "I can't read this. Why are the words so small?" _vision problems_

b. "Ow! My leg really hurts!" _____

c. "I feel sad all the time." _____

d. "What? Could you repeat that again, please?" _____

e. "Help! I have too much to do, and no time to do it!" _____

4. Circle the words to complete the pamphlets.

Do you have

(Vision Problems)/ Hearing Loss?
　　　　　　a.
_____

Are you having trouble reading this?

It may be time for new

glasses / hearing aids.
　　　b.
Or maybe you like contact lenses / fluids.
　　　　　　　　　　　c.
Visit an audiologist / optometrist and have
　　　　　　　d.
your eyes checked.

Are you feeling

tired and sad most of the time?
_____

Maybe you are one of the more than

20 million people suffering from

depression / stress. Don't despair!
　　　e.
See a physical therapist / therapist for
　　　　　　　　　　f.
physical / talk therapy. You can also
　　　g.
get immunized / join a support group.
　　　　　　　h.

5. What about you? What do you do when you feel stress?

Example: *When I feel stress, I exercise.*

Challenge How do you take care of your health? What do you do? What don't you do?
Write two paragraphs.

1. **Look in your dictionary. What happened? Complete each sentence.**

   a. The little girl in the laundry room _____*swallowed poison*_____ .

   b. The woman in the snow _____ .

   c. The man with the toaster _____ .

   d. The boy in the doctor's office _____ .

   e. The man boiling water in the kitchen _____ .

   f. After her car hit a tree, the woman on the ground _____ .

   g. The woman near the ambulance _____ when the paramedics arrived.

2. **Circle the words to complete the article.**

   ## How Safe Are You At Home?

   Not very. As you probably know, most accidents occur at home. The chart below shows the

   number of people who were injured at home in just one year using everyday products. More than

   two million people (fell)/ were in shock while using stairs, steps, or bicycles. Falls also caused
           a.

   some of the 301,375 injuries in the bathtub or shower. How else are people getting hurt?

   Some people drowned / choked or burned themselves / got frostbite while bathing. More than
           b.   **c.**

   30,000 people cut themselves and bled / couldn't breathe while using razors, and other people
                     d.

   burned themselves / overdosed on drugs or had a heart attack / an allergic reaction (such as a
           e.   **f.**

   skin rash) while taking medication.

Product	Estimated U.S. Injuries
stairs, steps	2,028,968
bicycles	539,642
bathtubs and showers	301,375
TVs	50,021
stoves and ovens	43,347
razors and shavers	33,532

   Chart based on information from: Consumer Product Safety Review, 2003. www.cpsc.gov.

   Challenge Look at the chart in Exercise 2. How do you think people hurt themselves using TVs and irons?

  See page 288 for listening practice.

1. Look in your dictionary. Complete the information from a first aid manual.

Always keep your medicine chest or first aid kit well supplied. Include:

a. _____gauze_____ for holding sterile pads in place, or (if sterile) for covering cuts

b. _____ for removing pieces of glass or wood from the skin

c. _____ for preventing movement of a broken or sprained arm, finger, etc.

d. _____ for covering large cuts and burns

e. _____ for holding pads and gauze in place

f. _____ for preventing infection of small cuts

g. _____ for covering small cuts

h. _____ for pouring on a new cut to help prevent infection

i. _____ for putting around a sprained ankle

j. _____ for treating rashes and allergic skin reactions

k. _____ for reducing pain and swelling

l. _____ for finding medical information

Note: A deep cut that continues to bleed may need _____ . Contact your doctor or go
m.
to a clinic or hospital emergency room. People with special medical conditions such as diabetes,
heart disease, or serious allergies, should wear a _____ to identify the problem.
n.

2. Write the name of the life-saving techniques. Use the words in the box.

| CPR | ~~Heimlich maneuver~~ | rescue breathing |

a. _Heimlich maneuver_ Named after the doctor who invented it, this technique is used on people who are choking on food or another object.

b. _____ Performed mouth to mouth, this technique is used on people who have stopped breathing.

c. _____ Involves mouth-to-mouth breathing and heart compression on people who have stopped breathing. Special training is needed.

Challenge Are there first aid items that you use that are not in your dictionary? Write about them.
Example: *I use vitamin E for small kitchen burns.*

See page 288 for listening practice. 117

1. Look in your dictionary. What are the people talking about?

a. "Can you please fill <u>this</u> out for me?"   _____*health history form*_____

b. "According to <u>this</u>, your pressure is fine."   _____

c. "Relax. <u>This</u> will only hurt for a second."   _____

d. "According to <u>this</u>, you have a low fever."   _____

e. "When I listen through <u>this</u>, your lungs sound clear."   _____

2. Complete the pamphlet. Use the words in the box.

~~appointment~~	check your blood pressure	draw blood
examination table	examine your eyes	examine your throat
health history form	health insurance card	listen to your heart
patient	nurse	receptionist

Dr. Gregory Sarett

What to Expect During Your ____*Appointment*____
a.

Before you see the doctor, the _____ will ask to see your
b.

_____. If you are a new _____, she will also ask you to
c. **d.**

complete a _____ . Then a _____ will check your
e. **f.**

height and weight. She will also _____ to see if it is too high or too low.
g.

Then, Dr. Sarett, using a stethoscope, will _____ while you are on the
h.

_____. He will use the stethoscope to listen to your lungs and abdomen,
i.

too. Next comes the vision exam. Using an ophthalmoscope (an instrument with a light), the

doctor will _____ . He will also _____ , nose, and ears.
j. **k.**

He may do other tests, too. He may, for example, _____ and send it to a lab
l.

for testing. At the end of the exam, he will discuss the results and make recommendations.

Challenge Look in your dictionary. Write about Mr. Zolmar's doctor's appointment.
Begin: *Andre had a doctor's appointment. First, the receptionist . . .*

1. Look in your dictionary. What is the dentist or dental hygienist doing?

a. "I'm getting all the plaque off." ___cleaning teeth___

b. "I'm almost finished. Then I'll fill it." _____

c. "This will give us a good picture of that tooth." _____

d. "You won't feel any pain after this." _____

e. "It's almost out now." _____

2. Complete the pamphlet. Use the words in the box.

cavities	crown	dental instruments	dentist	dentures
fillings	gum disease	hygienist	~~plaque~~	

COMMON DENTAL QUESTIONS

Q: What is _____plaque_____ ?
a.

A: A substance that forms on your teeth.

After it gets hard, only a

_____ or dental
b.

_____ using special
c.

_____ can remove it.
d.

Q: I never get _____.
e.

Do I still need to make appointments

every year?

A: Yes. Dentists also check for other

problems, including cancer and

_____, the main
f.

reason for tooth loss. The goal is to keep

your own teeth and avoid needing

_____.
g.

Q: I have a lot of old silver and gold

_____. Is there
h.

anything I can do about their

appearance?

A: Yes. Dentists can place a

_____ over a tooth
i.

with old fillings.

Challenge Write two more questions about dental care like the ones in Exercise 2. Try to find the answers.

See page 289 for listening practice. 119

1. **Look in your dictionary.** *True* or *False*? **Correct the <u>underlined</u> words in the false sentences.**

   RN
   a. The ~~CNA~~ is checking the patient's IV drip. _____*false*_____

   b. The <u>administrator</u> is putting an ID bracelet on a new patient. _____

   c. The pediatrician's patient isn't wearing a <u>hospital gown</u>. _____

   d. The <u>surgical nurse</u> is discussing a patient's food. _____

   e. There's a medical waste disposal inside the <u>lab</u>. _____

   f. There's medication on the patient's <u>bed table</u>. _____

   g. The <u>bed pan</u> is next to the hospital bed. _____

   h. The <u>volunteer</u> is drawing blood for a blood test. _____

2. **Circle the words to complete the information from a hospital pamphlet.**

The Operation—What to Expect
Surgery is stressful, but it can help to know what to expect.

In most cases, orderlies will take you to the hospital's emergency / (operating) room on a
            a.
bed table / gurney. They will then carefully move you to the ambulance / operating table,
    b.   **c.**
where the surgery will take place. Your surgical team (the anesthesiologist, surgical

nurses, and, of course, the dietician / surgeon) will be there. In order to avoid infection,
           d.
they will wear surgical caps / gowns on their heads and sterile surgical gloves / stretchers
        e.   **f.**
on their hands. All the instruments will be sterilized, too. During

the operation, the administrator / anesthesiologist will monitor
           g.
all your medical charts / vital signs (blood pressure, breathing,
      h.
and heart rate). A call button / An IV, attached to a vein in
        i.
your arm, will provide you with fluids, and, if necessary,

medication. Ask your doctor how long it will take to recover

from your operation. Remember: Knowing what to expect

will help you feel better!

3. **Look at the chart. Write the numbers to complete the sentences.**

Doctors by Specialty and Sex in the United States		
Specialty	Male	Female
anesthesiology	30,452	8,370
cardiology	20,060	2,054
internal medicine	104,688	46,245
obstetrics / gynecology	24,801	17,258
ophthalmology	15,529	3,177
pediatrics	33,515	36,636
psychiatry	27,213	13,079
radiology	7,465	1,270

Based on information from: The American Medical Association, 2004 as reported by *The World Almanac and Book of Facts* 2007.

a. There are _____3,177_____ female eye doctors in the United States.

b. The number of male eye doctors is _____.

c. There are _____ female doctors who are X-ray specialists.

d. _____ male doctors are heart specialists.

e. _____ male doctors specialize in mental illness (for example, depression).

f. _____ female doctors specialize in women's health care.

g. _____ male doctors specialize in children's medicine.

4. **What about you? Who would you prefer? Check (✓) the columns.**

	Male	Female	No Preference
a. internist			
b. cardiologist			
c. psychiatrist			
d. ophthalmologist			
e. orderly			
f. obstetrician			
g. pediatrician			
h. nurse			

Challenge Find out the name of other kinds of medical specialists. What do they do?
Example: *An orthopedist is a bone doctor.*

Go to page 247 for Another Look (Unit 6). | See page 289 for listening practice.

1. **Look in your dictionary. *True* or *False*?**

   a. The <u>aerobics</u> class starts at 10:00.   _____true_____

   b. There's a <u>fat-free</u> cooking demonstration.   _____

   c. The health fair opened at <u>9:00</u>.   _____

   d. An acupuncture treatment is <u>free</u>.   _____

   e. You can buy <u>vitamins</u> at the Good Foods booth.   _____

   f. The medical screening is <u>free</u>.   _____

   g. A nurse is <u>taking</u> a woman's <u>temperature</u>.   _____

   h. The eye exam is <u>$2.00</u>.   _____

   i. There's a nutrition label <u>demonstration</u>.   _____

2. **Write the letter of the false sentences in Exercise 1. Make them true.**

   <u>b.</u>   There's a sugar-free cooking demonstration. _____

   ____   _____

   ____   _____

   ____   _____

   ____   _____

3. **Circle the words to complete the journal entry.**

   Today, I went to a <u>booth</u> / <u>health fair</u> at a local <u>clinic</u> / <u>demonstration</u>. I am so glad I went!
                  a.   **b.**
   At the <u>hatha yoga</u> / <u>medical screening</u> booth, I found out that my <u>blood pressure</u> / <u>pulse</u> is a little
                   c.   **d.**
   high—135 over 80. The nurse told me that exercise helps, so I watched a very interesting

   <u>acupuncture</u> / <u>aerobic exercise</u> class. It looked easy and fun, and I'll ask my doctor if it's OK for me.
                   e.
   Next, I had an <u>ear</u> / <u>eye</u> exam and found out I can see perfectly—no problems there! I wanted to
                   f.
   try an acupuncture <u>exam</u> / <u>treatment</u>, but the needles scared me a little. Maybe next time. The last
                       g.
   booth had a lecture about <u>nutrition labels</u> / <u>vitamins</u>—very interesting! I'm going to start reading
                             h.
   them when I shop for food.

4. **What about you? Do you exercise? Is exercise important to you? Why or why not?
   Tell a classmate.**

5. Look in your dictionary. Complete the flyer.

Come to the _____Health Fair_____ !
a.

Where: Fadool _____   **When:** _____ , 9–4
b.   c.

Learn and have fun at these booths:

1 _____   We'll check your blood pressure and
d.
_____ your _____ for only $2.00.
e.   f.

2 _____   Can you see the big *E*? How about
g.
the little *c*? Find out here—it's _____ !
h.

3 _____   Are you getting enough protein?
i.
Listen and learn about _____ .
j.

4 _____   Exercise and
k.
relax the gentle way. 2–3 p.m.

5 _____   Chef Bill will
l.
show you how to cook sugar-free desserts.

6 _____   Headaches?
m.
Sore feet? Feeling blah? Try a treatment
for only $5.00.

See you there!

---

6. Where can you hear . . . ? Match.

__2__ **a.** "Bend your left leg. Raise your right arm."   **1.** nutrition lecture

____ **b.** "Now cover your left eye, and read the first row."   **2.** yoga class

____ **c.** "Seventy-two beats a minute. Excellent."   **3.** acupuncture treatment

____ **d.** "You can make this delicious dessert with no sugar!" **4.** medical screening

____ **e.** "Notice the serving size. It's only a half cup."   **5.** cooking demonstration

____ **f.** "Just relax. The needle won't hurt."   **6.** eye exam

---

Challenge Work with a classmate. Imagine you are planning a health fair. Look at the activities in the word box below and the ones in your dictionary. What are some activities that you will include? Why?

bicycle safety	talking to your doctor	quitting smoking
having a healthy back	making a first aid kit	having healthy teeth

See page 289 for listening practice. **123**

1. **Look in your dictionary. *True* or *False*? Correct the underlined words in the false statements.**

   a. The post office is across from the ~~bank~~. ⎯courthouse⎯   _____*false*_____

   b. The bank is on Main Street next to the <u>police station</u>.   _____

   c. The Chinese restaurant is between the courthouse and the <u>fire station</u>.   _____

   d. The gas station is on 6th Street, across from the <u>office building</u>.   _____

   e. The parking garage is next to the <u>hotel</u>.   _____

   f. The <u>city hall</u> is on the corner of Grand Avenue and Main Street.   _____

   g. The <u>bus station</u> is on the corner of Elm Street and Grand Avenue.   _____

2. **Complete the ads. You can use the words in Exercise 1 for help.**

   a.
   > **INTOWN** _Parking Garage_
   > **Your car is safe with us.**
   > **Park long- or short-term.**
   > **Low rates.**
   > **130 Washington Place**

   b.
   > **Down City** _____
   > 201 Elm Street
   > International Cooking
   > Open for dinner
   > Tues–Sun 6:00–9:00
   > Reservations suggested
   > Tel 555-2634   Fax 555-2635

   c.
   > *Miram* _____
   > *Medicine with a Heart*
   > *Patient information 555-4313*
   > *Emergency service 555-4310*
   > *Visit our website at www.mh.us.*

   d.

   > *Parkside* _____
   > 12 minutes from the airport
   > 100 new non-smoking rooms
   > Free breakfast
   > Free cable TV and Internet connection
   > 555-2956 www.ps.us

   e.
   > **Rick's** _____
   > Open every day from 6 a.m. to midnight.
   > Best car wash in town!
   > Just 2 minutes from the highway

   f.

   > **The People's Savings** _____
   > "Where your money is our business!"
   > **Downtown Branch:**
   > **210 Main Street**
   > **24-hour ATM**
   > **555-6666**

3. **Look in your dictionary. Where can you go to . . . ?**

   a. have lunch   <u>   the restaurant   </u>

   b. borrow a book or DVD   <u>   </u>

   c. visit a sick friend   <u>   </u>

   d. spend the night   <u>   </u>

   e. get the 8:04 p.m. to Boston   <u>   </u>

   f. apply for a driver's license   <u>   </u>

   g. report a crime   <u>   </u>

   h. get married   <u>   </u>

4. **Circle the words to complete the notes.**

   a.
   > I went to the (bank) / city hall
   > to get some money.
   > I'll be home around 4:00.
   >
   > Dan

   b.
   > I'm driving Suzie to the
   > bus station / hospital.
   > She's taking the 8:40 to
   > Greenville. See you soon.
   >
   > Alicia

   c.
   > It's now 3:00. I'm going to the
   > gas station / parking garage.
   > The tires need air.
   > I'll be back soon.
   >
   > M

   d.
   > I needed to go to the
   > office building / post office
   > to buy some stamps.
   > Also, your Mom called.
   >
   > R

5. **What about you? Work with a partner. Complete the chart with information about your community.**

Place	Street Location
library	
courthouse	
bus station	
city hall	
fire station	
police station	
post office	

Challenge Look in a phone book or at an online phone directory.
Find the names of a hotel, a bank, a library, and a hospital in your community.

See page 290 for listening practice. 125

City Streets

1. **Look in your dictionary. Where can you find . . . ? (Do not use *supermarket* or *shopping mall*.)**

   a. a sandwich   _coffee shop_

   b. a cake   _____

   c. paper and pens   _____

   d. the best view of the city   _____

   e. tickets for a football game   _____

   f. English classes   _____ or _____

   g. a new couch   _____

   h. a used car   _____

   i. paint for your living room   _____

   j. a room for the night   _____

   k. a place to exercise   _____

2. **Complete the tourist information. Use the words in the box.**

   | cemetery | church | convention center | school |
   | shopping mall | ~~skyscraper~~ | stadium | theater |

PLACES OF INTEREST IN NEW YORK CITY

Empire State Building Over 1,250 feet tall, this building is the most famous _skyscraper_ in
a.
New York City. Go to the top for a wonderful view.

Yankee _____ Located in the Bronx, this is home to one of the best teams in baseball
b.
history—the New York Yankees.

Trump Tower Inside this modern building at Fifth Avenue and 56th Street, you will find five floors of

excellent (and very expensive) stores from around the world in a large _____.
c.

Jacob K. Javits Center Thousands of businesspeople and tourists go to this _____ called "The Marketplace for the World," to see exhibits such as the New York International Auto Show and Book Expo America.

d.

Trinity _____ This is one of the oldest and most beautiful houses of worship in the city. Many historically important people, such as Alexander Hamilton and Robert Fulton, are buried in its _____.

e.

f.

Cooper Union Completed in 1859, this _____ is one of the oldest in the United States. Free classes were given day and night to fit working people's schedules. Students of all ages still study there today.

g.

Broadway and 42nd Street This is a great location if you want to go to the _____. On every night (except Monday), you can choose between more than 30 shows around this famous intersection.

h.

3. **What about you? Would you want to live near a . . . ? Check (✓) the boxes.**

	Yes	No	Why?
construction site	☐	☐	_____
school	☐	☐	_____
supermarket	☐	☐	_____
factory	☐	☐	_____
Other: _____	☐	☐	_____

Challenge Make a list of places for tourists to visit in your city or town. Include information about each of the places.

1. **Look in your dictionary. Where can a shopper use these coupons?**

BARGAIN PACK COUPON
FREE
Burger, Fries, and
Medium Drink
When you buy a lunch combo
at the regular price.

a. _____fast food restaurant_____

MANUFACTURER'S COUPON
SAVE $1.50 When you buy two boxes of
Nuts 'n Bran or
Apple Oatmeal Cereal
Apple Oatmeal **CEREAL**   **Nuts 'n Bran**

b. _____

BRITE AID
CHILDREN'S COLD MEDICINES
1/2 PRICE   Savings Coupon
This Month Only
Offer expires 11/30

c. _____

STORE COUPON
Men's Haircuts
Just
$15
with this coupon
(first time customers only)

d. _____

BARGAIN PACK COUPON
Fall Special
20% OFF
All shirts cleaned and pressed
Not valid after 11/30

e. _____

Buy 12 Get 1 FREE   STORE COUPON
(with a FREE cup of coffee) Baked Fresh Daily!

f. _____

2. **Where can you hear . . . ? Use your dictionary if you need help.**

Dad: I can't read the menu.

Tim: Drive forward a little.

a. _drive-thru window_

Bob: Where's the bleach?

Kim: On top of the dryer.

c. _____

Anne: How much change do I need?

Clerk: Two quarters for ten pages.

b. _____

Pete: Do you get Spanish papers?

Owner: *El Diario* comes on Tuesdays.

d. _____

128

3. Look at the picture. <u>Underline</u> six more mistakes in the newspaper article.

LOCAL NEWS

Last week, Fran Bates rode her bike into Mel Smith's <u>car</u>. There were no injuries. A pedestrian entered the video store with a dog and was asked to leave. Two children opened the mailbox on Elm Street. Fire Chief Dane closed it and called their parents. A shopper parked a car at the crosswalk on Main Street and received a parking ticket.

The town council met yesterday and voted to fix the parking space at Main and Elm. Pedestrians say they cannot cross the street safely. Officer Dobbs reported that the parking meter on that corner should also be fixed. Finally, the council voted for another street vendor. Shoppers complained about long lines for the only one in service in front of the photo shop.

4. Look at the picture in Exercise 3. Rewrite the article correctly.

Example: *Last week, Fran Bates rode her bike into Mel Smith's cart.*

Challenge Look at the picture in Exercise 3. Write about other problems.

See page 290 for listening practice.

A Mall

1. **Look in your dictionary. Check (✓) the activities you can do at this mall. Write the kind of store you can do them in. (Do not use *department store*.)**

   ☐ buy cough syrup   _____

   ✓ buy a birthday card   _____*card store*_____

   ☐ look at DVD players   _____

   ☐ get clothes dry-cleaned   _____

   ☐ plan a vacation   _____

   ☐ get new eyeglasses   _____

   ☐ get a hamburger   _____

   ☐ buy flowers   _____

   ☐ buy a dictionary   _____

   ☐ buy a dog   _____

   ☐ mail letters   _____

   ☐ buy chocolates   _____

2. **Two teenagers are shopping at a mall. Look at the mall directory on page 131 of this book. Read the conversations and write the kind of place for each one.**

   a. **Server:** What flavor?
      Emma: Strawberry, please.   _____*ice cream shop*_____

   b. **Amy:** What do you think? Too curly?
      Emma: No. It's a terrific perm.   _____

   c. **Amy:** I love that new song by King.
      Emma: Let's go buy the CD.   _____

   d. **Emma:** Hey! Do you want to take the elevator?
      Amy: No. Let's take this instead. It'll be faster.   _____

   e. **Emma:** Let's go here for your high heels.
      Amy: Good idea. I usually don't like shopping at Crane's.   _____

   f. **Amy:** Do you like these earrings?
      Emma: Yeah. You look good in gold.   _____

   g. **Emma:** I need to get a new cell phone.
      Amy: Well, there's Cell Town right over there.   _____

   h. **Amy:** Excuse me. Where's the main entrance?
      Clerk: Right over there. Next to the restrooms.   _____

3. **Look at Exercise 2. Circle the numbers and symbols on the map and draw Amy and Emma's route.**

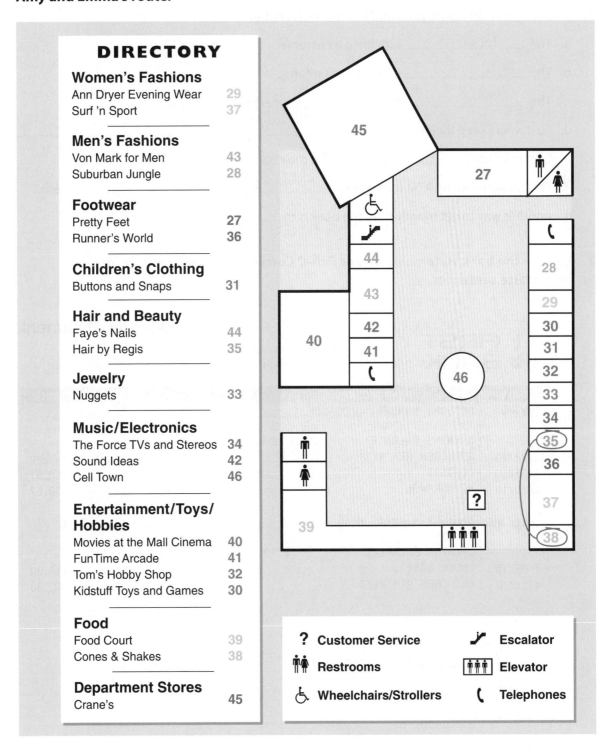

DIRECTORY

Women's Fashions
Ann Dryer Evening Wear	29
Surf 'n Sport	37

Men's Fashions
Von Mark for Men	43
Suburban Jungle	28

Footwear
Pretty Feet	27
Runner's World	36

Children's Clothing
Buttons and Snaps	31

Hair and Beauty
Faye's Nails	44
Hair by Regis	35

Jewelry
Nuggets	33

Music/Electronics
The Force TVs and Stereos	34
Sound Ideas	42
Cell Town	46

Entertainment/Toys/Hobbies
Movies at the Mall Cinema	40
FunTime Arcade	41
Tom's Hobby Shop	32
Kidstuff Toys and Games	30

Food
Food Court	39
Cones & Shakes	38

Department Stores
Crane's	45

? Customer Service   **Escalator**

Restrooms   **Elevator**

Wheelchairs/Strollers   **Telephones**

4. **What about you? Look at the mall in Exercise 3. Where would you like to go? Why?**

Challenge Where do you prefer to shop—downtown (the business center of a town or city) or a shopping mall? Think about weather conditions, the transportation you can use to get there, the kinds of stores, prices, and entertainment. Write at least five sentences.

See page 291 for listening practice.

The Bank

1. **Look in your dictionary. Complete the sentences.**

   a. The ____teller____ is helping a customer.

   b. The _____ is wearing a uniform.

   c. The _____ is helping two customers open an account.

   d. Customers keep their valuables in a _____ in the bank's _____.

   e. Customers can _____ with their computers.

   f. The customer at the ATM is using his _____ to _____ cash.

   g. Another way to get money from the bank is to _____ a check.

2. **Look at the bank statement. *True* or *False*? Correct the <u>underlined</u> words in the false sentences.**

Monthly Statement

FIRST BANK

JAMAL AL-MARAFI
MARCH 31–APRIL 30, 2010

DATE	TRANSACTION		AMOUNT	BALANCE
SAVINGS	ACCOUNT NUMBER: 0125–00			
	OPENING BALANCE: $1117.20.00			
3/31/10	QUIKCASH ATM #123	W	50.00	1,067.20
4/01/10	DEPOSIT	D	1,283.47	2,350.67
4/20/10	WITHDRAWAL	W	100.00	2,250.67
CHECKING	ACCOUNT NUMBER: 0135–08			
	OPENING BALANCE: $849.00			
4/05/10	CHECK #431	W	732.00	117.00
4/11/10	QUIKCASH ATM #123	W	75.00	42.00

   checking

a. Jamal's ~~savings~~ account number is 0135-08.   ___false___

b. On 3/31, he <u>withdrew cash</u>. _____

c. On 4/01, he <u>made a deposit</u>. _____

d. On 4/05, he used his <u>check book</u>. _____

e. On 4/11, the balance in his checking account was <u>$849.00</u>. _____

f. On 4/11, he used a <u>deposit slip</u>. _____

Challenge Compare the balances and transactions in Jamal's savings and checking account.
Example: *Jamal made one deposit in his … .*

1. Look in your dictionary. Complete the sentences.

a. You can look up the Nile River in an _____atlas_____.

b. The little girl and her mother are looking at a _____.

c. You'll need a _____ to check out library books.

d. The library clerk is at the _____.

e. If you keep a book too long, you have to _____.

2. Complete the librarian's answers. Use the words in the box.

author	biography	~~DVD~~	magazines	newspaper
online catalog	periodicals	reference librarian	title	

Patron: Do you have the movie *Crash* on videocassette?

Librarian: No, but we have it on _____DVD_____.
   a.

Patron: I'm looking for a job. Do you have this weekend's

   job ads?

Librarian: The Sunday _____ is over there
   b.

   along with the other _____.
   c.

Patron: Where can I find information about fashion and makeup?

Librarian: We get several fashion _____ every month. Try those.
   d.

Patron: I'm looking for a novel by Jane Austen, but I can't remember what it's called.

Librarian: You don't need the _____. Just type the name of the
   e.

   _____ into the _____ and press *Enter*.
   f.   **g.**

Patron: Can you recommend a good _____ about John F. Kennedy?
   h.

   I have to write a report about his life.

Librarian: Sorry. I'm the library clerk. Ask the _____. She's over there.
   i.

Challenge Look at the library in your dictionary. What is each person doing? **Example**: *The reference librarian is showing a man an atlas.*

See page 291 for listening practice.   **133**

1. Look in your dictionary. Answer the questions.

a. What comes in books of 24?   *stamps*

b. What says *Newtown, New York*?   _____

c. What has a Los Angeles postmark?   _____

d. What tells you the weight of a package?   _____

e. Where can you buy stamps?   _____ , _____ ,

and _____

f. Who delivers the mail?   _____

2. Circle the words to complete the information about the U.S. postal services.

HOW TO SEND YOUR MAIL   *U.S. MAIL*

First-Class Letter / Package: For
             a.
envelopes weighing 13 oz. or less. Price: First

oz. $0.41, each additional oz. $0.17.

Post card / Postmark: Price: $0.26
         b.
small; $0.41 large.

Priority Mail®: Mail weighing more than

13 oz. Price: $4.60 and up.

Express Mail® / Certified Mail™: The
        c.
fastest way to send a letter or package.

The post office guarantees that it will

deliver / receive it overnight—365 days a year
  d.
including weekends. Price: $16.25 and up.

Ground post: for **scales / packages**
                e.
weighing from 1–70 lbs. Price: $4.50 and up.

Certified Mail™ / Priority Mail®: the safest
              f.
way to **address / mail** important, valuable letters
           g.
and packages. You get a mailing receipt, and the

receiver's post office also keeps a record.

You can find **postal forms / return addresses**
                  h.
for this service at your post office. Price: $2.65

plus postage.

Airmail / Media mail (Book Rate): For small
         i.
and large packages containing books, CDs, DVDs,

and other media. Price: $2.13 and up.

**Note: Rates change. Check your local post office or
go to www.usps.com.**

3. What about you? What kinds of mail service do you use? How much do they cost?

4. **Look at the information in Exercise 2. Answer the questions.**

a. You are mailing a very important document to a school. What's the safest way to mail it?
   <u>   Certified Mail™   </u>

b. Your letter must arrive tomorrow. What's the fastest way to send it? _____

c. You are mailing DVDs to your nephew. How should you send them? _____

d. You are mailing gifts to your family. They live in the same state as you. You need the package to arrive in 10 days. What's the cheapest way to send them? _____

e. You are mailing a 14-oz. envelope to a friend. It's OK if it doesn't arrive tomorrow. What's the cheapest way to send it? _____

5. **Complete this email. Use the words in the box.**

addressed	delivered	envelope	~~greeting card~~	letter carrier	mailbox
mailed	put on	received	return address	stamp	wrote

My Mail   — □ ×

To: LibraGuy@iol.us
Subject: Sorry!

Hi Enrique!

I really didn't forget your birthday on October 4! Two weeks ago, I went to the store and got you

a beautiful ____<u>greeting card</u>____. I _____ a note in the card, put the card in
                    a.   **b.**

the green _____, _____ the envelope, walked to the nearest
              c.   **d.**

_____, and _____ the card. Yesterday I was very surprised when the
         e.   **f.**

_____ _____ the card—to ME!!! Guess what! I forgot to_____
    g.   **h.**   **i.**

a stamp! (Luckily, I didn't forget to write my _____ on the envelope!) So, long story
                                                        j.

short, that's the reason you never _____ a card from me this year.
                                            k.

Next year I'll send you an e-card, so I won't need a _____!
                                                              l.

Challenge Use the information in Exercise 2 to calculate the postage within the United States for . . . .

a. a 3-oz. letter   _____   c. a 5-oz. certified letter   _____

b. a small post card _____   d. a 1-oz. letter for next day delivery _____

See page 292 for listening practice. **135**

1. **Look at the DMV office on page 136 in your dictionary. *True* or *False*? Correct the underlined words in the false sentences.**

   DMV handbook
   a. You can get a form or a <u>photo</u> at the information stand.   *false*

   b. Three people are taking a test in the <u>testing area</u>.   _____

   c. A DMV clerk is taking a man's <u>fingerprint</u>.   _____

   d. Another clerk is giving a man a <u>vision exam</u>.   _____

   e. One <u>window</u> is closed.   _____

2. **Look at the pictures. Answer the questions.**

PROOF OF INSURANCE	KEEP IN VEHICLE AS EVIDENCE OF INSURANCE	
POLICY HOLDER: ROSA RODRIGUEZ	POLICY NUMBER: 54323–45HG	**ABC** **AUTO INSURANCE**
ADDRESS: 79 MAIN ST HOUSTON, TX 77002	EXPIRATION DATE: 12/01/2010	14601 Young Street Houston, TX 77034
MAKE: HONDA CIVIC	YEAR: 2009	

   a. What is Rosa's license plate number?   *LVD 123*

   b. What is her driver's license number?   _____

   c. When is the expiration date for her license?   _____

   d. Are there registration stickers on her license plate?   _____

   e. When is the expiration date for her proof of insurance?   _____

3. Circle the words to complete the information from the website.

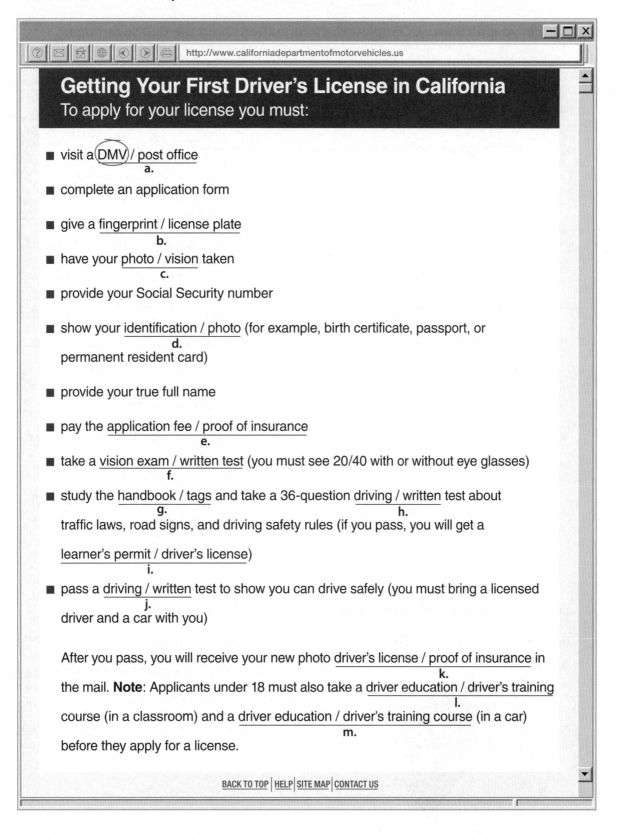

http://www.californiadepartmentofmotorvehicles.us

Getting Your First Driver's License in California
To apply for your license you must:

- visit a **DMV** / post office
  a.
- complete an application form
- give a fingerprint / license plate
  b.
- have your photo / vision taken
  c.
- provide your Social Security number
- show your identification / photo (for example, birth certificate, passport, or
  d.
  permanent resident card)
- provide your true full name
- pay the application fee / proof of insurance
  e.
- take a vision exam / written test (you must see 20/40 with or without eye glasses)
  f.
- study the handbook / tags and take a 36-question driving / written test about
  g.   **h.**
  traffic laws, road signs, and driving safety rules (if you pass, you will get a
  learner's permit / driver's license)
  i.
- pass a driving / written test to show you can drive safely (you must bring a licensed
  j.
  driver and a car with you)

  After you pass, you will receive your new photo driver's license / proof of insurance in
  k.
  the mail. **Note**: Applicants under 18 must also take a driver education / driver's training
  l.
  course (in a classroom) and a driver education / driver's training course (in a car)
  m.
  before they apply for a license.

BACK TO TOP | HELP | SITE MAP | CONTACT US

Challenge Compare getting a license in California to getting a license in your native country or another state in the United States. **Example:** *In Germany, you can sometimes get your driver's license when you are 17...*

See page 292 for listening practice.

1. **Look in your dictionary. Complete the information about the U.S. government.**

There are three _____branches_____ of government: the _____ , the
a.   b.

legislative, and the judicial. There is an election for _____ , the most important
c.

person in the executive branch, every four years. He or she lives in the _____
d.

and runs the country. The president chooses a _____ , which includes a
e.

Secretary of State. If the president dies or becomes too sick to work, the _____
f.

continues to do the job. The _____ branch, called Congress, makes the laws of
g.

the country. It has two "houses": the _____ and the House of Representatives.
h.

The Senate has 100 members called _____ . There are two from each state and
i.

they are elected for six-year terms. The House has 435 members called _____ .
j.

States with bigger populations have more representatives than states with smaller populations. These

representatives are elected for two-year terms. The third branch of government, the

_____ branch, reviews laws to make sure they follow the U.S. Constitution. The
k.

highest court is called the _____ . Its decisions are final. Eight
l.

_____ and one _____ "sit" on the Supreme Court. After
m.   n.

the Senate approves the judge that the president chooses, the judge can keep his or her job for life.

2. **Look at the pie chart. Circle the words to complete the sentences.**

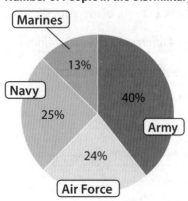

Number of People in the U.S. Military

Marines — 13%
Navy — 25%
Army — 40%
Air Force — 24%

a. The Army / Navy is the biggest branch of the military.

b. The Navy / Marines is bigger than the Air Force / Army.

c. The Air Force / Marines is the smallest branch.

d. The chart does not include the Coast Guard / Navy.

Based on information from: The Department of Defense Personnel & Procurement Statistics (2007)
http://siadapp.dmdc.osd.mil/personnel/MILITARY/Miltop.htm.

3. **Look in your dictionary. Answer the questions.**

a. What is the state capital of Florida? _____Tallahassee_____

b. Who is the head of the state government? _____

c. Who helps him or her? _____

d. Which branch of government does an assemblyperson work for? _____

e. Who else works there? _____

f. Who is the head of the city government? _____

g. Which branch of government does a councilperson work for? _____

4. **Complete the newspaper article. Use the words in the box.**

city council	councilperson	ran for office	debated	elected officials
got elected	opponent	political campaign	serve	~~election results~~

ELECTION COVERAGE *A3*

Dan Chen Wins!

By Roland Cormier
Smithfield, Wednesday, Nov 7

The __election results__ are in. The city of Smithfield has a new _____ ,
      a.   **b.**
forty-five year old Dan Chen. Mr. Chen, a Smithfield resident, _____ in
                                                      c.
yesterday's election. He beat his _____ , Martha Larson, by 35,000
                                      d.
votes. This was the first time Chen _____ . He led an excellent
                                        e.
_____ . Hundreds of people watched as he and Larson
     f.
_____ the issues last month at the Smithfield City College Auditorium.
     g.
Mr. Chen will _____ on the Smithfield _____ for a
                   h.   **i.**
term of four years. There are four other _____ on the council.
                                             j.

Challenge Compare a branch of the U.S. government with another country's government that you
know. **Example:** *In the U.S., a president runs the country. In Jordan, a king runs the country.*

See page 292 for listening practice.

1. Look in your dictionary. Complete the sentences.

a. To avoid a $500 fine, you must ____*obey the law*____.

b. Anne Johnson reads the newspaper in order to _____.

c. Alena Smolka decided to _____ *yes* in the election.

d. Charles Li uses a check to _____.

e. This year, Ana Guzman must _____ with eleven other citizens.

f. As an eighteen-year-old male, Todd McBain must _____.

2. Read the sentences. Which right is each person talking about? Use the words in the box.

~~fair trial~~ free speech freedom of the press freedom of religion peaceful assembly

"I know the jury will find me Not Guilty!"

"We can march in the park."

"We can say what we want."

a. ____*fair trial*____   b. _____   c. _____

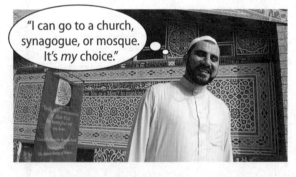
"I can go to a church, synagogue, or mosque. It's *my* choice."

"The newspaper can print what it wants."

d. _____   e. _____

3. Read the information. Who can take a citizenship test? Check (✓) the correct box.

a. ☐ Luisa is 17 years old. She has lived in the U.S. for 10 years.

b. ☐ Mehmet is 50 years old. He has lived in the U.S. for 4 years.

c. ☐ Mei-ling is 20 years old. She has lived in the U.S. for 6 years.

Challenge Which right of citizens is the most important to you? Why?

      See page 293 for listening practice.

1. Look in your dictionary. Who is . . . ?

a. wearing handcuffs _____the suspect_____

b. talking to the witness _____

c. typing _____

d. standing next to the defendant in the court room _____

e. sitting in jail _____

f. standing in a corner in the courtroom _____

2. Circle the words to complete the interview with a former convict.

A HARD LESSON

PS MAGAZINE: Tell us about your experience with the legal system.

You (went to prison) / stood trial for several years, didn't you?
a.

DAN LEE: Yes—for burglary. I was released / arrested three
b.
years ago. It was the happiest day of my life.

PS MAGAZINE: You didn't have a job when you were arrested.

How did you hire a lawyer / stand trial?
c.

DAN LEE: I didn't. The court gave me one. And she was good. In fact, when we appeared in

court / jail, she got the guard / judge to lower the bail to $1,000.
d.   e.

PS MAGAZINE: So what happened when you sentenced the defendant / stood trial?
f.

DAN LEE: She did her best, but the prosecuting / defense attorney had a lot of
g.
evidence / handcuffs against me.
h.

PS MAGAZINE: Were you surprised when the police officer / jury gave a verdict / witness
i.   j.
of "guilty"?

DAN LEE: No, but I *was* surprised when the judge sentenced / released me. Seven years!
k.
Now I tell young people what it's like to spend years in jail / court.
l.

Challenge Write the story of the man in the dictionary who was arrested.

Crime

1. **Look in your dictionary. Put each crime in the correct category.**

Crimes Against People	Crimes Against Property (buildings, cars, etc.)	Substance Abuse Crimes (drugs and alcohol)
_____	_____vandalism_____	_____
_____	_____	_____
_____	_____	
_____	_____	
_____		

2. **Look at the line graph. Complete the sentences. Use the words in the box.**
   (You will use two words more than once.)

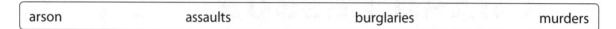

arson   assaults   burglaries   murders

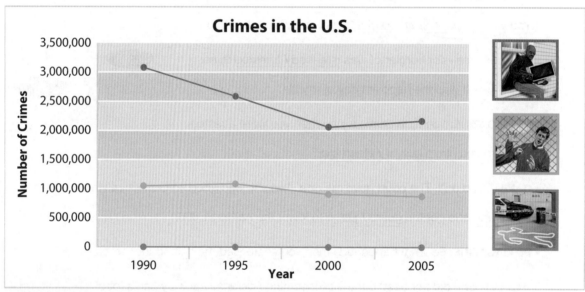

Based on information from: Crime in the United States (2006)
http://www.fbi.gov/ucr/cius2006/data/table_01.html.

a. In 1990, there were about one million _____assaults_____ in the U.S.

b. In 1990, there were about three million _____.

c. Between 2000 and 2005, the number of _____ went up.

d. The number of _____ has changed less than the other crimes.

e. Since 2000, the number of _____ has gone down.

f. The chart does not have information about _____.

Challenge Look at page 258 in this book. Follow the instructions.

  See page 293 for listening practice.

1. Look in your dictionary. Complete the poster with the correct advice.

Neighborhood Lookout *Safety Tips*

a. _____*Lock your doors.*_____ A dead-bolt is your best protection. Door chains are also good.

b. _____ Always ask, "Who's there?" If you don't know them, don't let them in!

c. _____ Who else is on the street? Notice other people.

d. _____ For men, the best place is an *inside* jacket pocket. For women, keep it *closed* and *close* to your body at all times.

e. ATMs are great, but be careful using one. _____

f. _____ There's safety in numbers. Remember: muggers usually look for *easy* victims.

g. _____ Remember: Criminals don't want witnesses, so lights are your friends.

h. _____ Whose suitcase is that? If its owner isn't there, contact the police.

i. Be careful on the Internet, too. Only _____ where you see the 🔒 symbol.

j. _____ If you witness a crime or become a crime victim, dial 911 immediately!

The East Village Neighborhood Lookout — Looking Out for You!

2. Look at the picture. What safety mistakes is the man making? Use the information in Exercise 1.

a. _He isn't staying on well-lit streets._

b. _____

c. _____

d. _____

e. _____

3. What about you? Which of the safety tips in Exercise 1 do you follow? Make a list.

Challenge Interview five people. Find out about the safety tips they follow.

1. **Look in your dictionary. Which disaster is the news reporter talking about?**

   a. "The same one erupted five years ago."   _volcanic eruption_

   b. "All homes near the beach were destroyed by the ocean water."   _____

   c. "The two vehicles were badly damaged, but the drivers
      were not hurt in the crash."   _____

   d. "Store detectives found the little girl sitting on the floor."   _____

   e. "The twister destroyed several farms in its path."   _____

   f. "The search and rescue team arrived at the house quickly."   _____

2. **Complete the news articles. Use the words in the box.**

airplane crash	avalanche	blizzard	drought
~~earthquake~~	explosion	fire	firefighters
hurricane	search and rescue team		

a.

DISASTER STRIKES KOBE, JAPAN

TOKYO, JAN 17 —An ___earthquake___ measuring 7.1 on the Richter scale hit the
city of Kobe, Japan killing more than 5,000 people and injuring 26,500 others. More
than 100,000 buildings were destroyed.

b.

_____ KILLS 109

Miami, May 11—A DC-9 jet en route to Atlanta went down in the Florida
Everglades just a few minutes after takeoff from Miami. All 109 passengers were
killed. The cause of the disaster is not yet known.

c.

INFERNO IN LONDON UNDERGROUND

London, November 18—Thirty died and thirty-one were seriously injured in a
_____ in one of the busiest subway stations in the world. "As soon as
I got on the escalator, I could smell burning," said one witness. Seconds later she saw
the red flames and dark smoke. _____ rushed to the scene.

d.

BOMB _____ in Oklahoma City Kills 169

Oklahoma City, April 19—A car bomb went off outside a federal office building, killing 168 people. A member of the _____ also died while trying to save the victims. The bomb destroyed most of the nine-story building and damaged many other buildings in the area.

e.

HIGH WINDS HIT THE YUCATAN

Cancun, October 22—_____ Wilma, the most powerful Atlantic storm ever recorded, struck the popular tourist resorts of Mexico's Yucatan Peninsula, leaving 8 dead and destroying many beach hotels. Winds of 150 miles per hour broke windows and caused trees to fall.

f.

THE _____ OF '93

Boston, March 22—Described as a "hurricane with snow," the giant storm hit the eastern third of the United States. The winds created snow drifts as high as 14 feet in New England.

g.

A LONG DRY WINTER

Santa Barbara, March 23—As a result of 73% less rain than usual over the last year, California is experiencing its worst _____ since the 1930's. The state is going to stop water deliveries to farms in an effort to save water.

h.

MAN RESCUED FROM _____

Banff, Canada, March 27—An employee at Sunshine Village ski resort was buried when a 200-meter-wide wall of snow hit him and caused him to fall. A rescue team reached him in less than four minutes. The employee is fine.

Challenge Write a paragraph about an emergency or natural disaster.

See page 294 for listening practice.

Emergency Procedures

1. **Look in your dictionary. Complete the sentences.**

   a. The Rivera family ___is planning for an emergency___.

   b. Their _____ is Aunt Maria in California.

   c. If there is a flood, they have two _____ out of their house.

   d. Their _____ is Rt. 102, a road near their house.

   e. Their _____ is at the corner of Oak and Elm.

   f. The _____ is in their basement.

2. **Complete the disaster kit checklist. Use the words in the box.**

batteries	blankets	bottled water	can opener	canned food
coins	important papers	packaged food	towelettes	~~warm clothes~~

EMERGENCY CHECKLIST

Clothing and Bedding
- ☐ _____warm clothes_____ (hat, gloves, etc.)
  - **a.**
- ☐ _____ or sleeping bags
  - **b.**

Tools and Supplies
- ☐ flashlight and extra _____
  - **c.**
- ☐ non-electric _____
  - **d.**
- ☐ _____ (1 gallon per person per day)
  - **e.**

Food
- ☐ ready-to-eat _____ (cereal, bread)
  - **f.**
- ☐ _____ (soup, juice)
  - **g.**

Sanitation
- ☐ toilet paper
- ☐ moist _____
  - **h.**

Special Items
- ☐ medication
- ☐ extra eyeglasses
- ☐ cash and _____
  - **i.**
- ☐ copies of _____
  - **j.**

146

3. Look in your dictionary. What are people doing? Write sentences.

a. Carlos is looking out the window.   *He's watching the weather.*

b. Rosa is packing her suitcase.   _____

c. The Riveras are listening to the radio and leaving.   _____

d. Carlos is carrying a woman's suitcase to the shelter.   _____

e. The family is leaving their home.   _____

f. They are entering a hurricane shelter.   _____

g. Kenji and his son are under the table.   _____

h. They are not looking outside at the weather.   _____

i. Kenji and his family are in their car.   _____

j. Rosa is on the phone with Aunt Maria.   _____

k. Kenji and Rosa are in their basements.   _____

l. Kenji is in his front yard.   _____

4. What about you? Are you ready? Look at the checklist in Exercise 2. Complete the chart.

Things I have	Things I don't have	Things I'm going to get
Other:	Other:	Other:

Challenge What things should you have in a first aid kit? Make a list.

Go to page 248 for Another Look (Unit 7). | See page 294 for listening practice.

Community Cleanup

1. **Look at the top row of pictures on pages 148 and 149 in your dictionary. Complete the chart. Check (✓) the columns.**

	Donuts	Hammers & More	Pharmacy	Flowers
a. This store has broken windows.	✓	✓	✓	✓
b. There is a streetlight in front.				
c. There is litter in front.				
d. There is graffiti on the store.				
e. It is next to the hardware store.				
f. It is across the street from the pharmacy.				

2. **Complete the conversation. Use the words in the box.**

streetlights	hardware store	litter	graffiti	street
change	free	give a speech	~~petition~~	

Marta: Excuse me. Would you please sign this ___*petition*___?
a.

We really need to _____ things here.
b.

Main Street is a mess. There's a lot of _____
c.

painted on the stores.

Customer: Yes, there is. And there's a lot of _____
d.

in the street. Is that what the petition is for?

Marta: No. I am going to talk about those things when I _____ to the city council,
e.

but the petition is to repair the _____. They don't work.
f.

Customer: Oh, of course, I'll sign it. This _____ is a mess.
g.

Marta: Thanks. And can you give some of your time?

We need volunteers to do the rest of the work.

Customer: Sure. I can help plant some flowers. And I work right next door

at the _____. I can ask the manager to give some _____ paint.
h. i.

Marta: Oh, great! Thank you.

148

3. Look in your dictionary. How many . . . do you see?

   a. stores on the street   _4_

   b. signatures on the petition   ___

   c. broken streetlights   ___

   d. city council members who are applauding   ___

   e. people who are giving a speech   ___

4. Read Amar's web post. Circle the words to complete the sentences.

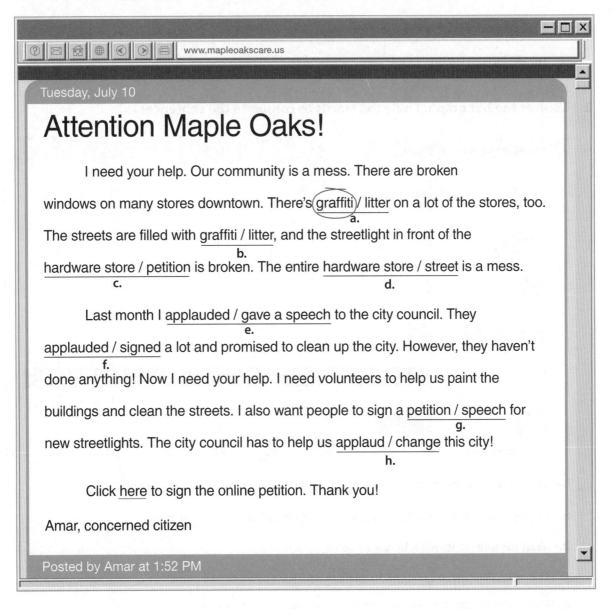

www.mapleoakscare.us

Tuesday, July 10

Attention Maple Oaks!

I need your help. Our community is a mess. There are broken windows on many stores downtown. There's (graffiti) / litter on a lot of the stores, too.
                                                    a.

The streets are filled with graffiti / litter, and the streetlight in front of the
                                             b.

hardware store / petition is broken. The entire hardware store / street is a mess.
                c.   **d.**

Last month I applauded / gave a speech to the city council. They
                                e.

applauded / signed a lot and promised to clean up the city. However, they haven't
     f.

done anything! Now I need your help. I need volunteers to help us paint the

buildings and clean the streets. I also want people to sign a petition / speech for
                                                          g.

new streetlights. The city council has to help us applaud / change this city!
                                                     h.

Click here to sign the online petition. Thank you!

Amar, concerned citizen

Posted by Amar at 1:52 PM

Challenge Imagine there are problems in your community. Write a web post. Tell people about the problems and ask for help. Use Exercise 4 as a model.

See page 295 for listening practice.

1. Look in your dictionary. *True* **or** *False*? **Correct the <u>underlined</u> words in the false sentences.**

a. A passenger is getting into the ~~truck~~. *taxi*   ___false___

b. There is one <u>motorcycle</u> on the street.   _____

c. The <u>helicopter</u> is flying over the airport.   _____

d. The subway station is around the corner from the <u>bus stop</u>.   _____

e. A <u>bicycle</u> rider is wearing a jacket.   _____

f. There are four people at the <u>subway station</u>.   _____

2. Look at the bar graph. Circle the words to complete the sentences.

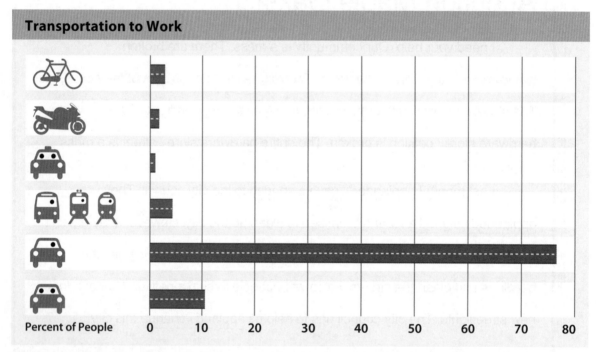

Based on information from: 2005 American Community Survey, U.S. Census Bureau.

a. Almost 5% of the population get to work by bus, train, or <u>car</u> / (subway).

b. Most people go to work by <u>car / train</u>.

c. The least popular way to get to work is by <u>motorcycle / taxi</u>.

d. More people go to work by <u>bicycle / taxi</u> than by motorcycle.

e. More than 75% of people ride to work <u>alone / as a passenger</u> in a car.

3. What about you? How do you get to work? school? the market? the airport? Use your own paper.

4. **Compare these types of transportation. Write sentences with *than* and the words in parentheses ( ).**

a. *The plane is safer than the car.*
(plane / car / safer)

b. _____
(bus / subway / faster)

c. _____
(plane / bus / more expensive)

d. _____
(bicycle / motorcycle / more dangerous)

e. _____
(bus / taxi / cheaper)

f. _____
(car / truck / more comfortable)

5. **Look at the chart. Complete the sentences.**

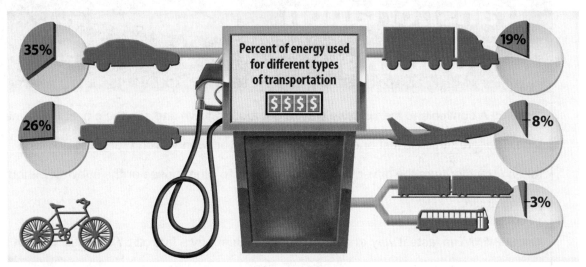

Based on information from: 2005 American Community Survey, U.S. Census Bureau
http://www.eia.doe.gov/kids/energyfacts/uses/transportation.html.

a. Small ___*trucks*___ use 26% of the total energy for all types of transportation.

b. At 19%, large _____ use less energy than small ones.

c. _____ use the most energy of all types of transportation.

d. _____ use only 8% of the total energy for transportation.

e. _____ and _____ together use just 3% of the total energy for transportation.

f. And, of course, _____ use no energy at all!

Challenge What are the advantages (positive points) and disadvantages (negative points)
of different types of transportation? Compare your answers with a classmate's list.
Example: *A bicycle is good exercise. It doesn't use gas, but it isn't very fast.*

See page 295 for listening practice.

1. Look in your dictionary. What are the people talking about? Where are they?

	What?	Where?
a. "<u>It</u> goes in this way."	fare card	subway station
b. "<u>This</u> says there's one at 6:30."		
c. "Use <u>this</u>, Miss, to change at Avenue A."		
d. "<u>It</u> says $22.00, so I'll tip $3.30."		
e. "Is <u>it</u> for a one-way trip or a round trip?"		

2. Circle the words to complete the pamphlet.

Public Transportation Options

THE BUS A convenient, inexpensive way to get around town and see the city at the same time. The (fare) / track is just one price—for one mile or twenty! Don't forget to ask for a
a.
token / transfer from the driver, so you can change to other buses or the subway without
b.
paying again.

THE SUBWAY The fastest way to get around town. Just buy a fare card / schedule from an
c.
automatic conductor / vending machine and put it in the meter / turnstile.
d. **e.**

TAXIS Convenient, but expensive. Watch the meter / shuttle as your driver / rider takes
f. **g.**
you to your destination. The faster you go, the faster it changes (and the more you pay)!

TRAINS For longer distances, a good form of public transportation. A round-trip ticket is sometimes less expensive than two one-way / round-trip tickets, so plan ahead! Buy
h.
one at the subway car / ticket window and then wait on the platform / track for your train.
i. **j.**

Challenge Describe the advantages and disadvantages of different types of public transportation.
Example: *The subway is fast, but you can't see the street from it.*

  See page 296 for listening practice.

1. **Look in your dictionary. *True* or *False*? Correct the <u>underlined</u> words in the false sentences.**

   a. A woman is walking <s>down</s> ~up~ the steps.   *false*

   b. A man is running <u>across the street</u>.   _____

   c. The yellow truck is going to <u>drive through the tunnel</u>.   _____

   d. The blue car is <u>getting off</u> the highway.   _____

2. **Look at the map of Toronto. Circle the words to complete the directions.**

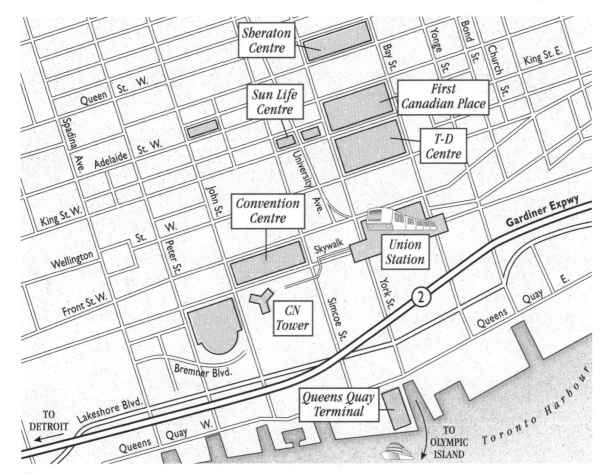

   a. To go from Union Station to Toronto Harbour, <u>get off</u> / <u>go under</u> the Expressway on York St.

   b. To go from the Convention Centre to the Sun Life Centre, get <u>into</u> / <u>out of</u> the taxi on King St.

   c. To go from Queen's Quay Terminal to Olympic Island, go <u>across</u> / <u>around</u> Toronto Harbour.

   d. To go from Union Station to Detroit, get <u>on</u> / <u>off</u> the Expressway at York Street.

   e. To go from CN Tower to Union Station on foot, go <u>over</u> / <u>under</u> the Skywalk.

Challenge Write directions from your home to:
school   the bus station   Other: _____

1. Look in your dictionary. Which signs have . . . ?

a. numbers   _speed limit_ and _____

b. letters, not words   _____ and _____

c. pictures of people   _____, _____, _____, and _____

d. arrows (→)   _____, _____, _____, _____

and _____

2. Complete the written part of a test for a driver's license. Circle the letters of the answers.

 **DRIVING TEST ANSWER SHEET**

1. When you see this sign, you must ____.

a. go more slowly

b. come to a complete stop

c. turn right

2. When you see this sign, you ____.

a. must drive exactly 45 mph

b. can drive 55 mph

c. can drive 60 mph

3. This sign means ____ crossing.

a. pedestrian

b. railroad

c. school

4. This sign means ____.

a. you can't enter the street

b. the street is very dangerous

c. the street ends

5. This sign means you should look for ____.

a. restrooms

b. rivers

c. trains

6. When you see this sign, you can make a ____.

a. left turn

b. right turn

c. U-turn

7. This sign means ____.

a. handicapped parking

b. a hospital

c. no parking any time

8. This sign means ____.

a. do not enter

b. the street ends

c. there's a cemetery nearby

Challenge Draw some other traffic signs. Explain their meanings.

1. Look in your dictionary. *True* or *False*? Correct the underlined words in the false sentences.

a. The car went ~~west~~ *east* on Elm Street.   _____*false*_____

b. It <u>didn't stop at the corner</u> of Elm and Main.   _____

c. It turned <u>right</u> on Pine.   _____

d. It continued to drive <u>south</u> on Oak.   _____

2. Look at the Internet map. Circle the words to complete the sentences.

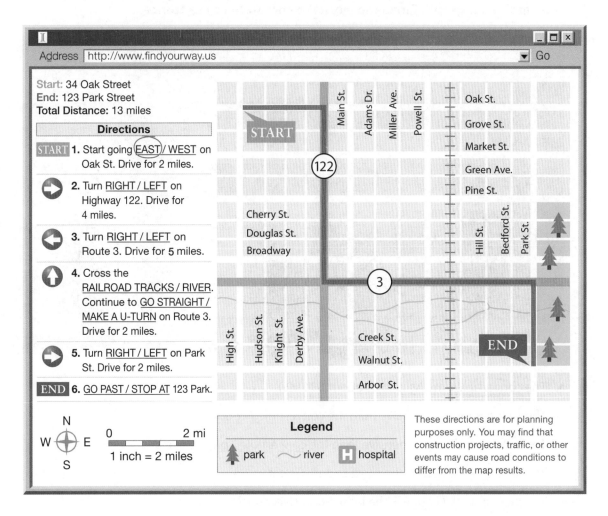

Address http://www.findyourway.us   Go

Start: 34 Oak Street
End: 123 Park Street
Total Distance: 13 miles

Directions

START **1.** Start going (EAST) / WEST on Oak St. Drive for 2 miles.

2. Turn RIGHT / LEFT on Highway 122. Drive for 4 miles.

3. Turn RIGHT / LEFT on Route 3. Drive for **5** miles.

4. Cross the RAILROAD TRACKS / RIVER. Continue to GO STRAIGHT / MAKE A U-TURN on Route 3. Drive for 2 miles.

5. Turn RIGHT / LEFT on Park St. Drive for 2 miles.

END **6.** GO PAST / STOP AT 123 Park.

N W ✛ E S   0   2 mi   1 inch = 2 miles

Legend

🌲 park   ～ river   H hospital

These directions are for planning purposes only. You may find that construction projects, traffic, or other events may cause road conditions to differ from the map results.

Street labels: Main St., Adams Dr., Miller Ave., Powell St., Oak St., Grove St., Market St., Green Ave., Pine St., Hill St., Bedford St., Park St., Cherry St., Douglas St., Broadway, High St., Hudson St., Knight St., Derby Ave., Creek St., Walnut St., Arbor St.

3. Look at the map in Exercise 2. Circle the words to complete the sentences.

a. The <u>Internet map</u> / (river) is blue.

b. According to the <u>scale</u> / GPS, one inch is 2 miles.

c. The map has a <u>symbol</u> / key for parks.

d. The <u>streets</u> / highways are orange.

Challenge Look at the map in Exercise 2. Give directions from 123 Park Street to 34 Oak Street.

See page 296 for listening practice.

1. **Look in your dictionary. Which car or truck . . . ?**

   a. takes furniture from one place to another   *moving van*

   b. takes children to school   _____

   c. helps move your car if it's in an accident   _____

   d. uses both gas and electricity   _____

   e. transports oil from one place to another   _____

   f. can pour sand on the ground   _____

2. **Look at the bar graph. Circle the words to complete the sentences.**

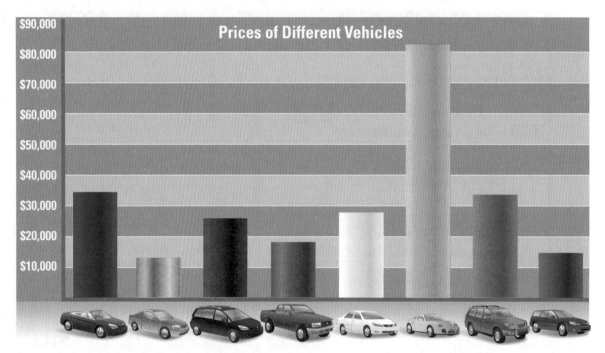

Prices of Different Vehicles

$90,000
$80,000
$70,000
$60,000
$50,000
$40,000
$30,000
$20,000
$10,000

   a. The ⟨convertible⟩/ minivan costs about $34,000.

   b. The sedan is more expensive than the <u>convertible / coupe</u>.

   c. The SUV is a little less expensive than the <u>convertible / pickup truck</u>.

   d. The <u>sports car / coupe</u> is the most expensive car.

   e. The <u>pickup truck / coupe</u> is the least expensive vehicle.

   f. The <u>minivan / station wagon</u> costs about $28,000.

3. **What about you? Look in your dictionary. Which car would you choose? Why?**
   Example: *I would choose a pickup truck. I carry a lot of things, but not many passengers.*

Challenge Look at newspaper or online ads. Find the price range of the car you chose in Exercise 3.

  See page 297 for listening practice.

1. **Look in your dictionary. Complete the sentences.**

    a. Juan wanted to buy __a used car_____.

    b. He _____ in the newspaper and online.

    c. When he _____, he learned how many miles were on the car.

    d. When he _____, he learned that it was in good condition.

    e. He _____ of $2,000.

    f. After he got the title from the seller, he _____.

2. **Look at the checklist. What did Juan do? What didn't he do? Write sentences.**

    ## Car Maintenance

    - ☑ Fill the tank with gas.
    - ☑ Check the oil.
    - ☐ Put in coolant.
    - ☐ Go for a smog check.
    - ☐ Replace the windshield wipers.
    - ☑ Fill the tires with air.

    a. __He filled the tank with gas._____

    b. _____

    c. __He didn't_____

    d. _____

    e. _____

    f. _____

Challenge List other things people do to maintain their cars. **Example:** *They check the spare tire and add air if necessary.*

1. Look in your dictionary. How many . . . does the car have?

a. hubcaps _____4_____

b. license plates _____

c. gauges _____

d. power outlets _____

e. sideview mirrors _____

f. tail pipes _____

g. rearview mirrors _____

h. spare tires _____

2. Complete the conversations. Use the words in the box.

| air conditioner | front seat | ~~gas gauge~~ | gas pedal | glove compartment |
| license plate | radio | rearview mirror | stick shift | temperature gauge |

a. **Passenger:** Look, the _____gas gauge_____ is almost on empty.

   Driver: There's a gas station. I'll stop there.

b. **Driver:** Where would you like to sit?

   Passenger: In the _____, next to you.

c. **Driver:** It would be good to hear a traffic report.

   Passenger: I'll turn on the _____.

d. **Passenger:** It's getting hot in here.

   Driver: We can turn on the _____.

e. **Passenger:** Do we have a map?

   Driver: There should be one in the _____.

f. **Passenger:** That truck is getting very close!

   Driver: Don't worry. I'm watching it in the _____.

g. **Passenger:** Step on the _____! You're going much too slow.

   Driver: OK.

h. **Passenger:** Look at the _____.

   Driver: Oh. The radiator needs coolant. It's much too hot.

i. **Passenger:** That car is leaving the accident scene!

   Driver: Quick! Let's call the police. Write down the _____ number!

j. **Passenger:** Do you like using a _____?

   Driver: Yes. I've always driven a car with a manual transmission.

3. **Circle the words to complete the information from a driver's manual.**

BASIC DRIVING

a. The bumper / steering wheel gives you control over your car.

b. Always have the correct amount of air in your hubcaps / tires. Check the air pressure.

c. When you step on your brake pedal / clutch, your car should stop quickly and smoothly.

d. Jumper cables / Turn signals tell other drivers which direction you are going to go.

e. Brake lights / Tail lights tell other drivers that you are slowing or stopping.

f. Your hood / horn lets other drivers and pedestrians hear that you are there.

g. Lug wrenches / Headlights are important in night driving, rainy weather, and in fog.

h. The heater / windshield should be free of cracks and breaks. Use your gear shift / windshield wipers to clean it.

PREVENTING INJURIES

i. Check your odometer / speedometer to see how fast you are going.

j. All new cars come with air bags / spare tires that open in case of an accident. They keep you from hitting your head against the dashboard / trunk or steering wheel.

k. Back seats / Seat belts help prevent injury or death in case of an accident. Always use them.

l. Use your jacks / door locks to keep your doors from opening in an accident.

m. Buy child safety seats / hazard lights for small children and always use them. It's the law!

AIR AND NOISE POLLUTION CONTROL

n. Make sure there is enough coolant in the battery / radiator.

o. If your car is making a lot of noise, you may need to replace your ignition / muffler.

Challenge Look in your dictionary. Choose five parts of the car that are not described in Exercise 3. What are they for? **Example**: *heater—to keep the inside of the car warm.*

See page 297 for listening practice.

1. **Look in your dictionary. Who's speaking? About what?**

		Who?	About what?
a.	"My other bag isn't on <u>it</u>!"	passenger	baggage carousel
b.	"Put your keys in <u>it</u>, too, with your briefcase."		
c.	"You didn't fill <u>it</u> out."		
d.	"Put <u>it</u> over your face."		

2. **Circle the words to complete the travel trips.**

ESL INTERNATIONAL TRAVEL TIPS

BEFORE YOUR FLIGHT

Arrive at <u>customs / (the airline terminal)</u> three hours before your flight.
   a.

Check the <u>departure monitor / tray table</u> for information about your flight.
   b.

If you don't have a <u>boarding pass / life vest</u>, check in electronically at the
   c.

<u>screening area / check-in kiosk</u> or show your e-ticket to the <u>pilot / ticket agent</u>.
   d.   e.

After going through the <u>cockpit / screening area</u>, go to your <u>bin / gate</u>.
   f.   g.

Wait in the <u>cockpit / boarding area</u>.
   h.

ON THE PLANE

After you find your <u>emergency card / seat</u>, <u>find / stow</u> your carry-on bag in the
   i.   j.

<u>overhead compartment / upright seat</u> near your seat.
   k.

Pay attention as your <u>flight attendant / TSA agent</u> shows you how to put on your
   l.

<u>oxygen mask / reclined seat</u> and gives you other important safety information.
   m.

<u>Fasten / Stow</u> your seat belt and keep it closed in case of turbulence.
   n.

<u>Take / Turn</u> off your cell phone.
   o.

Fill out <u>a declaration form / an arrival monitor</u> before you land.
   p.

AFTER YOU LAND

Go to the <u>check-in kiosk / baggage carousel</u> to <u>check in / claim</u> your baggage.
   q.   r.

Take your bags through <u>customs / the emergency exit</u>.
   s.

3. **Look at Taking a Flight on page 160 in your dictionary.** *Before or After?*
   Circle the words to complete the sentences.

   a. The passenger checked his bags before / (after) he checked in electronically.

   b. He stowed his carry-on bag before / after he found his seat.

   c. He turned off his cell phone before / after the plane took off.

4. **Look at the flight information.** *True or False?* **Write a question mark (?)**
   if the information isn't there.

MERLIN, JARED
PAGE 1 OF 1 FILE #142-34-02-54-2

Reconfirm reservations 72 hours prior to each flight. Failure to do so may result in missing
your flight or having the space canceled by the airline.

AIRWAY AIRLINES	FLIGHT 613	10 MAR SUN
DEPART 0755A	NEW YORK LGA	CHECK-IN REQUIRED
ARRIVE 1048A	MIAMI INTERNATIONAL	MEALS: SNACK
AIRWAY AIRLINES	FLIGHT 695	10 MAR SUN
DEPART 1115A	MIAMI INTERNATIONAL	SEAT 23D NON-SMOKING
ARRIVE 1215P	SAN JUAN	MEALS: SPECIAL LOW-SALT

a. The passenger bought his ticket from Happy Travel.   _____true_____

b. This is an e-ticket.   _____

c. The arrival time in Miami is 11:15 a.m.   _____

d. The departure time from New York is 7:55 a.m.   _____

e. Passengers will board flight 613 at 7:35 a.m.   _____

f. Passengers can have two carry-on bags.   _____

g. Flight 613 takes off on Sunday morning.   _____

h. It lands on Sunday afternoon.   _____

i. The passenger doesn't have to check in for flight 613.   _____

j. He is in seat 23D on flight 695.   _____

k. The seat is next to an emergency exit.   _____

l. The passenger requested a special meal.   _____

m. Passengers will claim their baggage at carousel 4.   _____

Challenge Write a paragraph about a plane trip you or someone you know took.

See page 298 for listening practice.

Taking a Trip

1. **Look in your dictionary. Number the sentences in the correct order. (Number 1 = the first thing that happened)**

   ____ **a.** They have a flat tire.

   ____ **b.** They get lost.

   ____ **c.** They run out of gas.

   ____ **d.** They look at scenery.

   ____ **e.** They arrive at their destination.

   ____ **f.** They ask a gas station attendant for directions.

   ____ **g.** They get a speeding ticket.

   _1_ **h.** Joe and Rob leave Seattle, their starting point.

   ____ **i.** Their car breaks down.

2. **What's happening? Match.**

   _2_ **a.** "Where are we? Was that our turn?"

   ____ **b.** "Go straight one mile. Then turn right."

   ____ **c.** "The car is stopping. We forgot to buy gas!"

   ____ **d.** "You were way over the speed limit."

   ____ **e.** "Our bags are in the car. Let's go to New York!"

   ____ **f.** "The mountains are beautiful!"

   ____ **g.** "There's smoke coming out of the engine!"

   ____ **h.** "Please send a truck. We're ten miles west of El Paso."

   ____ **i.** "I'm going to bring my bathing suit and suntan lotion."

   ____ **j.** "I'll take the flat tire off. Would you get the spare tire?"

   1. They're calling a tow truck.
   2. They're getting lost.
   3. They're running out of gas.
   4. They're getting a speeding ticket.
   5. They're packing.
   6. They're getting directions.
   7. They're leaving their starting point.
   8. They're looking at scenery.
   9. Their car is breaking down.
   10. They're changing a flat tire.

3. **What about you? Check (✓) the things that have happened to you. Tell a classmate about your experiences.**

   ☐ I forgot to pack something important.   ☐ I ran out of gas.

   ☐ I got a speeding ticket.   ☐ I got a flat tire.

   ☐ My car broke down.   ☐ I got lost.

162

4. Complete the story. Use the words in the box.

pack	get a speeding ticket	breaks down	get lost
~~destination~~	scenery	gas station attendant	run out of gas
road trip	tow truck	mechanic	

_____Destination_____ : **CHICAGO**
a.

"I'm tired of San Diego," Jane says. "Let's take a

_____ on spring break and visit Lia in Chicago." "Let's
b.

_____ our bags!" says Tonya. "I can't wait." A week later, Jane and Tonya
c.

are driving through the beautiful _____ in Nevada. But problems are still
d.

in front of them. They _____ in Utah, and they stop to ask a
e.

_____ for directions. They _____ in Colorado because
f.   g.

they are driving too fast. In Kansas, they _____. Jane walks to a gas station
h.

and buys some. Finally, their car _____ only fifty miles from Chicago.
i.

Tonya calls a _____, and the truck takes the car to a mechanic. "Your car
j.

will be ready in two days," says the _____. The friends rent a car. Two
k.

hours later, they're at Lia's door.

5. Complete the sentences about Jane and Tonya's trip home. Use the words in the box.

get a speeding ticket	~~have any problems~~	run out of gas
break down	get lost	have a flat tire

a. Jane and Tonya had a great trip home because they didn't _have any problems_____.

b. They always obeyed the speed limit, so they didn't _____.

c. A mechanic checked their car, so their car didn't _____.

d. They remembered to buy gas, so they didn't _____.

e. They bought some new tires, so they didn't _____.

f. They got good directions on the Internet, so they didn't _____.

Challenge Write a story about a road trip. Use your own experience or your imagination.

1. Look in your dictionary. Who . . . ? Check (✓) the columns.

	The Employer	The Receptionist	The Payroll Clerk	The Supervisor	All Employees
a. uses a time clock					✓
b. greets customers					
c. signs paychecks					
d. receives paychecks					
e. hands out paychecks					
f. gives instructions					

2. Complete the conversations. Use the words in the box.

customer	deductions	employee	entrance
payroll clerk	~~receptionist~~	time clock	pay stub

Receptionist : Irina's Computer Service. How can I help you?
    a.

_____ : I need to bring in my computer. Could you tell me your address?
    b.

_____ : This is my first day. I need to clock in, but I can't find the
    c.

                  _____ .
                d.

Supervisor: It's over there. To the right of the _____ where you
                                   e.

        come in.

Employee: I don't understand my _____ . Why are there so
                            f.

        many _____ ?
                  g.

_____ : Well, this one is for federal. This is for state. This is for Social Security.
    h.

**3. What about you? Look in your dictionary. Answer the questions.
Discuss your answers with a classmate.**

    a. Would you like to work at Irina's Computer Service? Why or why not?

    _____

    b. Would you prefer to work in the office or the room with the time clock? Why?

    _____

4. **Look in your dictionary. *True* or *False*? Correct the underlined words in the false sentences.**

   A customer
   a. ~~An employee~~ is standing in the entrance.   _false_

   b. Employees can find the <u>safety regulations</u> near the door   _____
      that says *Employees Only*.

   c. Irina Sarkov is in <u>the office</u>.   _____

   d. The <u>payroll clerk</u> is giving Kate Babic a paycheck.   _____

   e. The supervisor is talking to <u>the employer</u>.   _____

5. **Look at the pay stub and paycheck. Answer the questions.**

   a. What is the employee's name?
      Enrique Gutierrez

   b. What is the employer's name?
      _____

   c. What is the pay stub amount?
      _____

   d. What are the wages before deductions?
      _____

   e. How many deductions are there?
      _____

   f. Which is more, the state deduction or
      the Social Security deduction?
      _____

   g. What is the amount of the paycheck?
      _____

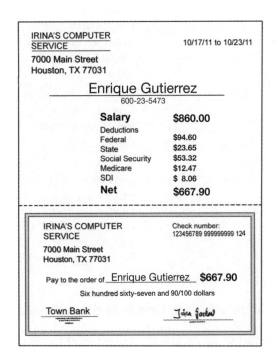

IRINA'S COMPUTER SERVICE   10/17/11 to 10/23/11
7000 Main Street
Houston, TX 77031

Enrique Gutierrez
600-23-5473

Salary	$860.00
Deductions	
Federal	$94.60
State	$23.65
Social Security	$53.32
Medicare	$12.47
SDI	$ 8.06
Net	**$667.90**

- -

IRINA'S COMPUTER SERVICE   Check number: 123456789 999999999 124
7000 Main Street
Houston, TX 77031

Pay to the order of _Enrique Gutierrez_ **$667.90**

Six hundred sixty-seven and 90/100 dollars

Town Bank   *Irina Sarkov*

Challenge Look at the pay stub in Exercise 5. What is *SDI*? Does the state you live in have this type of deduction? Look up *SDI* online or ask someone you know.

1. **Look in your dictionary. Write the job titles.**

JOBS $A3$

a. _____Baker_____ to make bread, pies, and cakes at our midtown restaurant. $9.67/hr. 555-2343

b. _____ to prepare and sell meat at our busy counter. S & W Supermarket. $28,000/yr. Call 555-4345

c. _____ to receive payment, give change and receipts to customers. Amy's Foods. Mineral Springs Road. 555-2243

d. _____ to plan and design public buildings at our growing firm. MCKAY, BROWN, & PETRILLO. 555-3451

e. _____ to watch our two preschoolers. Good storytelling skills a must! Excellent references required. $15/hr. 555-3406

f. _____ to put together parts in radio factory. On-the-job-training. $450/wk. Call Frank Collins. 555-9922.

g. _____ to repair and maintain cars at small garage. Part-time, weekends. 555-7396

h. _____ to help build shelves and doors in new building. $525/wk., 555-4345. Ask for Mr. Heller.

i. _____ to perform in plays for a small theater company. TV, stage, or movie experience. 555-8299

j. _____ to plan and organize appointments for busy business executive. H. Thomas & Sons. 555-8787

2. **Circle the words to complete the sentences.**

   a. A carpenter / childcare worker works with children.

   b. An auto mechanic / accountant needs to be good with numbers.

   c. An appliance repair person / assembler can fix refrigerators.

   d. An architect / artist enjoys painting.

   e. Many business owners / businesspeople have their own stores.

3. **What about you? Look at the ads in Exercise 1. Which job would you like? Which job wouldn't you like? Why?**

Challenge Look at page 258 in this book. Follow the instructions.

1. Look in your dictionary. *True* or *False*? Correct the underlined words in the false sentences.

    dental assistant

a. The home health care aide and the ~~customer service representative~~ work with patients.   _____*false*_____

b. The <u>graphic designer</u> uses a computer.   _____

c. The delivery person works for a <u>gardener</u>.   _____

d. The firefighter and the <u>dockworker</u> wear hard hats.   _____

2. Look at the bar graph. Circle the words to complete the sentences.

How Stressful* is the Job?

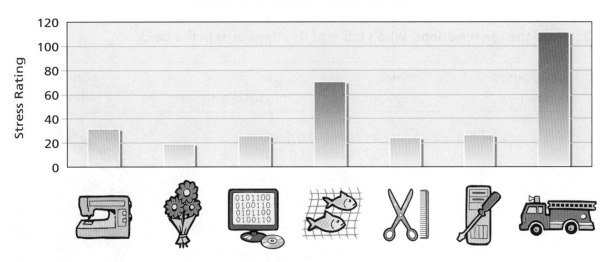

* A *stressful* job can make you feel nervous and not relaxed.
Based on information from: Krantz, L.: *Jobs Rated Almanac* (NJ: Barricade Books, 2002).

a. A <u>computer technician / (firefighter)</u> has the job with the most stress.

b. A <u>florist / computer software engineer</u> has the job with the least stress.

c. A garment worker's job is less stressful than a <u>computer technician's / commercial fisher's</u> job.

d. A hairdresser and a <u>computer software engineer / commercial fisher</u> have about the same amount of job stress.

e. A hairdresser has less job stress than a <u>florist / garment worker</u>.

3. What about you? Look in your dictionary. Which job do you think is the most stressful? the least stressful? Why?

Challenge Look at pages 166–169 in your dictionary. Find five other stressful jobs. Tell a classmate. Do you and your classmate agree?

See page 299 for listening practice.

1. Look in your dictionary. Cross out the word that doesn't belong. Give a reason.

a. homemaker   ~~musician~~   housekeeper

A musician doesn't work in the home.

b. machine operator   nurse   occupational therapist

_____

c. (house) painter   medical records technician   manicurist

_____

d. police officer   messenger   homemaker

_____

e. physician assistant   nurse   model

_____

2. Read the conversations. Who's talking? Use the words in the box.

interpreter	~~lawyer~~	manicurist	model
mover	musician	physician assistant	police officer

a. _____Lawyer_____: "Your honor, I object!
My client is not guilty!"

_____: "Monsieur le juge, je récuse!
Mon client n'est pas coupable!"

b. _____: "Where should we put this couch?"

_____: "Over there. That way our patients
can look out the window while
they're waiting."

c. _____: "I'll be wearing a red dress at the fashion show."

_____: "Well, this color nail polish will look great with it."

d. _____: "Where were you yesterday between 11:00 and 11:30 p.m.?"

_____: "I was at the Blue Note Club, detective. I was playing the piano."

Challenge Write three short conversations between a police officer and a house painter,
a homemaker and a mover, and a messenger and a physician assistant.
Use the conversations in Exercise 2 as an example.

1. **Look in your dictionary. Who said . . . ?**

   a. "These shoes are very comfortable. Would you like to try them on?" _____retail clerk_____

   b. "It can be difficult being a single mom, but we can help you." _____

   c. ". . . 18, 19, 20 . . . . That's 20 boxes of desk lamps." _____

   d. "You can get a very special offer, but you must order today!" _____

   e. "Ms. Davidson's office is through the glass doors to your left." _____

2. **Look at the chart. *True* or *False*?**

Occupation	Hours a week	$ a year
	45	40,000
	42.5	28,000
	42.5	20,000
	47.5	35,000
	35	16,000
	40	73,000
	45	31,000
	45	50,000

   Based on information from: Krantz, L.: *Jobs Rated Almanac* (NJ: Barricade Books, 2002).

   a. A truck driver works more hours a week than a sanitation worker. _____true_____

   b. A server works as many hours as a security guard. _____

   c. A veterinarian works the most hours and makes the most money. _____

   d. A server works the fewest hours and makes the least money. _____

   e. A welder works as many hours as a writer and makes almost as much money. _____

   f. A reporter makes two times as much money as a security guard. _____

Challenge Look at job ads online or in the newspaper. Find four jobs. Make a chart like the one in Exercise 2. Then write four sentences comparing the jobs.

See page 300 for listening practice. **169**

Job Skills

1. **Look in your dictionary. Complete the job descriptions.**

   a. A cashier _____ *uses a cash register* _____.

   b. A childcare worker _____.

   c. A garment worker _____.

   d. A carpenter _____.

   e. A server _____.

   f. An interpreter _____.

2. **What about you? Complete the questionnaire. Check (✓) the job skills you have.**

Can you...?	Kim	Alexis	Carlos	Diana	Your name: _____
solve math problems	✓				
program computers	✓			✓	
type	✓		✓	✓	
sell cars		✓		✓	
repair appliances				✓	
operate heavy machinery			✓		
drive a truck		✓			
teach	✓				
do manual labor	✓		✓		
assemble components		✓	✓		

3. **Look at the chart in Exercise 2. *True* or *False*?**

   a. Kim could apply for a job as a teacher. _____ *true* _____

   b. Carlos could get a job as a truck driver. _____

   c. Only Diana could apply for a job as a repair person. _____

   d. Both Kim and Alexis could get jobs as assemblers. _____

   e. Alexis could apply for a job as a salesperson, but not as a repair person. _____

   f. Kim, Carlos, and Diana could be administrative assistants. _____

   g. You and Kim could work as accountants. _____

   h. You and Carlos can both work with your hands. _____

Challenge Look at page 258 in this book. Follow the instructions.

  See page 300 for listening practice.

1. **Look in your dictionary. What does the administrative assistant need to do to follow the boss's instructions?**

   a. "Please put these files in alphabetical order."   _organize materials_

   b. "I'd like to meet with Mr. Lorenzo next Friday, if possible."   _____

   c. "Could you send this report to Amy Ma at 555-3523?"   _____

   d. "We need enough copies for thirty people."   _____

2. **Read the conversations. Circle the words to complete the sentences.**

   a. **Ana:**   J & R Associates. Good morning.
      Caller 1: Hello. Can I speak to John Smith, please?

      Ana is <u>putting the caller on hold</u> / (greeting the caller.)

   b. **Caller 2:** Is Marta Rodriguez there?
      Ana: Yes. I'll connect you.

      Ana is <u>checking messages / transferring the call</u>.

   c. **Caller 3:** Can I speak to Tom Chen, please?
      Ana: I'm sorry. Mr. Chen isn't in.
      Caller 3: OK. Please tell him that I called.
      Ana: Sure. What is your name and number, please?

      Ana is <u>leaving a message / taking a message</u>.

   Ana

3. **Look at the pictures. Write what the office assistant can do.**

   a. _____He can transcribe notes._____   c. _____

   b. _____   d. _____

Challenge Look in your dictionary. Make a list of the office and telephone skills you have.

Career Planning

1. **Look in your dictionary. Complete the sentences.**

   a. _Vocational training_ gives you "hands on" experience.

   b. One woman is taking an _____ in medical transcription.

   c. One man is getting _____ from his supervisor.

   d. Ms. Diaz recently got a _____. Now she's a manager.

2. **Complete the FAQs (Frequently Asked Questions) from a website. Use the words in the box.**

~~career counselors~~	internship	interest inventory	job fair
on-the-job training	resource center	recruiters	skill inventory
vocational training			

   Career Counseling Center

   Q. I'm not really sure about the kind of job I want. Can you help me?

   A. Yes! Come and talk to one of our _career counselors_. An _____ will
                                 a.   **b.**

   help you find out the kinds of jobs you will enjoy. A _____ will show you the
                                                  c.

   kinds of jobs you will be good at.

   Q. What if I'm interested in a job but don't have the necessary skills?

   A. Many jobs offer _____. You learn the skills <u>after</u> you are hired.
                                       d.

   Q. How can I learn skills <u>before</u> I'm hired?

   A. There are several possibilities. _____ teaches practical skills for a specific
                                             e.

   job, for example a car mechanic or a computer programmer. But you can also get an

   _____ with a company before you graduate from school.
                        f.

   Q. How can I get more information about a specific job?

   A. Our _____ has hundreds of books and brochures about different jobs.
                      g.

   And you can speak to _____ from various companies at our yearly
                                      h.

   _____ .
         i.

   Challenge When is it good to have vocational training? List four jobs. Tell a classmate.

1. **Look in your dictionary.** *Before* **or** *After*? **Circle the words to complete the sentences.**

   a. Dan checked Internet job sites (before) / after he went to an employment agency.

   b. He wrote a cover letter <u>before / after</u> he wrote a resume.

   c. <u>Before / After</u> he looked in the classifieds, he talked to friends.

   d. <u>Before / After</u> he went on an interview, he filled out an application.

2. **Complete the information. Use the words in the box.**

set up an interview	check Internet job sites	send in your resume
write a resume	~~talk to friends~~	go on the interview
fill out an application	get hired	go to an employment agency
look in the classifieds	look for help wanted signs	

---

http://www.jobtips/default.us

Looking for a Job
It can take a lot of time—and work—to find a job. Here are some tips.

Tell everyone that you are looking for work. Begin close to home. <u>   Talk to friends   </u>,
a.

relatives, teachers, and classmates. Keep your eyes open. When you're walking down the street,

_____ in store windows. Get the newspaper every day and be sure to
b.

_____. Go online to _____. If you want someone to help
c.   **d.**

you with the process, _____. They can even help you _____ by
e.   **f.**

listing all your work experience and education.

Applying for a job: When you apply for a job, _____ and a cover letter. Interested
g.

employers will call you to _____. Then, you will probably have to
h.

_____. This gives the employer basic information about your skills and experience.
i.

When you _____, you will have the chance to talk about your experience in more
j.

detail. It's a long process. Remember: Be patient and don't give up. You may have to try many different

approaches before you finally _____ and get that first paycheck!
k.

Challenge Look at page 259 in this book. Follow the instructions.

See page 301 for listening practice. **173**

Interview Skills

1. Look in your dictionary. Write the interview skill.

a. "I worked there for four years."   <u>talk about your experience</u>

b. "Is there health insurance?"   _____

c. "Nice to meet you."   _____

d. "Hmm. This website says GBG has 100 employees."   _____

2. Look at the pictures. Circle the words to complete the interviewer's notes.

GLOBAL IMPORTERS   Amy Cho Interview   4/23

Ms. Cho (dressed appropriately) / prepared in a suit, and she **was / wasn't** very
              a.   b.

neat. The interview was at 10:00, but she was **late / on time**. She didn't
                                                        c.

bring her resume / turn off her cell phone. Ms. Cho **greeted me / shook hands,**
                 d.   e.

but she didn't **listen carefully / make eye contact**. She **asked questions / talked**
                                      f.   g.

about her work experience. I liked that she **asked / brought** questions about
                                                  h.

our company. At the end of the interview, she **didn't thank / thanked** me, but
                                                        i.

a few days later she **brought her resume / wrote a thank-you note**.
                                                    j.

Challenge Look at Exercise 2. Would you give Amy Cho a job? Why or why not?

  See page 301 for listening practice.

1. Look in your dictionary. Complete the factory newsletter.

THE LAMPLIGHTER

"WE LIGHT UP YOUR LIFE" Vol. 25, no. 2 June 7, 2012

T. J. Rolf, President
and ___factory owner___
a.

"As we enter our 25th year of business, I want to thank the following people for their dedication and hard work."

WELCOME TO LAMPLIGHTER

Jan Larson,
_____
d.
Jan has been hired to
_____
e.
a new desk lamp. We will begin
to _____
f.
this new product in September.
WELCOME JAN!

20 YEARS

Pete Johnson,
Shipping Clerk

Pete has been with us for more than 20 years. He has stood on the
_____ carefully
b.
checking the orders that we
_____ to over
c.
32 states. Congratulations, Pete!
Employee of the Month!

15 YEARS

Ivonne Campis,
Assembler

For 15 years, Ivonne has assembled the _____
g.
that make our lamps. Her skills and care have contributed to the high quality of our product.

10 YEARS

Doug Wilson,
_____
h.
For 10 years, Doug has watched over the assembly line, assuring the highest product quality. He helps create a friendly and productive work environment.

5 YEARS

Alice Carver,
_____
i.
Alice Carver has worked in the
_____ for 5 years,
j.
taking finished lamps off the conveyor belt and putting them in boxes ready for shipment.

Challenge Look in your dictionary. Write short paragraphs about the shipping clerk and the order puller for the factory newsletter in Exercise 1. Use your imagination.

See page 302 for listening practice. **175**

1. Look in your dictionary. Complete the sentences.

a. The _____*trowel*_____ is to the left of the hedge clippers.

b. The gardening crew leader is talking to the _____.

c. You can use a _____ or a _____
to remove leaves from your lawn.

d. You can use a _____ to remove weeds.

e. You need a _____ to plant a tree.

f. You can cut the grass with a _____.

g. You can use a _____ to move dirt or plants.

h. You can water the lawn by hand, or you can install a _____.

2. Look at the picture. Complete the note to the gardening crew.

> Carlos,
>
> I ___*fertilized*___ the plants and
>   **a.**
> _____ the hedges, but please:
>   **b.**
> _____
>   **c.**
> _____
>   **d.**
> _____
>   **e.**
> _____
>   **f.**
> _____
>   **g.**
>   Thanks!!

Challenge Compare a shovel to a trowel and hedge clippers to pruning sheers. How are they the
same? How are they different? What can you use them for?

1. Look in your dictionary. Cross out the word that doesn't belong. Write the category.

a.   _Place for animals_   barn   corral   ~~vegetable garden~~

b.   _____   hired hand   field   orchard

c.   _____   vineyard   soybeans   wheat

d.   _____   farmer   rancher   tractor

e.   _____   hay   livestock   cattle

2. Circle the words to complete the blog.

myspot.us   <<back   MySpot.us | rss 🔊 | sign in | sign out

SAMANTHA'S TRAVELS

JULY 10: **My First Day on the Farm**

When I got up, it was still dark. John Johnson, the

(farmer) / hired hand who owns the place, was already
        a.

in the corral / barn. He was harvesting / milking the
        b.   **c.**

cows. My job was to feed / plant the chickens and
                        d.

other cattle / livestock.
        e.

Breakfast here is great! We have fresh eggs and ham along with tomatoes from

the vegetable garden / vineyard and fruit from the barn / orchard. After breakfast, it
        f.   **g.**

is time to work in the fence / field. John says that in the old days horses pulled most
        h.

of the farm equipment / steers. Today, a hired hand / tractor does the job. John and
        i.   **j.**

his farm workers / ranchers planted rows of corn and other crops / wheat. They also
        k.   **l.**

grow alfalfa / cotton for animal feed. I'd like to come back when they harvest / milk
        m.   **n.**

the corn in the summer. I like life on the farm.

POSTED BY SAMANTHA AT 1:52 PM   [REPLY TO THIS]

Challenge Would you like to spend some time on a farm or a ranch? Write a paragraph explaining
your opinion.

Construction

1. **Look in your dictionary. *True* or *False*? Correct the underlined words in the false sentences.**

   a. There are ~~eight~~ *thirteen* construction workers on the site.   *false*

   b. One worker is climbing a <u>ladder</u>.   _____

   c. Two construction workers are helping move the <u>plywood</u>.   _____

   d. The worker in the <u>cherry picker</u> is not hammering.   _____

   e. One worker is using a <u>sledgehammer</u>.   _____

2. **Complete the sentences. Use the words on the bricks.**

   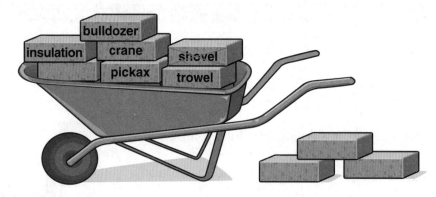

   a. You can use a _____*shovel*_____ to dig a small hole in the ground.

   b. A _____ moves earth or large rocks from one place to another.

   c. _____ keeps a house warm.

   d. A _____ can lift and place beams on high floors.

   e. A _____ is used to lay bricks.

   f. A _____ is used to dig in very hard ground.

3. **What about you? Check (✓) the materials that your school and home are made of.**

	School	Home
bricks		
shingles		
stucco		
wood		
Other:		

   Challenge Look for pictures of buildings in your dictionary, newspaper, or in a magazine. What building materials are used? **Example:** *The condominium on page 52 is made of brick.*

  See page 303 for listening practice.

1. Look in your dictionary. *True* or *False*?

a. The man listening to music is a careful worker.   *false*

b. The frayed cord is near the slippery floor.   _____

c. There's a fire extinguisher near the flammable liquids.   _____

d. Poisonous fumes are coming from the radioactive materials.   _____

2. Circle the words to complete the safety poster.

⚠ **WARNING**

PROTECT YOURSELF
from Head to Toe!

Protect your head: A (hard hat) / respirator can protect you from falling objects. Don't forget
          a.
your hair. If it's long, wear your hair back so it won't get caught in machinery.

Protect your eyes: Always wear safety glasses / work gloves or earmuffs / safety goggles.
                                    b.   **c.**
Protect your ears: Noise can cause hearing loss. Wear ear plugs / safety goggles or safety
                                                              d.
earmuffs / particle masks if you work near loud machinery.
          e.
Protect your hands: Always wear work gloves / back support belts when handling
                                        f.
knee pads / radioactive materials.
          g.
Protect your feet: Knee pads / Safety boots protect you from falling objects.
                            h.
Avoid dangerous situations: Don't use power tools in wet locations or near

radioactive / flammable liquids or gases. Keep a fire extinguisher / respirator on the wall
          i.   **j.**
in case of fire. And have a frayed cord / two-way radio so you can communicate with
                                        k.
other workers. Remember: Better safe than sorry!

3. What about you? What safety equipment do you use? When do you use it?

Example: *I wear ear plugs when I go to a loud concert.*

Challenge Look at page 259 in this book. Follow the instructions.

See page 303 for listening practice.

1. **Look in your dictionary. Cross out the word that doesn't belong.**
   Then write the section of the hardware store.

   a. ___Hardware___   nail   bolt   ~~C-clamp~~   wood screw

   b. _____   ax   plunger   pipe   fittings

   c. _____   circular saw   2 × 4   router   electric drill

   d. _____   paintbrush   paint roller   spray gun   chisel

   e. _____   wire stripper   drill bit   extension cord   wire

   f. _____   hacksaw   chain   adjustable wrench   mallet

2. **Complete the conversations. Use the words on the toolbox.**

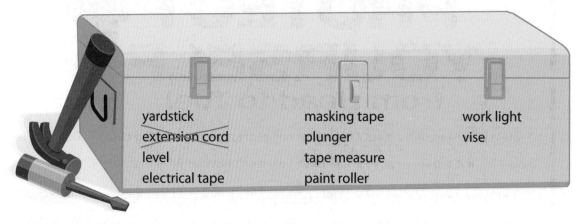

yardstick   masking tape   work light
~~extension cord~~   plunger   vise
level   tape measure
electrical tape   paint roller

a. **Ty:**   I want to use this electric drill over there, but the cord is too short.
    Jade: No problem. Use this ___extension cord___.

b. **Ian:**   I've been painting for hours, and I still have three more walls to do.
    Tina: Why don't you use this _____? It's faster than a paint brush.

c. **Lily:**   Oh, no. The toilet is stopped up again.
    Dan: Here. Use this _____. It always works.

d. **Kim:**   Do you know how long the shelf in the dining room is?
    Lian: No. Use the _____ or _____ to find out.

e. **Eva:**   Help! I could use a third hand here!
    Jana: Use the _____ to hold the wood in place.

f. **Jules:**   Don't get paint on the glass!
    Lyle: I won't. I always put _____ around the panes before I start.

g. **Nico:**   That wire doesn't look very safe.
    Iris: Don't worry. I'll put some of this _____ on before using it.

h. **Olga:**   Does this shelf look straight?
    Boris: Hmm. I'm not sure. Let's use the _____. Then we'll know for certain.

i. **Enzo:**   It's so dark behind here. I can't see what I'm doing!
    Pia: Here. Use the _____.

3. **Look at the pictures. Each situation shows a mistake. Describe the mistake and tell the people what they need to do the job right.**

a.

You can't paint on that wall.
You need to use a scraper first.

b.

_____
_____

c.

_____
_____

d.

_____
_____

e.

_____
_____

f.

_____
_____

4. **What about you? Check (✓) the tools you or someone you know has used. What did you use them for?**

☐ hammer _____

☐ ax _____

☐ handsaw _____

☐ screwdriver _____

☐ pliers _____

☐ plane _____

☐ wrench _____

☐ vise _____

☐ electric drill _____

☐ Other: _____

Challenge Imagine you can have only three tools from the ones in Exercise 4. Which would you choose? Explain your choice.

See page 303 for listening practice.

1. Look in your dictionary. Answer the questions.

a. Who is in the reception area? _the receptionist_

b. Who is working in the cubicle next to the conference room? _____

c. Who is walking to the supply cabinet? _____

d. Who is cleaning the floor? _____

e. Where is the presentation? _____

f. Who is standing at the file cabinet? _____

2. Match the word parts.

_5_ **a.** paper   **1.** bands

___ **b.** correction   **2.** book

___ **c.** postal   **3.** scale

___ **d.** rubber   **4.** pad

___ **e.** appointment   **5.** shredder

___ **f.** legal   **6.** fluid

3. Read the notes. What do you need to do the job? Use the words from Exercise 2.

> Please collate these pages, but don't staple them.
> Thanks.
> L.

> There are some mistakes in this report. Please correct them before you make copies.

> * This is for your eyes only!
> Please read and destroy.

a. _rubber bands_   b. _____   c. _____

> Please let me know when my next meeting with L. J. Inc. is.

> I'll be out of the office on Friday. Please take notes at the staff meeting.
> Thanks.
> R.F.

> Mail two packages to Anne Miles.

d. _____   e. _____   f. _____

4. **Look in your dictionary. Cross out the word that doesn't belong. Give a reason.**

   a. janitor   file clerk   ~~mailer~~   receptionist   <u>A mailer isn't a person.</u>

   b. scanner   desk   file cabinet   supply cabinet   _____

   c. envelope   ink pad   letterhead   sticky note   _____

   d. rubber band   paper clip   paper cutter   staples   _____

   e. calculator   computer   fax machine   stapler   _____

5. **Circle the words to complete the instructions.**

MEMO

To: Alice Rader

From: Marta Lopez *ML*

_____

* The electric pencil sharpener / (photocopier) is broken again. Please call the repair
  a.
  person. You'll find the phone number in the laser printer / rotary card file under "p."
  b.

* The book on my desk goes to A. Olinski at 354 Main Street. The mailing label / stamp
  c.
  is already filled out. Please use glue / clear tape so you can read the address through it.
  d.

* The Thompson report is more than 500 pages. Use the stapler / laser printer so it prints
  e.
  out faster. Before you file it, use the paper cutter / shredder to make it 8 × 10 inches.
  f.
  The paper in the printer is too long now.

* Please stamp all letters to Japan "air mail." (The legal / ink pad is in the top
  g.
  left drawer.)

* Please order more rubber bands / clear tape. (I like the ones that come in different
  h.
  colors and sizes.)

Thanks.

Challenge Look at the office supplies in your dictionary. Which items can you use for the same job?

Example: *You can use an inkjet printer or a laser printer to print out computer files.*

See page 304 for listening practice.   **183**

1. Look in your dictionary. Read these job descriptions. Write the job.

a. Register and check out guests: _____desk clerk_____

b. Carry the guests' luggage on a luggage cart: _____

c. Take care of the guests' cars: _____

d. Clean the guests' rooms: _____

e. Repair and service hotel equipment: _____

2. Circle the words to complete the hotel website.

Address http://www.greatwoodhotel.us

Greatwood Hotel

GUEST ROOM | POOL | GYM | MEETING ROOM | BALLROOM | RESTAURANTS

As soon as you come through our hallway/(revolving door) you'll be our doorman/guest!
  a.   b.

For business or pleasure — we have everything you need…

Accommodations: 285 comfortable guest/meeting rooms with double or king-size
  c.
beds/housekeeping carts and 10 larger pools/suites with tables and couches
  d.   e.
(non-smoking available). Cable TV, A/C, VCR, and free Internet access in all rooms.

Food: Eat at our excellent restaurant or call our 24-hour pool/room service.
  f.

Recreation: Swim in our heated outdoor ballroom/pool. Work out in our gym/meeting rooms.
  g.   h.

Services/Features: Driving here? Enjoy our free parking. Shop at our beautiful

gift shop/luggage cart. And take the elevator/front desk up to our roof for a great view!
  i.   j.

Challenge Imagine you are staying at the hotel in your dictionary. Write a post card.
Describe the hotel.

 See page 304 for listening practice.

1. **Look in your dictionary. Read these job descriptions. Write the job.**

http://www.restaurantopening.us

Large Hotel Restaurant Now Hiring for the Following Positions:

____*caterer*____ : to prepare and serve food for large banquet room events
a.

_____ : to plan menus
b.

_____ : to help the head chef
c.

_____ : to bring food and drinks to the diners
d.

_____ : to clear the tables
e.

_____ : to prepare hamburgers and other fast food
f.

_____ : to supervise servers
g.

_____ : to carry food from the walk-in freezer and storeroom
h. into the kitchen

_____ : to greet guests and show them to their tables
i.

_____ : to wash dirty glasses and plates
j.

To apply, please visit our website at www.hotelgrand.us

2. **What about you? Would you like to be a . . . ? Check (✓) Yes or No. Give a reason.**

	Yes	No	
a. short-order cook	☐	☐	_____
b. dishwasher	☐	☐	_____
c. food preparation worker	☐	☐	_____
d. sous chef	☐	☐	_____
e. server	☐	☐	_____
f. headwaiter	☐	☐	_____
g. bus person	☐	☐	_____
h. caterer	☐	☐	_____
i. runner	☐	☐	_____

Challenge Write a job ad for a restaurant worker. Use the job descriptions in Exercise 1 as an example.

1. **Look in your dictionary. How many . . . do you see?**

   a. accidents that have happened or will happen   _7_

   b. bricklayers   ____

   c. dates on the schedule   ____

   d. electrical hazards   ____

   e. budgets   ____

   f. notes about people who called in sick   ____

   g. floor plans   ____

2. **Look in your dictionary. Answer the questions.**

   a. How much will the drywall cost?   _$200,000_

   b. When did construction start?   _____

   c. Who called in sick?   _____ and _____

   d. How much will the wiring cost?   _____

   e. When will the walls be put up?   _____

   f. Who is the contractor?   _____

3. **Circle the words to complete the conversation.**

   Sam: Hello. Lopez Contracting.

   Pat: Hello, Mr. Lopez. It's Pat. I'm (calling in sick) / worried today.
   　　　　　　　　　　　　　　　　　　　　　　　　　a.

   Sam: Oh, no. I need you to help me with the budget / floor plan. We're over by $50,000.
   　　　　　　　　　　　　　　　　　　　　　　　　　　　　　b.

   Pat: Could you email the budget? I can look at it at home. I think it would be

   　　　　an electrical hazard / dangerous for me to come to work today. I'm really sick.
   　　　　　　　　　　c.

   Sam: OK. I'll send it right now. See if we can cut costs with the wiring / bricklayer.
   　　　　　　　　　　　　　　　　　　　　　　　　　　　　　　　　d.

   Pat: Hmm . . . Well, I don't think so. That could be a contractor / an electrical hazard.
   　　　　　　　　　　　　　　　　　　　　　　　　　　　　　　e.
   　　　　I'll look at the budget. Maybe we can pay the bricklayers / clinics less.
   　　　　　　　　　　　　　　　　　　　　　　　　　　　　f.

   Sam: No, we can't do that! They're the best.

   Pat: Maybe we could pay the floor plan / contractor less.
   　　　　　　　　　　　　　　　　　　g.

   Sam: You know what, you're sick and need to rest. I'll ask Sue to help me.

4. **Complete the notes. Use the words in the box.**

called in sick	budget	wiring	electrical hazard
floor plan	~~bricklayer~~	clinic	

Mr. Lopez:

A ___bricklayer___ got hurt on
       a.
the job. I took him to

the _____.
       b.
I'll be back after lunch to finish

the plumbing.

Daniel

Mr. Lopez:

Mrs. Simone called.

The _____ is an
       c.
_____. Her
       d.
company will charge $40,000

to repair it in the building.

     Mark

Mr. Lopez:

The steel will cost $840,000.

That makes us $30,000 over

_____.
       e.

Lilia

Mr. Lopez:

Todd _____.
       f.
He'll be back tomorrow. He

said the _____
       g.
is on his desk if you need it.

     Pat

5. **What about you? Look in your dictionary. Which job do you think would be the hardest? the easiest? the most dangerous? Why?**

Challenge Write a report about the construction site in your dictionary. Write about the problems that happened that day.

See page 305 for listening practice.

1. Look at page 188 in your dictionary. Where are the students learning . . . ?

    a. to teach preschool   *in community college*

    b. to add numbers   _____

    c. to repair a car   _____

    d. to count to four   _____

    e. about biology   _____

    f. about history   _____, _____,

                     and _____

2. Look at page 188 in your dictionary. Which school do students of these ages usually attend?

Age	Type Of School
a. 11–14 years old	_____middle school_____
b. 18–22 years old	_____, _____, _____, or vocational school
c. under 5 years old	_____
d. 14–18 years old	_____ or vocational school
e. 22 years old and older	_____, _____, _____, or vocational school
f. 5–11 years old	_____

3. Complete this journal entry. Use Exercise 2 for help.

It's the end of Tommy's first week in _elementary school_ ! It seems like yesterday that I
                                    a.

took him to _____ . His first grade class went to a farmers' market this week
              b.

and brought home things beginning with the letters A and B—apples, beans, bananas. He's

learning to read! In just six years, he'll be in _____ studying geography and history.
                                            c.

After that, he'll be a teenager in _____ , and we'll really have to think about his
                                d.

future. After graduation, will he go to _____ like his Dad? Or go to
                                    e.

_____ and study computers, like I did? Wait a minute. He's just starting his second
      f.

week of first grade now. Let's just enjoy this year.

4. Look at page 189 in your dictionary. In which class are students . . . ?

a. painting _____ *arts* _____

b. exercising _____

c. singing _____

d. learning about the Civil War _____

e. doing experiments in a group _____

f. studying the novel *Moby Dick* _____

g. speaking French and Spanish _____

h. repeating words in English _____

5. Look at the things Katia needs for school. Complete her schedule.

MONDAY

language arts

TUESDAY

WEDNESDAY

THURSDAY

FRIDAY

Student Planner

6. What about you? Check (✓) the classes you would like to take.

☐ math

☐ science

☐ history

☐ physical education

☐ music

☐ world languages   If *yes*, which? _____

☐ arts   If *yes*, which type? _____

☐ Other: _____

Challenge Explain your choices in Exercise 6.
Example: *I would like to take history because I like to learn about the world.*

See page 305 for listening practice.

1. **Look in your dictionary.** *True* or *False*? **Correct the <u>underlined</u> words in the false sentences.**

   body
   a. The ~~conclusion~~ of the essay has three paragraphs.   ___false___

   b. The <u>title</u> of the essay has four words.   _____

   c. The student indented the first <u>sentence</u> in each paragraph.   _____

   d. There's a quotation in the <u>introduction</u>.   _____

   e. The period comes <u>after</u> the last quotation mark.   _____

   f. The student capitalized <u>names</u>.   _____

   g. The <u>footnote</u> tells us where the student got his information.   _____

   h. The student used parentheses in the first <u>sentence</u>.   _____

2. **Look at the punctuation rules. Complete the sentences.**

   ## Some Punctuation Rules

   a Use a __question mark__ at the end of a question. *Where do you come from?*

   b Use a _____ at the end of a statement. *I come from Ecuador.*

   c Use an _____ to show a strong feeling. *I love Quito!*

   d Use an _____ in a contraction. *It's a beautiful city.*

   e Use a _____ before a list. *I miss a lot of things: my home, my friends, my school.*

   f Use a _____ between items in a list. *I email Ana, Enrique, and Tomas every week.*

   g Use _____ around additional information. *I like Los Angeles (especially the beach), and I'm beginning to feel more at home here.*

   h Use a _____ between parts of a word. *We live in a three-year-old building.*

   i Use _____ around a person's exact words. My mother says, *"There's no place like home."*

3. **What about you? Write three sentences about your experience in this country. Use . . .**

   a. a period   _____

   b. quotation marks   _____

   c. an exclamation mark   _____

4. **Look in your dictionary. What is Miguel doing?**

   a. "For this draft, I'll just use my notebook."   _writing a first draft_

   b. "Oh, it should be *came*, not *come*!"   _____

   c. "Here it is, Mr. Wilson."   _____

   d. "I'll write *work* in this circle."   _____

   e. "What do you think of the title, Mindy?"   _____

   f. "Hmmm . . . Maybe I could write about my first day at work."   _____

   g. "For this draft, I'll use my computer."   _____

   h. "Paragraph 3 will be about success."   _____

5. **Find and circle seven more mistakes in this student's essay.**

   ## Things Get Better

   I arrived in chicago in 1997. I came with my parents: my brother, and my little sister. At first I wasn't very happy. I didn't know anyone besides my family, and I missed my friends a lot. My mother told me, "Dont worry! Things will get better.

   When I began school; things improved a little. I made friends right away? Because we were all from different countrie's we had to speak English. That really (helped) a lot! Now I can even write a composition in English. I guess my mother was right.

6. **Look at the essay in Exercise 5. Describe the mistakes.**

   a. _The student didn't capitalize Chicago._

   b. _The student used a colon after "parents" instead of a comma._

   c. _____

   d. _____

   e. _____

   f. _____

   g. _____

   h. _____

   Challenge Write an essay about how you felt when you came to this country or started this school. Write a first draft, edit it, get feedback, rewrite it, and turn it in to your teacher.

See page 305 for listening practice.

1. **Look in your dictionary. Cross out the word that doesn't belong. Write the category.**

a. ___Types of math___   algebra   calculus   geometry   ~~solution~~

b. _____   even   negative   numerator   odd

c. _____   add   divide   equation   subtract

d. _____   circle   curved   perpendicular   straight

e. _____   acute   diagonal   obtuse   right

f. _____   cone   cylinder   parallelogram   sphere

g. _____   cube   rectangle   square   triangle

2. **Complete the test. Circle the letter of the correct answer.**

Mathematics test

Name: _____

Date: _____

School: _____

1. The number 12 is ___.
  ⓐ even
  b. odd
  c. negative

2. The ___ of $8 \times 3 = 24$.
  a. sum
  b. difference
  c. product

3. An equation always has ___.
  a. an equal (=) sign
  b. a fraction
  c. pi

4. In an equation, x is called ___.
  a. an endpoint
  b. a graph
  c. a variable

5. The first odd number after 7 is ___.
  a. 5
  b. 8
  c. 9

6. The number -20 is ___.
  a. positive
  b. negative
  c. odd

7. You can use ___ to solve a word problem.
  a. a dictionary
  b. an equation
  c. a ruler

8. In the fraction 2/3, 3 is the ___.
  a. denominator
  b. numerator
  c. quotient

3. **What about you? Which operations or types of math do you use? When do you use them?**
Example: *I multiply to change dollars to Mexican pesos.*

4. Look in your dictionary. Complete the sentences.

    a. A _____ *triangle* _____ has three straight lines.

    b. Perpendicular lines have two _____ angles.

    c. An _____ angle is bigger than a right angle.

    d. A square is a _____ with four equal sides.

    e. A cube has six _____.

    f. The diameter of a circle is two times longer than the _____.

    g. The distance between two _____ lines is always equal.

    h. _____ lines look like the letter *T*.

5. Complete the analogies.

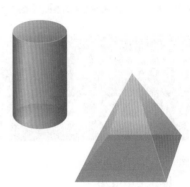

    a. circle : sphere = square : _____ *cube* _____

    b. triangle : three = rectangle : _____

    c. add : subtract = multiply : _____

    d. triangle : shape = pyramid : _____

    e. divide : quotient = subtract : _____

    f. circle : circumference = rectangle : _____

    g. straight line : square = curved line : _____

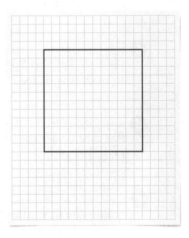

6. Follow the instructions.

    a. Draw a circle inside the square.

    b. Draw the diameter.

    c. Draw a diagonal line from the top left corner of the square to the bottom right corner.

    d. Draw a line parallel to the left side of the square.

    e. Draw a line parallel to the right side of the square.

    f. Draw a line perpendicular to the top line of the square. Begin your line at the middle point of the top line of the square, and end your line at the bottom line of the square.

Compare your drawing with a classmate's. Are they the same?

Challenge Look at page 101 in your dictionary. Find examples of lines, shapes, and solid forms.
      Example: *The dryer door is a circle.*

See page 306 for listening practice.

1. Look in your dictionary. Complete each sentence.

a. The _____*biologist*_____ is using a microscope to examine a leaf.

b. The nucleus is in the center of the _____.

c. Plants make oxygen through the process of _____.

d. Many _____ live in the desert.

e. Many _____ live in the ocean.

f. The ocean is the _____ of many invertebrates.

2. Look at the science book. Complete the definitions.

THE PARTS OF A MICROSCOPE

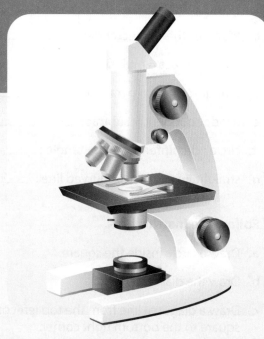

a _____*eyepiece*_____: the part you look through

b _____: the large piece on the side that you turn to make the image clear

c _____: the small piece on the side that you turn (after b.) to make the image clearer

d _____: the large flat area under the objectives where you place the slide

e _____: a lens that makes the image larger—there are usually 3 or 4 different sizes

f _____: the part that holds the objectives—it turns so you can change the power

g _____: the parts that hold the slide on the stage

h _____: the bottom of the microscope

i _____: the part that sends light through the diaphragm

j _____: the round part under the stage—it has different sized holes that control the amount of light

k _____: the part you hold when you carry the microscope

3. Look in your dictionary. *True* or *False*? Correct the underlined words in the false sentences.

        chemist

a. The ~~physicist~~ is discussing a molecule.   *false*

b. A molecule has different <u>atoms</u> in it.   _____

c. An <u>electron</u> is positive.   _____

d. The <u>neutron</u> is in the center of the atom.   _____

e. The physicist is using <u>the periodic table</u> to show that c = the speed of light.   _____

f. The physicist drew a picture of a prism and a <u>molecule</u> on the board.   _____

4. Look at the lab experiment. Complete the student's notes.

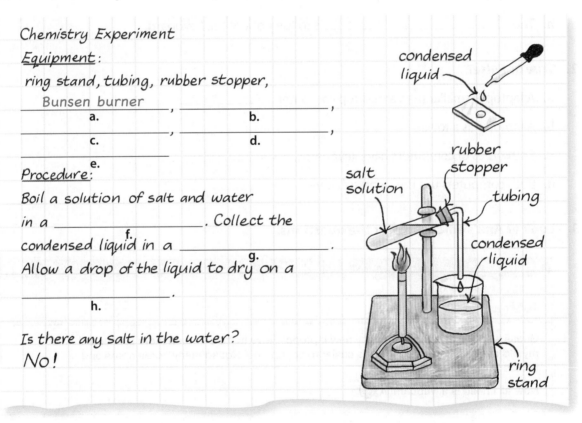

Chemistry Experiment
Equipment:
ring stand, tubing, rubber stopper,
    Bunsen burner
_____ , _____ ,
        a.   b.
_____ , _____ ,
        c.   d.
_____
        e.
Procedure:
Boil a solution of salt and water
in a _____ . Collect the
            f.
condensed liquid in a _____ .
                          g.
Allow a drop of the liquid to dry on a
_____ .
        h.

Is there any salt in the water?
No!

condensed liquid —
salt solution
rubber stopper
tubing
condensed liquid
ring stand

5. Look at the student's notes in Exercise 4. Check (✓) the things the student did.

✓ use a Bunsen burner   ☐ observe

☐ state a hypothesis   ☐ record the results

☐ do an experiment   ☐ draw a conclusion

Challenge Describe the use of crucible tongs, forceps, a graduated cylinder, a balance, and a funnel.
        Example: *You use crucible tongs to pick up hot objects.*

See page 306 for listening practice.

Computers

1. Look in your dictionary. Complete the sentences.

a. There are two _____USB ports_____ on the front of the tower.

b. The DVD and CD-ROM drive is in the _____.

c. A _____ drive is in one of the ports.

d. The microprocessor, _____, and _____ are inside the tower.

e. The power cord goes from the tower into the _____.

f. The webcam is on top of the _____.

g. Cables go from the monitor to the _____ and to the _____.

h. The _____ is to the right of the keyboard.

2. True or False?

a. A laptop is smaller than a desktop computer.   _____true_____

b. A laptop has a tower.   _____

c. Both types of computers have keyboards.   _____

d. Both computers use the same software.   _____

3. Look at Ana's email. Answer the questions.

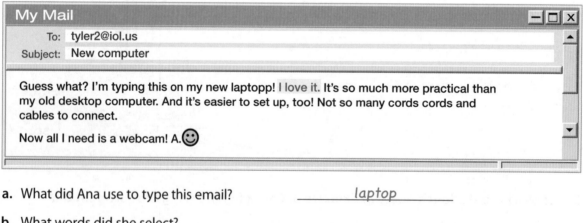

My Mail	− □ ✕
To: tyler2@iol.us	
Subject: New computer	

Guess what? I'm typing this on my new laptopp! I love it. It's so much more practical than my old desktop computer. And it's easier to set up, too! Not so many cords cords and cables to connect.

Now all I need is a webcam! A.☺

a. What did Ana use to type this email?   _____laptop_____

b. What words did she select?   _____

c. What word does she need to delete?   _____

d. What letter does she need to delete?   _____

e. How many times did she go to the next line?   _____

Challenge Do an Internet search or ask your classmates. Give three examples of software. What do they do?

   See page 306 for listening practice.

1. **Look in your dictionary. Circle the words to complete the sentences.**

   a. You can find "File" in the (menu bar) / search box.

   b. You start typing at the pointer / cursor.

   c. To return to a website you just visited, click on the back / forward button.

   d. A drop-down menu / URL begins with http://.

   e. To move up and down a webpage, use the scroll bar / tab.

   f. To watch a movie, you need a search engine / video player.

   g. To research information on the Internet, you use a search engine / link.

   h. When you sign in, you type your password into a search / text box.

2. **Look at Jason's email. What did he do right (☺) ? What did he do wrong (☹) ?**
   Use the words in the box.

address the email	attach a file	attach a picture
check the spelling	type the message	~~type the subject~~

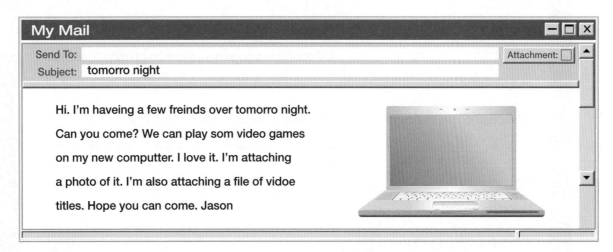

   My Mail — □ ✕

   Send To: _____ Attachment: ☐ ▲
   Subject: tomorro night

   Hi. I'm haveing a few freinds over tomorro night.
   Can you come? We can play som video games
   on my new computter. I love it. I'm attaching
   a photo of it. I'm also attaching a file of vidoe
   titles. Hope you can come. Jason

   a. _He typed the subject._   d. _____

   b. _____   e. _____

   c. _____   f. _____

Challenge Do you think it's important to check your spelling in an email? Why or why not?
Write a paragraph about your opinion.

1. Look in your dictionary. Complete the information.

DID YOU KNOW...?

★ Thomas Jefferson wrote the <u>Declaration of Independence</u>, and on July 4, 1776, the
   a.
   _____ adopted it. The thirteen colonies were a free country—the
   b.
   United States of America!

★ The _____ consisted of New Hampshire, Massachusetts,
   c.
   Rhode Island, Connecticut, New York, Pennsylvania, New Jersey, Maryland, Delaware,

   Virginia, North Carolina, South Carolina, and Georgia. The _____
   d.
   who lived there came from Spain, France, Sweden, Holland, and England, but they were all

   under British control.

★ George Washington was elected _____ of the United States.
   e.
   He stopped going to school when he was only 15 years old!

★ The first amendment (or changes) to the U.S. Constitution is called the

   _____ . These rights guarantee freedom of religion, speech,
   f.
   and the press.

★ When Europeans first came to North America, there were around 10 million

   _____ living there. By the year 2000, there were only 4.1 million.
   g.

★ The _____ between the thirteen colonies and Great Britain
   h.
   lasted for 8 years.

★ A British soldier was called a _____ because of the color of
   i.
   his uniform.

★ A _____ was an American soldier. He got this name because
   j.
   he had to be ready in a minute in order to be among the first to arrive at a battle.

★ The U.S. _____ was written in 1787 in fewer than 100 days! It
   k.
   was signed by 55 _____ , also called the "Fathers of our Country."
   l.

Challenge Look at page 260 in this book. Follow the instructions.

  See page 307 for listening practice.

1. **Look in your dictionary. Circle the words to complete the sentences.**

   a. The Egyptian pyramids are a product of (an ancient) / a modern civilization.

   b. An emperor / A president is the ruler of a group of countries.

   c. A dictator / prime minister is the leader of a country who controls everything and has all the power.

   d. A dictator / monarch is a king or a queen.

   e. An activist / army fights during a war.

   f. Invention / Immigration is moving from one country to another.

2. **Complete the chart.**

Category	Person		Country	Famous for...
composition	J.S. Bach (1685–1750) _composer_ **a.**		Germany	He is considered the greatest writer of Baroque music.
invention	Alessandro Volta (1745–1827) _____ **b.**		Italy	In 1800, he invented the first electric battery.
_____ **c.**	Vasco da Gama (1469?–1524) explorer		Portugal	In the late 1400s, he was the first to sail from Europe around the Cape of Good Hope in Africa to India.
_____ **d.**	Rosa Parks (1913–2005) _____ **e.**		U.S.A.	Known as the "Mother of the Civil Rights Movement," in 1955 she refused to give up her seat on a bus to a white passenger.
architecture	I.M. Pei (1917–) architect		U.S.A. _____ **f.** (from China)	He is famous for his modern skyscrapers, museums, and government buildings.

Challenge Do an Internet search or use an encyclopedia or history book. Find another example of an explorer, an inventor, a composer, an immigrant, or an activist. Give information like the information in the chart in Exercise 2.

1. Look in your dictionary. Cross out the word that doesn't belong. Complete the chart.

a	States in Mexico	~~Louisiana~~	Durango	Sonora	Jalisco
b	_States_ in the United States	Florida	Hawaii	Michigan	Baja California
c	Provinces in _____	Alberta	Alaska	Nova Scotia	Québec
d	_____ in Central America	Belize	Guatemala	Ontario	Panama
e	Regions in Mexico	Atlantic Provinces	Yucatan Peninsula	Chiapas Highlands	Gulf Coastal Plain
f	_____ of the United States	Midwest	Prairie Provinces	West Coast	Rocky Mountains
g	Bodies of Water	Gulf of Mexico	Southern Uplands	Atlantic Ocean	Caribbean Sea
h	_____	Costa Rica	Puerto Rico	Cuba	Bahamas

2. Look in your dictionary. Complete the sentences.

a. Texas is in the _____ _southwest_ _____ region of the United States.

b. Nicaragua lies between _____ and _____ in Central America.

c. _____ and the Dominican Republic share the same Caribbean island.

d. This island, _____, is the smallest Canadian province.

e. _____, Mexico is northwest of Coahuila.

f. The west side of the U.S. state of _____ lies on the Gulf of Mexico.

g. _____ is southwest of the U.S. state of Nebraska.

h. The U.S. state of _____ is made of many islands.

i. Campeche lies in the _____ region of Mexico.

j. _____ is the largest island in the Caribbean Sea.

3. What about you? What state, province, or country are you in? Where is it?

Example: *I'm in British Columbia. It's in the southwest part of Canada. It's north of the United States and south of the Yukon Territory.*

4. Look at the map. It shows where some products in Mexico come from. *True* or *False*? Correct the underlined words in the false sentences.

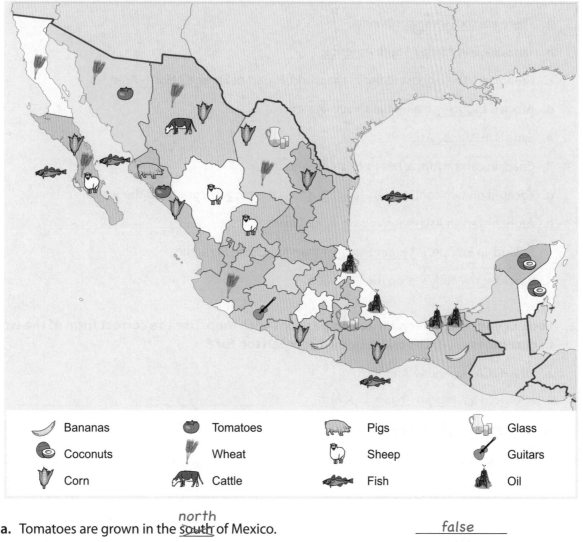

Bananas		Tomatoes		Pigs		Glass	
Coconuts		Wheat		Sheep		Guitars	
Corn		Cattle		Fish		Oil	

a. Tomatoes are grown in the ~~south~~ *north* of Mexico.   _____false_____

b. Coconuts grow in the <u>Yucatan Peninsula</u>.   _____

c. Bananas grow in the <u>north</u> of Mexico.   _____

d. Fishing is done in both the <u>Gulf of Mexico</u> and the <u>Pacific Ocean</u>.   _____

e. Oil is found in the <u>west</u>.   _____

f. There is <u>more</u> wheat in the north than in the south.   _____

g. Guitars are made in <u>Michoacán</u>.   _____

5. What about you? Draw a map showing some of the products from your native country. Write eight sentences.

Challenge Look at the map in Exercise 4. Write five more sentences about Mexican products.

See page 308 for listening practice.

1. **Look in your dictionary. Circle the words to complete the sentences.**

    a. There are six / (seven) continents.

    b. Tanzania is in Africa / South America.

    c. Greenland, the biggest island in the world, is part of Europe / North America.

    d. Africa is bigger / smaller than South America.

    e. Syria is in Africa / Asia.

    f. Chad, in central Africa, has five / six neighbors.

    g. Located on two continents, China / Russia is the biggest country in the world.

    h. Afghanistan, in Asia, has five / six neighbors.

    i. Poland, in Europe, is bigger / smaller than the Czech Republic.

    j. Kazakhstan / Turkey is on the Black Sea.

2. **Look in your dictionary. Write comparisons with _than_. Use the correct form of the words in parentheses ( ). Choose your own comparison for _f_.**

    a. IN AFRICA: Uganda / Angola (big)

    Angola is bigger than Uganda.

    b. IN EUROPE: Italy / Finland (warm)

    _____

    c. IN ASIA: Thailand / Laos (small)

    _____

    d. IN SOUTH AMERICA: Chile / Argentina (wide)

    _____

    e. AUSTRALIA / ANTARCTICA (cold)

    _____

    f. IN NORTH AMERICA: _____ / _____ (_____)

    _____

3. **Look in your dictionary. For each continent, find a country that is "landlocked" (it has no ocean around it).**

    Africa: _____ Chad _____   South America: _____

    Europe: _____   Asia: _____

4. **Look in your dictionary. Complete these world facts. Write the names of the continents, countries, and bodies of water.**

a. _____ Mexico _____

Location: southern North America

Borders: U.S. to north, Gulf of Mexico to east, Belize and Guatemala to south, _____ Ocean to west

b. _____

Location: island off southeast Africa in western _____ Ocean

Borders: about 300 miles (500 km) east of Mozambique

c. _____

Location: central Europe

Borders: Germany and Czech Republic to north, Hungary and Slovakia to east, Slovenia and _____ to south, Switzerland and Liechtenstein to west

d. Laos

Location: southeast Asia

Borders: Burma to northwest, _____ to north, Vietnam to east, Cambodia to south, _____ to southwest

e. _____

Location: western Africa

Borders: Guinea to north, Atlantic Ocean and _____ to west, Ivory Coast to east

f. _____

Location: northwestern South America

Borders: Colombia to north, Peru to east and south, _____ to west

g. Belarus

Location: northeastern Europe

Borders: Lithuania and _____ to north and northwest; Russia to north, northeast, and east; _____ to south, Poland to west

h. _____

Location: southwestern Asia

Borders: Turkmenistan to northwest, Uzebekistan and Tajikistan to north, China to northeast, Pakistan to east and south, _____ to west.

5. **What about you? Write a description of your country like the ones in Exercise 4. (If your country is in Exercise 4, choose a country you have visited.) Use your own paper.**

Challenge Choose five other countries. Write descriptions like the ones in Exercise 4.

1. **Look in your dictionary. *True* or *False*? Correct the underlined words in the false sentences.**

   a. There's a waterfall in the ~~forest~~. *rain forest*   _____false_____

   b. An ocean is larger than <u>a pond or a bay</u>.   _____

   c. There's a <u>beach</u> around the lake.   _____

   d. There's a canyon between the <u>mountain ranges</u>.   _____

   e. There are flowers in the <u>valley</u>.   _____

   f. Hills are lower than <u>mountain ranges</u>.   _____

2. **Complete the descriptions. Use the words in the box. Look at the world map on pages 202 and 203 in your dictionary if you need help.**

desert	island	lake	mountain peak	ocean	river	~~waterfall~~

   # WORLD FACTS

   a **Angel Falls** (3,212 feet) is the highest _____waterfall_____ in the world. It is located on the Churun River in southeast Venezuela.

   b The **Pacific** is the largest (64,186,300 square miles) and the deepest (12,925 feet) _____ in the world. It covers almost one third of the earth's surface.

   c Located in Tibet and Nepal, **Everest** (29,028 feet) is the highest _____ in the world. In 1953, Hillary and Norgay were the first to reach the top.

   d At 4,160 miles, the **Nile**, in Africa, is the longest _____ in the world. Its water supplies electricity and helps agriculture in Egypt and Sudan.

   e The **Sahara** in Africa is the biggest _____ in the world. At 3,500,000 square miles, it is almost as large as the United States. It gets only five to ten inches of rain a year and sometimes has dry periods that last for years.

   f Surrounded by water, **Greenland** (840,000 square miles) is the largest _____ in the world. It lies in the Arctic Circle and is a part of Denmark, although it is 1,300 miles away.

   g The **Caspian Sea** (144,000 square miles) is the largest _____ in the world. It's called a sea because its water is salty.

Challenge Look online, in an encyclopedia, or almanac. Write some facts about a rain forest, a canyon, and plains.

1. **Look in your dictionary. Complete the chart.**

PLANET NAME	DISTANCE FROM THE SUN (IN MILES)	SYMBOL	DIAMETER (IN MILES)
a. Mars	142 million	♂	4,220
b.	67 million	♀	7,521
c.	93 million	⊕	7,926
d.	888 million	♄	74,975
e.	484 million	♃	88,732
f.	1.8 billion	♅	31,763
g.	2.8 billion	♆	30,755
h.	36 million	♄	3,031

2. **Circle the words to complete the sentences. You can use your dictionary for help.**

   a. There are eight moons / (planets) / stars in the solar system.

   b. Uranus was the first planet discovered using a comet / solar system / telescope.

   c. The astronaut / astronomer / space station William Herschel first observed Uranus in 1781.

   d. Constellations / Observatories / Comets look like pictures in the sky.

   e. The Earth's galaxy / orbit / space (a group of billions of stars) is called the Milky Way.

   f. It takes 27 days for the moon to go from a new moon to a full moon and then back to a crescent moon / new moon / quarter moon again.

3. **What about you? Describe what you can see when you look at the night sky. Use your own paper.**

   Example: *I can see the constellation called the Big Dipper, . . .*

Challenge Look online, in an encyclopedia, almanac, or science book. Find out more about three planets. How long does a day last? How long does it take to orbit the sun?

See page 309 for listening practice. 205

A Graduation

1. **Look in your dictionary.** *True* or *False*?

   a. Adelia is wearing a cap and gown in <u>six</u> photos.   _____false_____

   b. Adelia's <u>mother</u> is taking pictures.   _____

   c. The guest speaker is <u>the mayor</u>.   _____

   d. The photographer is taking a picture of <u>ten</u> people.   _____

   e. <u>The photographer</u> is crying.   _____

   f. <u>Adelia</u> is speaking at the podium.   _____

2. **Look in your dictionary. Write the letters of the false sentences from Exercise 1. Make them true.**

   _a._   _Adelia is wearing a cap in five photos._ _____

   ____   _____

   ____   _____

   ____   _____

   ____   _____

3. **Look in your dictionary. Who said . . . ? Match.**

   _3_ **a.** "Adelia, I want to take a photo of you with your diploma."

   ____ **b.** "OK, everyone. I want this one to be a serious photo."

   ____ **c.** "Adelia, you look so beautiful in your cap and gown. It makes me cry."

   ____ **d.** "Welcome, students, teachers, and parents. I am happy to speak at this year's ceremony."

   ____ **e.** "I'll miss being in band with you, Adelia!"

   ____ **f.** "I graduated!"

   1. Adelia

   2. Adelia's mother

   3. Adelia's father

   4. Adelia's classmate

   5. the guest speaker

   6. the photographer

4. **Complete the comments on Adelia's webpage. Use the words in the box.**

celebrate	funny	caps	guest speaker	~~takes~~
cry	gown	photographer	podium	

People		Comments
Tamara		Congratulations! Your Dad ____*takes*____ great pictures. **a.** You look great in your cap and _____! **b.**
Jeff		Hey, Adelia. What a great day. I like the _____ photo. **c.** The _____ was so upset, but it's a great memory! **d.**
Wendy		I thought the _____ gave a great speech. **e.** Of course, she's my mother. She didn't _____ until **f.** after her speech!
Dan		We finally graduated! I almost fell when I got my diploma at the _____ . Now it's time to _____ ! I'm **g.** **h.** having a party on Saturday.
Marcos		Great pictures! I love the one where we are throwing our _____ in the air! **i.**

5. **What about you? Imagine you were at the graduation. Tell a partner about it. Answer these questions:**

   a. Were you a graduate or a friend or relative of a graduate?

   b. How did you feel? Did you cry?

   c. What photos did you take?

   d. Who did you talk to?

   e. How did you celebrate?

Challenge Write comments to Adelia. Tell her what you think of the photos on her webpage on pages 206 and 207 of the dictionary. Write at least six sentences.

See page 309 for listening practice.

1. **Look in your dictionary.** *True* **or** *False***? Correct the <u>underlined</u> words in the false sentences.**

a. A man is painting a picture of ~~rocks~~ trees.   _____false_____

b. Seven people are on the <u>path</u>.   _____

c. The <u>sun</u> is in the sky.   _____

d. There's a nest on a <u>rock</u> in the water.   _____

e. A man is examining four kinds of <u>fish</u>.   _____

f. There's a sign with pictures of five different types of <u>insects</u>.   _____

2. **Complete the pamphlet. Use the words in the box.**

birds	~~fish~~	flowers	insects	mammals	plants	rocks	trees

Did you know...?

a. _____fish_____ These animals are vertebrates (they have spines). They live in the water and can swim. Most of them lay eggs. There are more than 20,000 types, and many of them live ten to twenty years.

b._____ These animals are invertebrates (they don't have spines) and there are more than a million types! Their bodies have three parts, and they have six legs. Most of them eat plants.

c._____ There are about 260,000 types, and you can find them on land, in the ocean, and in rivers and lakes. They have chlorophyll, a green material that helps them make oxygen that people and animals breathe.

d._____ They are warm-blooded and when they are babies, they drink their mother's milk. Most of these animals have hair on all or part of their body. We belong to this animal group!

e._____ They are combinations of minerals (solid material that is not living). They come from deep inside the earth or from the oceans, rivers, and lakes. Many are millions of years old!

f. _____ These are very large plants! The "rings" in their trunk tell us their age. They provide oxygen, food, wood, and other important products.

g._____ They are the parts of plants that help the plant reproduce (make new plants). People like to grow them because of their beautiful colors and nice smell.

h._____ They can walk on their legs, and almost all of them can fly. There are more than 8,000 types of these feathered animals, and each type sings a different song!

❃ LILLO ❃
Nature Center

3. **Look in your dictionary. Cross out the word that doesn't belong.**

   a. Things that need water   trees   plants   ~~rocks~~

   b. Things that can fly   insects   nests   birds

   c. Things above the earth   soil   sun   sky

   d. Things that can swim   mammals   flowers   fish

   e. Things you can stand on   path   water   rocks

   f. Things with legs   insects   mammals   fish

4. **Circle the words to complete the pamphlet.**

LILLO Nature Center

PLANTS

Please . . .

❀ walk on our (paths)/ soil.
               a.

❀ take pictures of our beautiful flowers / sun.
                                b.

❀ read about our many different types of
trees / water.
    c.

❀ buy plants / nests to take home.
          d.

Please don't . . .

❀ feed the fish / insects or mammals / rocks.
                  e.   **f.**

❀ pick the flowers / trees.
                g.
(Leave them so everyone can enjoy them!)

❀ throw bottles or trash on the paths / birds.
                               h.
(Use the garbage cans and recycling bins.)

5. **What about you? Look in your dictionary. Imagine you are at the Lillo Nature Center. What will you do? Compare answers with a classmate.**

   Example: *I'll take pictures of the trees and flowers.*

   Challenge Find the names of three types of birds, flowers, mammals, fish, and insects.

See page 309 for listening practice.

Trees and Plants

1. **Look in your dictionary. What has...? You will use some answers more than once.**

Flowers	Berries	Needles	Leaves That Can Give You a Rash
dogwood	_____	_____	_poison ivy_
_____	_____	_____	_____
_____	_____		_____
	_____		

2. **Circle the words to complete the article. You can use your dictionary for help.**

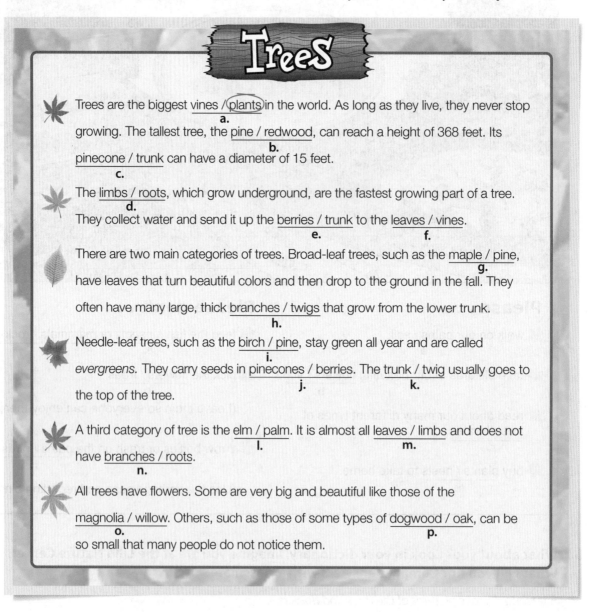

Trees

Trees are the biggest vines / (plants) in the world. As long as they live, they never stop
a.
growing. The tallest tree, the pine / redwood, can reach a height of 368 feet. Its
b.
pinecone / trunk can have a diameter of 15 feet.
c.

The limbs / roots, which grow underground, are the fastest growing part of a tree.
d.
They collect water and send it up the berries / trunk to the leaves / vines.
e. **f.**

There are two main categories of trees. Broad-leaf trees, such as the maple / pine,
g.
have leaves that turn beautiful colors and then drop to the ground in the fall. They

often have many large, thick branches / twigs that grow from the lower trunk.
h.

Needle-leaf trees, such as the birch / pine, stay green all year and are called
i.
evergreens. They carry seeds in pinecones / berries. The trunk / twig usually goes to
j. **k.**
the top of the tree.

A third category of tree is the elm / palm. It is almost all leaves / limbs and does not
l. **m.**
have branches / roots.
n.

All trees have flowers. Some are very big and beautiful like those of the

magnolia / willow. Others, such as those of some types of dogwood / oak, can be
o. **p.**
so small that many people do not notice them.

Challenge Make a list of five tree products. **Example:** _apples_

  See page 310 for listening practice.

1. Look in your dictionary. Complete the order form for this bouquet.

WESTSIDE Florist   **ORDER FORM**

1 mixed bouquet:

a. *4 red tulips*

b. *pink*

c. *3*

d. *1 yellow*

e. *purple*

f. *red*

g. *1*

2. Look in your dictionary. Complete the sentences with information from the chart.

Flower	Grown from	Season	Comments
		spring–fall	remove thorns for bouquets
		late spring–late summer	water often
		summer–early winter	plant seedlings in June
		early spring	very short stems
		winter–spring	good houseplant
		spring–summer	lovely perfume

a. _____*Lilies*_____ and _____ grow from bulbs.

b. _____, _____, and _____ grow from seeds.

c. _____ have thick white petals and smell very nice.

d. Don't hurt your finger when you make a bouquet of _____!

Challenge Write about flower traditions in your country. **Example:** *In the United States, men often give red roses to their wives or girlfriends on Valentine's Day.*

See page 310 for listening practice. **211**

1. **Look in your dictionary. Match the animals that look similar.**

   _3_ **a.** frog   **1.** garter snake

   ____ **b.** salamander   **2.** porpoise

   ____ **c.** dolphin   **3.** toad

   ____ **d.** tortoise   **4.** crocodile

   ____ **e.** alligator   **5.** lizard

   ____ **f.** eel   **6.** sea lion

   ____ **g.** walrus   **7.** turtle

2. **Complete the conversations. Use the words in the box. Use your dictionary for help.**

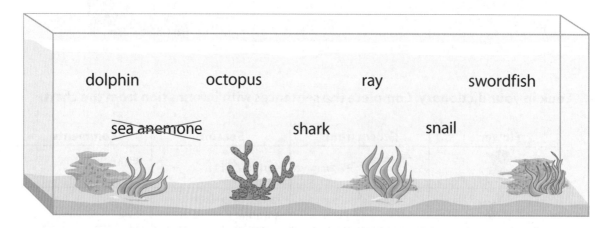

dolphin   octopus   ray   swordfish

~~sea anemone~~   shark   snail

   a. Kim: Wow! This aquarium is great. Is that a flower?
   Teacher: No, it's an animal. It's called a _____sea anemone_____.

   b. Silvia: What's that flat, blue and gray fish with the long tail?
   Viktor: I think it's a _____.

   c. Yi-Wen: What a long nose! Is it sharp?
   Teacher: Sure. That's why that fish is called a _____.

   d. Teacher: Look, Josette. That animal doesn't have any gills. Is it a fish?
   Josette: No, it's a _____. That's a kind of mammal.

   e. Teacher: How many legs does the _____ have?
   Ho-Jin: Eight.

   f. Omar: What's that large fish with the fin on the middle of its back?
   Teacher: It's a _____.

   g. Roman: Is that sea animal with the black shell dead?
   Teacher: No, it just moves very slowly. That's why people sometimes say
   "as slow as a _____."

3. Circle the words to complete the article.

Animal Defenses

Animals have many ways of protecting themselves. One fish, the cobra / (flounder) can

a.

change its color. Two sea animals, the squid / starfish and the sea otter / octopus, squirt ink into

b.   c.

the water and hide in its dark cloud.

Some poisonous amphibians / seals and reptiles warn enemies to keep away. The bright

d.

colors of some cod / frogs tell other animals they are not safe to eat. The garter snake / rattlesnake

e.   f.

makes a loud sound with its tail before it bites. The turtle's / tuna's hard shell and the sharp needles

g.

of the sea urchin / scallop are another kind of protection.

h.

Sea mammals like dolphins / newts use language to warn each other of danger. Scientists

i.

have recorded the songs that whales / worms sing to each other. Other members of this group,

j.

such as walruses and sea lions / seahorses, live in large groups to protect their babies.

k.

4. Circle the correct letter for each sentence. Write the letters in the circles below.

		True	False
a.	Mussels are sea mammals.	A	(O)
b.	Whales can sing.	L	Z
c.	All sea mammals have gills.	J	O
d.	Some mammals have fins.	R	L
e.	Rattlesnakes are poisonous.	E	B
f.	Crabs don't have legs.	G	C
g.	Bass have scales.	D	P
h.	Scallops and shrimp are black.	E	I
i.	Jellyfish look like fish.	T	C

_O_ ___ ___ ___ ___ ___ ___ ___ ___

Now unscramble the letters to find the name of an animal: _____

Challenge Look at page 260 in this book. Follow the instructions.

See page 310 for listening practice.

1. **Look in your dictionary. Write the name of the bird, insect, or arachnid.**

   a. It makes honey from flowers. Unlike the wasp, it dies after it stings.   *honeybee*

   b. It looks like a big duck and is raised for food and feathers.   _____

   c. It's very small. It eats blood and often lives in the fur or skin of mammals. It can make people sick.   _____

   d. It's brown with an orange breast.   _____

   e. It's very small and red, and it has black polka dots.   _____

   f. It has sharp claws and big eyes in the front of its head.   _____

   g. It begins its life as a caterpillar.   _____

   h. It has a long bill for eating nectar from flowers. It moves its wings 1,000 times a second.   _____

   i. It catches insects by making holes in trees with its beak.   _____

   j. It doesn't fly, but swims in icy water to catch fish.   _____

   k. It lives near water. It flies and bites people for blood.   _____

   l. It looks like a small grasshopper and eats cloth like a moth. It makes music by rubbing its wings together.   _____

   m. It has beautiful blue feathers and eats insects and fruit.   _____

   n. It likes human food and causes many diseases. A spider often catches it in its web.   _____

   o. It's very big with long, colorful feathers.   _____

2. **Write comparisons with *than*.**

   a. fly / tick (small) *A tick is smaller than a fly.*

   b. peacock / sparrow (colorful) _____

   c. beetle / scorpion (dangerous) _____

   d. pigeon / eagle (large) _____

   e. butterfly / moth (beautiful) _____

3. **What about you? Make a list of some common birds, insects, and arachnids where you live. Use your own paper.**

   Challenge Look up information about a bird, insect, or arachnid in your list from Exercise 3. Where does it live? What does it eat? How does it help or hurt people?

       See page 311 for listening practice.

1. Look in your dictionary. Which animals . . . ?

a. eat nuts _____*chipmunks*_____ and _____

b. are babies _____ and _____

c. have wings _____, _____, and _____

d. live in holes _____ and _____

e. give us milk _____, _____, and _____

f. carry people _____ and _____

2. Look at the magazine article. Complete the sentences.

Care and Cost of Common Pets

✓ a lot of care	$ very expensive
✓ moderate care	$ moderately expensive
✓ not much care	$ not expensive

a. _____*Dogs*_____ need the most care. In addition to giving them food and water, you need to train them and play with them. They are also the most expensive.

b. _____ need less care than dogs. With enough water and food, they can be alone during the day. They are less expensive than dogs, but more expensive than other pets.

c. If you like birds, think about getting one or more _____. They aren't expensive and don't need much care. They like to climb, so give them a tall cage with a ladder.

d. Perhaps the easiest and cheapest pets are _____. They can live long and healthy lives in a big bowl of fresh water with plants and room to swim.

e. Don't be afraid of these rodents. Mice and white _____ (not the ones that live in the city!) make nice pets. They don't cost much, and they don't need a lot of care.

f. Bushy-tailed and long-eared, _____ aren't expensive, but they do need moderate care and special food. No carrots!

Challenge Compare a rooster and a hen, a dog and a prairie dog, and a pig and a guinea pig.
Example: *A hen lays eggs, but a rooster doesn't. A rooster is bigger than a hen.*

See page 311 for listening practice.

1. **Look in your dictionary. Circle the words to complete the sentences.**

   a. The lion has a <u>pouch</u> / (<u>mane</u>) and <u>hooves</u> / <u>paws</u>.

   b. The <u>opossum</u> / <u>raccoon</u> has a striped <u>tail</u> / <u>trunk</u>.

   c. The <u>moose</u> / <u>mountain lion</u> has <u>antlers</u> / <u>quills</u> and <u>hooves</u> / <u>whiskers</u>.

   d. The <u>coyote</u> / <u>koala</u> has a grey <u>coat</u> / <u>hump</u>.

   e. The <u>baboon</u> / <u>buffalo</u> has <u>horns</u> / <u>tusks</u>.

   f. The chimpanzee and the <u>orangutan</u> / <u>platypus</u> are in the same animal family.

   g. The <u>beaver</u> / <u>hyena</u>, the <u>panther</u> / <u>skunk</u>, and the <u>antelope</u> / <u>deer</u> live in North America.

2. **Look at the bar graph. Complete the sentences.**

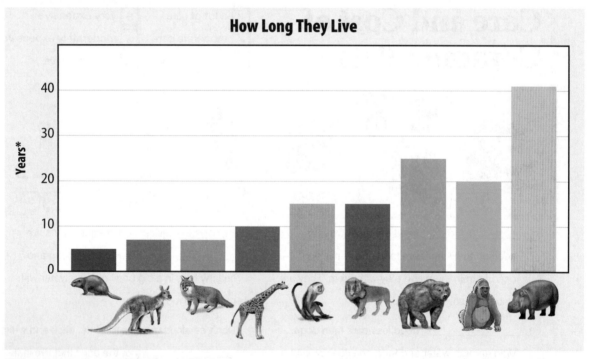

How Long They Live

*Years = average number of years in a zoo.
Based on information from: *The World Almanac and Book of Facts, 2007.* (NY: World Almanac Education Group, 2007).

   a. The grizzly _____*bear*_____ lives 25 years.

   b. The red fox lives as long as the _____.

   c. The _____ lives as long as the lion.

   d. The gorilla lives 10 years longer than the _____.

   e. The _____ lives the longest life.

   f. The _____ lives the shortest life.

   g. The _____ lives twice as long as the beaver.

3. Look at the maps. Make a list of endangered* animals and the continents where they live.

*Endangered = there are very few of these animals and they may not continue to live.
Based on information from: U.S. Fish & Wildlife Service http://ecos.fws.gov/tess_public/SpeciesReport.do?dsource=animals

_____wolf, North America_____   _____

_____   _____

_____   _____

_____   _____

_____   _____

Challenge List reasons why some animals are endangered. Search online or in an encyclopedia for "endangered species." **Example**: _People kill elephants for their tusks_

See page 311 for listening practice. **217**

Energy and Conservation

1. **Look in your dictionary. Circle the words to complete these sentences.**

   a. Nuclear / (Solar) energy comes directly from the sun.

   b. Coal, oil, and natural gas / radiation are sources of energy.

   c. Another source of energy is acid rain / wind power.

   d. Hydroelectric power / Geothermal energy comes from water.

   e. A danger of nuclear energy is air pollution / radiation.

   f. Old batteries are examples of biomass / hazardous waste.

   g. Acid rain / Fusion kills trees.

   h. Water pollution and oil spills / smog hurt the oceans.

2. **Look at the pie chart.** *True* or *False*?

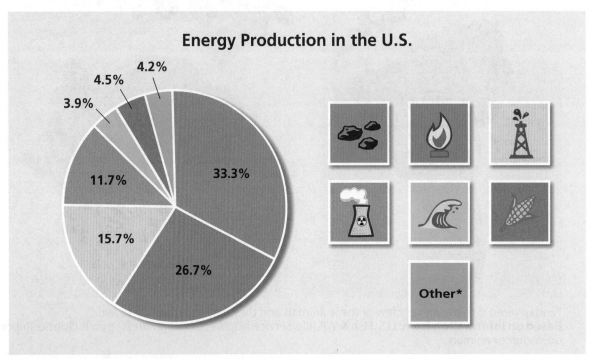

*Other sources include geothermal, solar, and wind.
Based on 2005 information from: The Energy Information Administration, U.S. Department of Energy
http://www.eia.doe.gov/aer/txt/stb0102.xls.

   a. More than 30% of energy produced in the United States is from coal.   _true_

   b. Almost 27% of energy produced is from oil.   _____

   c. The United States produces more energy from oil than from natural gas.   _____

   d. Almost 12% of its energy production is from nuclear energy.   _____

   e. It produces more energy from hydroelectric power than from biomass sources.   _____

   f. It doesn't produce much energy from wind power or solar energy.   _____

3. **Look in your dictionary. Complete the sentences.**

a. The streets will look better if people ___don't litter___ .

b. You can _____ by using a "regular" coffee cup instead of a paper one.

c. You can _____ by turning off the faucet when you brush your teeth.

d. If you _____ bottles and cans, you help reduce garbage and improve the quality of the earth at the same time!

4. **Look at the chart. Check (✓) the correct column(s).**

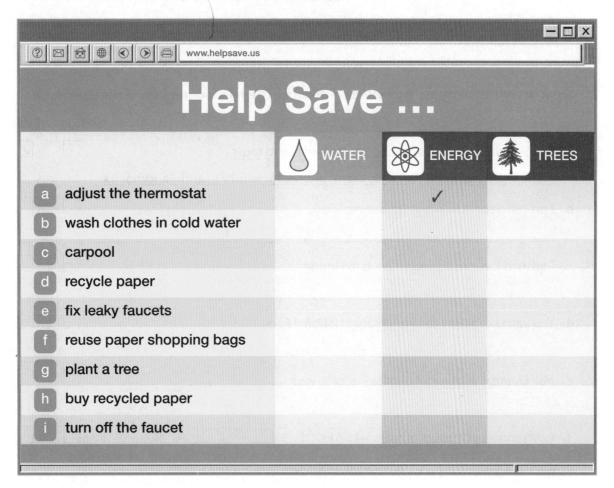

Help Save ...	WATER	ENERGY	TREES
a adjust the thermostat		✓	
b wash clothes in cold water			
c carpool			
d recycle paper			
e fix leaky faucets			
f reuse paper shopping bags			
g plant a tree			
h buy recycled paper			
i turn off the faucet			

www.helpsave.us

5. **What about you? List the things in Exercise 4 you do.**

Example: *I carpool to work to save energy.*

Challenge List other things people can do to help conserve energy and resources.
Example: *They can recycle batteries or use rechargeable batteries.*

Go to page 252 for Another Look (Unit 11). | See page 312 for listening practice.

U.S. National Parks

1. **Look in your dictionary. Which brochures show . . . ? Check (✓) the columns.**

	Yosemite	Dry Tortugas	Carlsbad Caverns
a. water	✓	✓	
b. coral			
c. wildlife			
d. a cave			
e. a ferry			
f. park rangers			

2. **Look in your dictionary. *True* or *False*? Rewrite the false sentences. Make them true.**

	True	False

a. The U.S. National Park system protects <u>ferries and tours</u>. ☐ ✓

   The U.S. National Park system protects wildlife and landmarks.

b. Fort Jefferson is in <u>Yosemite</u> National Park. ☐ ☐

_____

c. Carlsbad Caverns National Park is in <u>Florida</u>. ☐ ☐

_____

d. You can take a ferry to <u>Dry Tortugas</u> National Park. ☐ ☐

_____

e. Half Dome is a <u>cave</u> in Yosemite National Park. ☐ ☐

_____

f. <u>Park rangers</u> give tours of national parks. ☐ ☐

_____

3. **What about you? Tell a partner about your experiences.**

   a. What place have you gone to or lived in that is famous for its natural beauty?

   b. Was it in the U.S. or in another country?

   c. Was it near a river, a forest, a mountain, or a waterfall?

   d. Why is it famous (for example, caves, coral, islands, or wildlife)?

4. Complete the article. Use the words in the box.

caverns	park ranger	landmarks	~~wildlife~~
coral	caves	ferry	take a tour

PLAN A VISIT TO A NATIONAL PARK

Denali National Park is in Alaska. There is a lot of ___wildlife___ in the park, like bears,
a.

moose, and deer. You can _____ of the park with a _____ or see the park
b.   **c.**

on your own. You can't drive your car through the park. You must take the park buses.

Mammoth Cave National Park is in Kentucky. It has the longest system of _____
d.

and _____ in the world. In fact, over 365 miles of this underground system have
e.

been explored. You can see _____ such as Frozen Niagara and Rainbow Dome on
f.

cave tours.

Virgin Islands National Park is on Saint John, an island in the U.S. Virgin Islands. You can take

a _____ from Saint Thomas, a larger island, to Saint John. It's a 20-minute ride and
g.

leaves every hour. You can snorkel and see _____ in the ocean in this beautiful
h.

national park.

5. Match the photos with the parks. Use the information in Exercise 4.

Denali National Park	Mammoth Cave National Park	Virgin Islands National Park

a. _____   b. _____   c. _____

Challenge Write a paragraph about a U.S. National Park or another park or special outdoors place
you know about.

1. **Look in your dictionary. Where can you go to . . . ?**

   a. hear music _____rock concert_____, _____,

      or _____

   b. see sharks and starfish _____

   c. see flowers, trees, and plants _____

   d. hear people sing _____ or _____

   e. see paintings _____

   f. go on rides _____

   g. dance _____

   h. buy old clothes _____

   i. see a film _____

   j. see elephants _____

   k. play alone or on a team _____

2. **Look in your dictionary. Recommend places to go for these people.**

   a. David wants to be a gardener. _____botanical garden_____

   b. Julia needs some things for her home. _____

   c. Tina likes looking at quilts and farm animals. _____

   d. Amy enjoys seeing a "live" performance in a theater. _____

   e. Karl wants to be an artist. He likes paintings. _____

3. **What about you? Look at the places in your dictionary. Where do you go? Why?**
   Complete the chart.

	Places I go . . .	Why?
Often		
Sometimes		
Never		
Never, but I'd like to go.		

4. Look in your dictionary. Complete the newspaper listings below.

WHAT'S HAPPENING

ART

NEWPORT <u>Art Museum</u>
a.
Special exhibit of sculpture and paintings by local artists. Through August 25. **Tickets $5**.

MUSIC

CITY CENTER

Adriana Domingo sings the leading role in Antonio Rivera's new _____,
b.
Starry Night. 8:00 p.m., August 14 and 15.

Tickets $10–$30.

PLM HALL

Oakland Chamber Orchestra, with Lily Marksen at the piano, performs a _____
c.
featuring works by Beethoven, Bach, and Brahms. 8:00 p.m., August 15.

Tickets $20-$30.

THEATER

CURTAINS UP

The Downtown Players perform *The Argument*, a new _____ by J.L. Mason, starring
d.
Vanessa Thompson and Tyrone Williams as a married couple. Through August 20. **Tickets $20**.

CHILDREN

CROWN_____
e.
Roller coaster, merry-go-round, and other rides provide fun for kids and adults. Open daily 10:00 a.m. to 5:00 p.m. **Free admission**.

GENERAL INTEREST

Newport _____ Food, exhibitions,
f.
and prizes for best cow, quilt, and more. August 14–15, 10:00 a.m. to 7:00 p.m. **Free**.

SAL'S _____
g.
Dance to the music of rock band, Jumpin' Lizards. 8:00 p.m. to midnight. Must be 18 or older (ID required). **$10.00 (includes 1 beverage)**.

5. Look at the events in Exercise 4. *True* or *False*?

a. The play is free. ___*false*___

b. You can see an opera at City Center. _____

c. The county fair is open until 10:00 p.m. _____

d. A seventeen-year-old can go to Sal's. _____

e. There's an evening concert at PLM Hall on August 15. _____

f. Tickets to the amusement park are expensive. _____

g. You can see the special art exhibit on August 24. _____

Challenge Look in a local newspaper, an online website of weekend events, or the listings in Exercise 4. Talk to two classmates and agree on a place to go. Write your decision and give a reason.

See page 312 for listening practice. **223**

1. **Look in your dictionary. Where can you hear . . . ?**

   a. "I love playing in the sand."   _____sandbox_____

   b. "OK. Now try to hit this to left field."   _____

   c. "Here. Have some more chicken."   _____

   d. "We're the only cyclists here today."   _____

   e. "Push me higher, Mommy!"   _____

   f. "Bring your racquet all the way back when you serve the ball."   _____

2. **Read about the children. What should they use?**

   a. Toby likes to jump.   _____jump rope_____

   b. Jennifer is a little too young to ride a bicycle.   _____

   c. Jason is thirsty.   _____

   d. Cindi likes to climb bars.   _____

   e. Shao-fen likes to play on things that go up and down. _____

   f. Carlos is tired and just wants to sit down and rest.   _____

3. **What about you? Look at the park in your dictionary.**
   What would you like to do there . . . ?

   a. alone

      I'd like to ride my skateboard.

   b. with three of your classmates

      _____

   c. with a three-year-old child

      _____

   d. with a ten-year-old child

      _____

   e. with a seventy-five-year old relative

      _____

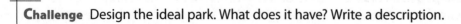

Challenge Design the ideal park. What does it have? Write a description.

  See page 313 for listening practice.

1. **Look in your dictionary. Complete the sentences.**

   a. The boy with the diving mask has _____*fins*_____ on his feet.

   b. There's a pink _____ hanging from the lifeguard station.

   c. The little girl in the red bathing suit is listening to a _____.

   d. A _____ is "catching" a wave on his surfboard.

2. **Circle the words to complete the hotel ad.**

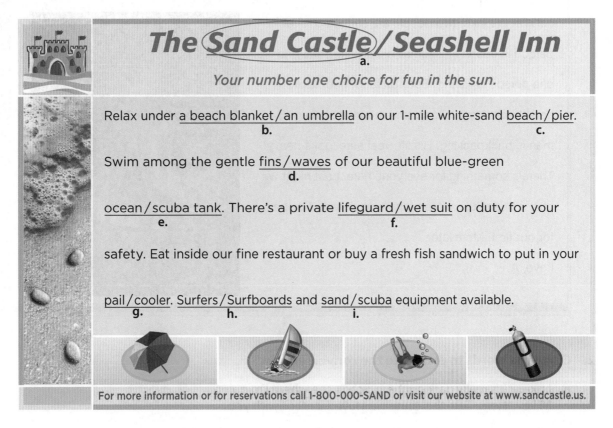

The ⟨Sand Castle⟩/Seashell Inn
a.

Your number one choice for fun in the sun.

Relax under a beach blanket / an umbrella on our 1-mile white-sand beach / pier.
b. c.

Swim among the gentle fins / waves of our beautiful blue-green
d.

ocean / scuba tank. There's a private lifeguard / wet suit on duty for your
e. f.

safety. Eat inside our fine restaurant or buy a fresh fish sandwich to put in your

pail / cooler. Surfers / Surfboards and sand / scuba equipment available.
g. h. i.

For more information or for reservations call 1-800-000-SAND or visit our website at www.sandcastle.us.

3. **What about you? What would you take to the beach? What would you buy or rent? Check (✓) the columns.**

	Take	Buy / Rent
surfboard		
beach chair		
beach umbrella		
blanket		

	Take	Buy / Rent
sunscreen		
cooler		
fins		
Other:		

Challenge Imagine you are at the beach in your dictionary. Write a postcard describing it.
   Example: *I'm sitting . . .*

See page 313 for listening practice.

1. Look in your dictionary. Find and correct five more mistakes in the email.

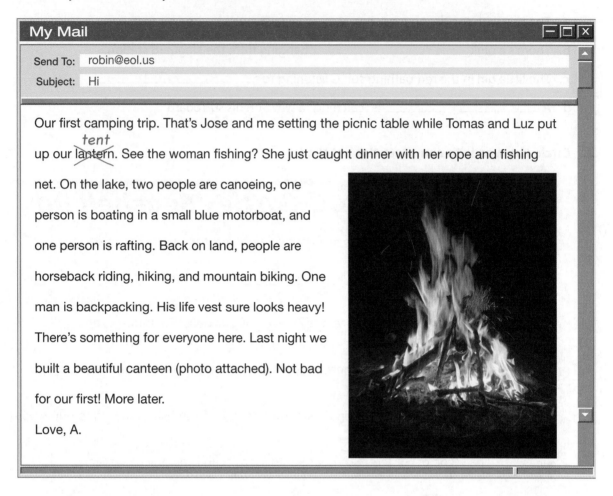

My Mail	− □ ✕
Send To:	robin@eol.us
Subject:	Hi

Our first camping trip. That's Jose and me setting the picnic table while Tomas and Luz put

up our ~~lantern~~ *tent*. See the woman fishing? She just caught dinner with her rope and fishing

net. On the lake, two people are canoeing, one

person is boating in a small blue motorboat, and

one person is rafting. Back on land, people are

horseback riding, hiking, and mountain biking. One

man is backpacking. His life vest sure looks heavy!

There's something for everyone here. Last night we

built a beautiful canteen (photo attached). Not bad

for our first! More later.

Love, A.

2. Circle the words to complete the conversations.

a. **Luke:** It's really dark out here. I can't see where I'm going.
   Mike: Here. Take this camping stove / (lantern) with you.

b. **Ming:** *Brrr.* It's getting cold out here.
   Sue: Hand me the canteen / matches. I'll light the fire.

c. **Jose:** Ow! These mosquitoes are driving me crazy.
   Ana: Here's some foam pad / insect repellent. That'll keep them away.

d. **Mia:** This rope is too long.
   Tom: You're right. What did we do with that multi-use knife / sleeping bag?

3. What about you? Would you like to go camping? Why or why not?

Example: *I'd like to go camping. I like sleeping outside.*

Challenge Look in your dictionary. Imagine you are on a camping trip. List the five most important
items to have. Give reasons.

1. Look in your dictionary. For which sports do you need . . . ?

a. a motorboat _____ *waterskiing* _____

b. waves _____

c. wind _____ and _____

d. a mask and fins _____ and _____

2. Look at the chart. Complete the sentences.

2006 WINTER OLYMPICS IN TURIN, ITALY

		GOLD (First Place)	SILVER (Second Place)	BRONZE (Third Place)
	MEN	Antoine Deneriaz France 1:48.80	Michael Walchhofer Austria 1:49.52	Bruno Kernen Switzerland 1:49.82
	WOMEN	Michaela Dorfmeister Austria 1:56.49	Martina Schild Switzerland 1:56.86	Anja Paerson Sweden 1:57.13
	MEN (15 km)	Andrus Veerpalu Estonia 38:01.3	Lukas Bauer Czech Republic 38:15.8	Tobias Angerer Germany 38.20.5
	WOMEN (10 km)	Kristina Smigun Estonia 27:51.4	Marit Bjorgen Norway 28:12.7	Hilde G. Pedersen Norway 28:14.0
	MEN	Yevgeny Plushenko Russia	Stephane Lambiel Switzerland	Jeffrey Buttle Canada
	WOMEN	Shizuka Arakawa Japan	Sasha Cohen United States	Irina Slutskaya Russia
	MEN (500 m)	Joey Cheek United States 1:09.76	Dmitry Dorofeyev Russia 1:10.41	Lee Kang Seok South Korea 1:10.43
	WOMEN (500 m)	Svetlana Zhurova Russia 1:16.57	Wang Manli China 1:16.78	Ren Hui China 1:16.87

a. China won two medals in _____ *speed skating* _____ .

b. Russia won a gold and a bronze medal in _____ .

c. The United States won one gold medal in _____ .

d. Estonia won the gold medal in both men's and women's _____ .

e. Bruno Kernen lost the silver medal in _____ by less than half a second.

f. _____ is not a timed event.

Challenge Which winter sports or water sports are best for where you live? Why?

See page 314 for listening practice.

1. Look in your dictionary. Cross out the word that doesn't belong. Give a reason.

a. billiards   ~~martial arts~~   table tennis   *It doesn't use a ball.*

b. fencing   gymnastics   wrestling   _____

c. boxing   inline skating   skateboarding   _____

d. cycling   horse racing   badminton   _____

2. Look at the line graph. Circle the words to complete the sentences.

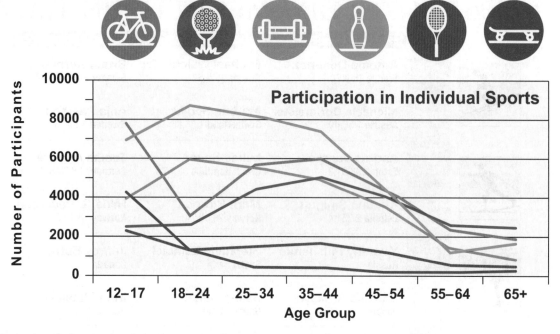

Based on information from: a survey of homes by the National Sporting Goods Association (2004) as reported by U.S. Census Bureau, *Statistical Abstract of the United States, 2007.*

a. (Bowling)/ Cycling is the most popular sport for people 18 to 24 years old.

b. Skateboarding / Tennis is the least popular sport for people over 25.

c. Golf / Cycling is the most popular sport for people over 65.

d. Participation in tennis / weightlifting goes down after the age of 24.

e. Between the ages of 64 and 65, the participation of bowling / golf goes up.

f. Participation in cycling / skateboarding goes down after the age of 12, but then it goes up again.

3. What about you? How has your participation in sports changed? Write sentences.

Example: *I started to play more soccer in high school.*

╆ **Challenge** Write five more sentences using information from the line graph in Exercise 2.

        See page 314 for listening practice.

1. **Look at the basketball court in your dictionary. Circle the words to complete the sentences.**

   a. There are two <u>players / (teams)</u> on the basketball court.

   b. The <u>coach / official</u> is on the court, too.

   c. The home <u>fan / score</u> is 83.

2. **Look at the bar graph. *True* or *False*? Correct the <u>underlined</u> words in the false sentences.**

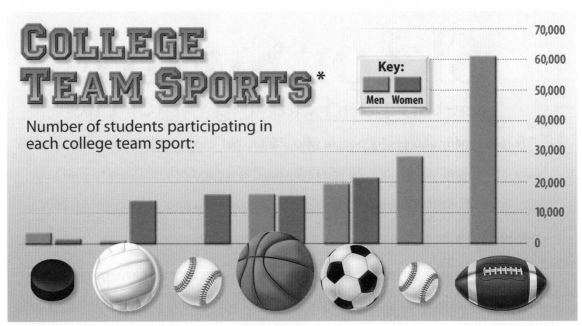

COLLEGE TEAM SPORTS*

Number of students participating in each college team sport:

Key: Men Women

*Note: These teams are in colleges which are members of the National Collegiate Athletic Association, an organization that governs college sports competitions in the United States.

Based on information from: U.S. Census Bureau, *Statistical Abstract of the United States, 2008*.

   Football
   a. ~~Baseball~~ is the most popular team sport among college men. _____ *false* _____

   b. More women than men play <u>soccer</u>. _____

   c. College men don't play on <u>volleyball</u> teams. _____

   d. Women don't play on college baseball and <u>football</u> teams. _____

   e. About 20,000 women play college <u>basketball</u>. _____

   f. Not many men or women participate in college <u>ice hockey</u>. _____

   g. More college students play baseball than <u>softball</u>. _____

Challenge Look at page 260 in this book. Follow the instructions.

1. **Look in your dictionary. Cross out the word that doesn't belong.**

a. with your feet   ~~catch~~   kick   jump

b. with a ball   hit   serve   bend

c. in water   swim   skate   dive

d. with other people   serve   tackle   pass

2. **Circle the words to complete the article.**

Ski or Swim?
Getting and Staying Fit for Life

There are many choices for people who want to get and stay fit. Some sports require very little special equipment. All you really need is a good pair of shoes to walk your way to good health. But you can also (dive) / dribble into a pool and ski / swim your
       a.   b.
way to fitness.

Want to exercise / serve with other people? Many communities have gyms that you
       c.
can join. There you can tackle / work out alone or with others. Bending / Pitching and
                                 d.   e.
hitting / stretching help firm muscles and keep your body flexible.
       f.

For those people who enjoy competing, there are many opportunities to race / pass in
                                                                                    g.
city marathons. But remember: Winning isn't everything. Even if you don't finish / start
                                                                                         h.
the race, you should feel good that you participated.

It's not really important which sport you choose. You can throw / shoot a baseball
                                                                        i.
or kick / swing a golf club. Just start slowly and be careful. Most of all, enjoy what you
       j.
do and do it regularly. In order to get and stay fit, sports should be a part of your

everyday life.

Challenge Look in your dictionary. Where else can a person swim, work out, ski, or race?
Write two sentences for each verb. **Example:** *You can swim in the ocean. You can swim in . . .*

  See page 315 for listening practice.

1. **Look in your dictionary. Which pieces of equipment are customers talking about?**

   a. "These are a little too heavy for me." _____weights_____

   b. "Oh, I see them now. They're under the target and next to the bow." _____

   c. "There's one. Under the volleyball." _____

   d. "They look like ice skates with wheels!" _____

   e. "Great! It's blue and white—the same as my team's colors." _____

   f. "I'd love to throw one of those around. I'd like red, maybe pink." _____

   g. "Well, this will really protect my head." _____

   h. "Wow! These will make me look really big!" _____

   i. "Oh, there they are. Between the snowboard and the ski poles." _____

   j. "Do you have one for left-handed pitchers?" _____

   k. "I have to wear them to protect my legs during soccer games." _____

2. **Make comparisons with *than*. Use the words in parentheses.**

   a. volleyball / basketball (big)

   ___A basketball is bigger than a volleyball.___

   b. golf club / hockey stick (long)

   _____

   c. ice skates / ski boots (warm)

   _____

   d. baseball / football (small)

   _____

   e. bowling ball / soccer ball (heavy)

   _____

3. **What about you? Look in your dictionary. What sports equipment would you buy from the store? Why?**

   Example: *I'd buy a bat for my niece because she wants to play baseball.*

Challenge Look online or at a newspaper ad. Find the prices of these pieces of sports equipment.

   a baseball glove _____   a tennis racket _____

   Other: _____

1. Look in your dictionary. Complete the crossword puzzle.

			¹W	a	t	²e	r	c	o	l	o	r		
³													⁴

(crossword grid with numbered cells: 3, 4, 5, 6, 7, 8, 9, 10, 11, 12, 13, 14, 15, 16, 17, 18, 19)

ACROSS

1. It's not oil paint
6. This one looks like a kitten
8. It comes in a stick
9. Red, but not hearts
10. A board game
11. Black, but not spades
13. Type of paint
17. Type of game
18. It holds a canvas
19. I like to _____ games

DOWN

2. It has a flower on it
3. Collect _____
4. You use them to knit
5. These are cubes
7. You can build these with a kit
10. It's on the easel
12. Type of figure
14. A board game
15. You can make one from paper
16. Type of paint

2. Cross out the word that doesn't belong. Give a reason.

a. checkers	chess	~~crocheting~~	*It's not a board game.*
b. dolls	diamonds	clubs	_____
c. watercolor	acrylic	quilt block	_____

3. **Look at the bar graph. Circle the words to complete the sentences.**

Fun and Games

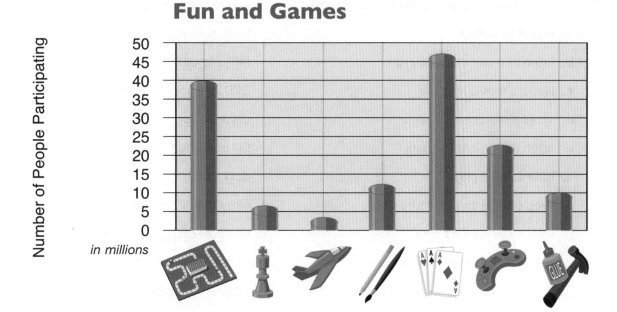

Based on information from: U.S. Census Bureau, *Statistical Abstract of the United States, 2008* (information is for 2006).

a. Playing (cards) / video games was the most popular of the seven activities.

b. About 12 million people drew or painted / played board games.

c. Almost 10 million people used a model / woodworking kit.

d. The least popular of the seven activities was chess / model making.

e. Playing cards was about two times as popular as playing board / video games.

4. **What about you? How often do you . . . ? Check (✓) the columns.**

	Every week	Every month	Never
play cards			
play board games			
use a video game console			
do crafts			
play with model trains			
paint			
quilt			
Other:			

Challenge Make a list of things to collect. Compare your list with your classmates.

See page 315 for listening practice.

1. Look in your dictionary. What can you use to . . . ? Circle the answers.

a. watch TV outside   flat screen / ⟨portable TV⟩

b. listen to music while you run   MP3 player / turntable

c. watch a movie at home   DVD / personal CD player

d. show pictures on a screen   battery charger / LCD projector

e. listen to music in the park   CD boombox / tuner

f. hold an MP3 player   dock / plug

g. keep photos on a memory card   film / digital camera

h. watch a movie on a train   portable cassette / DVD player

i. keep your paper photos in one place   photo / digital photo album

j. listen to music without headphones   adapter / speakers

k. record your own voice   battery pack / microphone

2. Look at the chart. Complete the sentences.

Percent of U.S. Homes with Electronic Devices

54%	88%	32%	84%	62%
2004	2006	2007	2007	2007

Based on information from: *New York Times Almanac* (2006) (for camcorder), Adweek (2006) http://allbasics.com (for CD player), and ITFacts (2007) http://www.itfacts.biz (for MP3 player, digital camera, and DVD player).

a. In 2004, only a little more than half the homes in the U.S. had _____camcorders_____.

b. In 2006, almost 90% had _____.

c. In 2007, 62% had _____.

d. In 2007, 52% more homes had _____ than _____.

3. Look at instructions for a universal remote control. Complete the sentences.

Operation Buttons

INSTRUCTIONS

a. _____play_____ : to watch a DVD

b. _____ : to go back

c. _____ : to stop the DVD for a short time during playing or recording

d. _____ : to record a program (You must press PLAY at the same time.)

e. _____ : to go to the end quickly

4. Look at the pictures. Circle the words to complete the sentences.

a. The (photo)/ screen is out of focus.

b. She didn't use a camera case / tripod.

c. The photo is overexposed / underexposed.

d. He didn't use a film camera / zoom lens.

5. What about you? Look at the electronic devices in Exercise 2. Which is the most important to you? Why?

Challenge Write instructions for using a portable cassette player, a CD boombox, an MP3 player, or another electronic device.

See page 316 for listening practice.

1. Look in your dictionary. Where can you hear . . . ?

a. "And now a look at what's happening today in Europe." <u>news program</u>

b. "Goodbye girls, goodbye boys. See you tomorrow." _____

c. "And now, for $50,000 . . ." _____

d. "Don't be afraid. I come from a friendly planet." _____

e. "This beautiful dress can be yours for just $55.99!" _____

f. "I love you and only you! Not your sister!" _____

g. "Pandas live in the forest of central China." _____

h. "Lopez is trying to get the ball from Jackson!" _____

i. "I'm almost finished brushing my teeth." _____

2. Circle the words to complete the TV movie listings.

Movie Listings
This Week's Highlights

Titanic*** (1997)	Rich girl (Kate Winslet) meets poor boy (Leonardo DiCaprio) on the historic sinking ship, and it's love at first sight. Don't miss this beautiful <u>mystery /</u> (romance.) (194 minutes) a.	Fri 8:00 P.M. Ch 7
Jurassic Park III* (2001)	Dinosaurs attack (again) in this scary <u>horror story</u> / western with Sam Neill, William H. Macy, and Téa Leoni. b. You'll be scared out of your seat. (92 minutes)	Fri 9:00 P.M. Ch 4
Spider Man 3* (2007)	Tobey Maguire stars again as the superhero Spider Man in this exciting <u>action story</u> / comedy. Great special effects. (140 minutes) c.	Fri 10:00 P.M. SCI
Romeo and Juliet (1996)	Starring Leonardo DiCaprio as Romeo and Claire Danes as Juliet, this modern version of Shakespeare's <u>mystery / tragedy</u> will bring tears to your eyes. (120 minutes) d.	Sat 9:00 P.M. ENT
Mr. & Mrs. Smith** (2005)	An "average" husband (Brad Pitt) and wife (Angelina Jolie) live secret and surprising lives in this very funny <u>comedy / tragedy.</u> (120 minutes) e.	Sat 10:00 P.M. Ch 7

3. **Look in your dictionary. Label the CDs. Then look at the pie chart.** *True* or *False*?

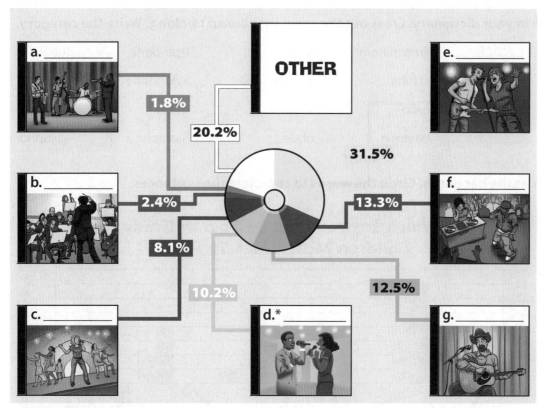

a. _____

e. _____

OTHER

1.8%

20.2%

31.5%

b. _____

f. _____

2.4%

13.3%

8.1%

10.2%

12.5%

c. _____

d.* _____

g. _____

* includes reggae, blues, soul

Based on information from: *The World Almanac and Book of Facts*, 2007. (NY: World Almanac Education Group, Inc. 2007.)

a. At 31.5% of all sales, rock sold the most out of all types of music.   _*true*_

b. At just 1.8% of sales, pop sold the least.   _____

c. Country music sold more than classical music.   _____

d. Jazz sold more than hip hop.   _____

e. 10.2% of sales came from R&B, blues, reggae, and soul together.   _____

4. **What about you? How often do you listen to . . . ? Check (✓) the column.**

	Often	Sometimes	Never
classical music			
jazz			
gospel			
reggae			
world music			

Challenge Write two short reviews of television programs or movies. Give them a one to six star (*) rating.

See page 316 for listening practice.

Music

1. Look in your dictionary. Cross out the word that doesn't belong. Write the category.

a. ___Brass___ French horn ~~bass~~ trombone tuba

b. _____ clarinet tambourine xylophone drums

c. _____ cello violin guitar organ

d. _____ bassoon oboe harmonica saxophone

2. Look at the bar graph. Circle the words to complete the sentences.

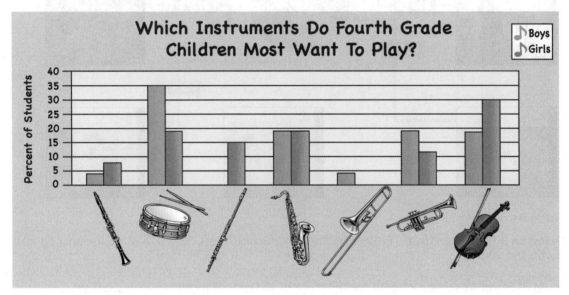

Based on information from: A study by S. Pickering, "Modifying children's gender-typed musical instrument preferences: the effects of gender and age," Sex Roles: *A Journal of Research* (Nov. 2001).

a. The (drum) / violin was the favorite instrument among boys.

b. 30% of girls chose the flute / violin as their favorite instrument.

c. 19% of both boys and girls chose the saxophone / trumpet.

d. No boys chose the flute / trumpet as their favorite instrument.

e. No girls chose the clarinet / trombone as their favorite instrument.

f. The graph does not include the harmonica or the electric keyboard / saxophone.

3. What about you? Can you . . . ? *Yes* or *No*?

play an instrument? _____   If *yes*, which one? _____

sing a song? _____   If *yes*, what is your favorite? _____

conduct an orchestra? _____   play or sing in a rock band? _____

Challenge Ask your classmates about the instruments they play. Draw a bar graph like the one in Exercise 2.

   See page 316 for listening practice.

1. Look in your dictionary. Complete the holiday cards.

a.

I looked really hard to find this

_____card_____, just to say
  a.

on this special day—that you're

always a part of my _____ .
       b.

Happy _____ .
     c.

I think we're a great _____ !
       d.

b.

Resolutions are made,

here comes the _____ .
       e.

I'm more than ready,

so throw the _____ !
       f.

The time is now near

to say Happy New _____ !
       g.

c.

As _____
   h.

light up the sky, the red, white,

and blue _____ will proudly
     i.

fly! Happy _____ !
      j.

d.

I hope that there will always

be _____ and
   k.

candy _____ on your tree!
    l.

Merry _____ .
     m.

e.

It's late November — time to

remember to give thanks for the

good things this year and, not the

least, a delicious _____
      n.

where _____ and stuffing
   o.

appear. Happy _____ !
      p.

f.

_____ burning bright, on a cool
 q.

October night. In scary costumes and a

_____ , for _____ treats
 r.   **s.**

the children ask. Happy _____ !
       t.

2. What about you? Check (✓) the cards you send. Who do you send them to?

☐ New Year's _____

☐ Valentine's Day _____

☐ Christmas _____

☐ Other: _____

Challenge Make a card for one of the holidays in your dictionary or for any other event.

1. Look in your dictionary. Match.

 _5_ **a.** There are presents   **1.** wrapping Lou's gift.

 ____ **b.** Lou is making a wish for   **2.** on a long table.

 ____ **c.** There are two cakes   **3.** from the deck.

 ____ **d.** A woman is videotaping the party   **4.** a new car.

 ____ **e.** Gani is   **5.** on a round table.

 ____ **f.** Amaka is   **6.** blowing out the candles.

2. Lou's Mom videotaped birthday messages for Lou and Gani. Circle the words to complete the messages.

a. "Hi, Lou. Happy 18th birthday! Did you ⟨make a wish⟩/ blow out the candles for a new car? I hope you get it. You can take me for a ride!"

b. "Happy birthday, Gani. Eighty years old! Wow! You have a lot of candles to <u>wrap / blow out</u>!"

c. "Hey, Lou. Have a great day. I hope you like the present I <u>videotaped / brought</u>."

d. "Happy birthday, Gani. Open my present first! I <u>sang / wrapped</u> it in some pretty red paper."

e. "Lou, happy birthday! I <u>hid / brought</u> your present in the yard. I hope you can find it!"

f. "Enjoy the party, Lou! Your Mom did a great job with the <u>decorations / videotape</u>. They look beautiful!"

3. What about you? How do you celebrate birthdays in your family? Compare your list with a partner's.

☐ have a party

☐ have a cake with candles

☐ put up decorations

☐ make a wish

☐ videotape the party

☐ bring gifts

☐ Other: _____

4. Look at the picture. *True* or *False*?

a. The present isn't for Lou. _____false_____

b. The present is from Paul. _____

c. He hid the present. _____

d. The present is wrapped in blue and red paper. _____

e. The present isn't a new car. _____

5. What happened first? Number *1* and *2* for each pair.

a. _2_ I blew out the candles.   _1_ I made a wish.

b. ___ We videotaped the party.   ___ We watched the videotape.

c. ___ He gave me the present.   ___ He wrapped the present.

d. ___ I found my present on the deck.   ___ My Mom hid my present.

e. ___ My Dad cut the cake.   ___ We ate the cake.

6. Complete the card. Use the words in the box.

| hid | presents | ~~make~~ | blow | decorations | brought | wrapped |

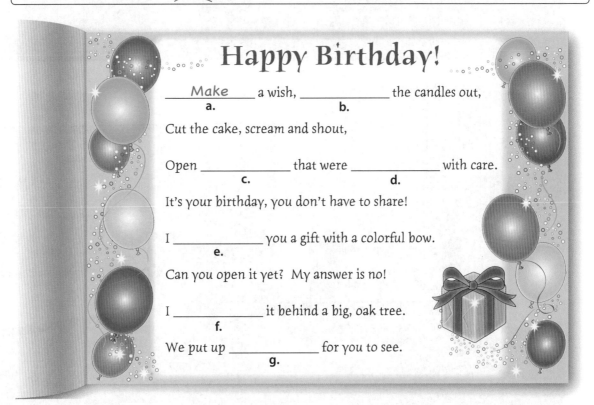

Happy Birthday!

_____Make_____ a wish, _____ the candles out,
    a.   **b.**

Cut the cake, scream and shout,

Open _____ that were _____ with care.
       c.   **d.**

It's your birthday, you don't have to share!

I _____ you a gift with a colorful bow.
    e.

Can you open it yet? My answer is no!

I _____ it behind a big, oak tree.
    f.

We put up _____ for you to see.
         g.

Challenge Write a birthday message for a greeting card. It can rhyme, but it doesn't have to.

See page 317 for listening practice.

Picture Comparison

Write about the two classrooms. How are they the same? How are they different?
Example: *Both classes are ESL classes. One class is ESL 101, the other class is ESL 102. Both classes have six students. In class 101, half the students are women, but in 102…*

A Picture is Worth a Thousand Words

These are photographs by Alfred Eisenstaedt and other photographers.
Write about the people in the photographs.

Describe the people.

What is their relationship?

Where are they?

What are they doing?

How do they feel?

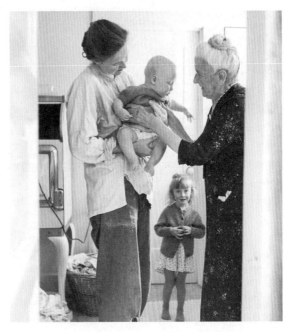

243

Word Map

Complete the diagram. Use the words in the box.

bathroom	bathtub	bed	bedroom	blanket
counter	dining area	dishes	drawer	dresser	end table
entertainment center		faucet	food processor	~~house~~	hutch
~~kids' bedroom~~	kitchen	lamp	living room	medicine cabinet
~~napkin~~	~~pillow~~	placemat	pot	~~rubber mat~~
~~stereo system~~	~~stove~~	~~stuffed animals~~	table	toothbrush	~~toy chest~~

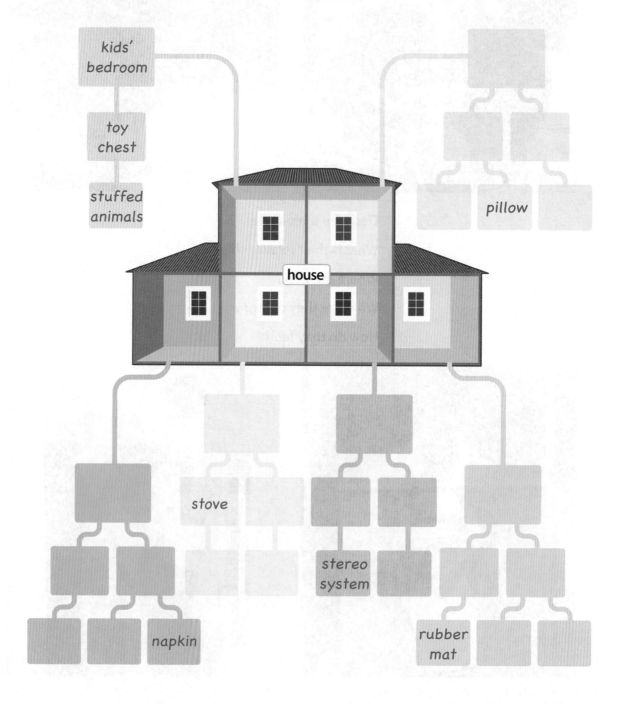

"C" Search

Look at the picture. There are more than 15 items that begin with the letter *c*. Find and circle them. Then, write at least 8 sentences describing the picture. Use the circled words in your sentences.

Example: *One man is eating a cheeseburger.*

Pack It Up!

Imagine that you are going away for the weekend. What clothing and accessories will you take for each place? Put at least six items in each suitcase. Use your dictionary for help.

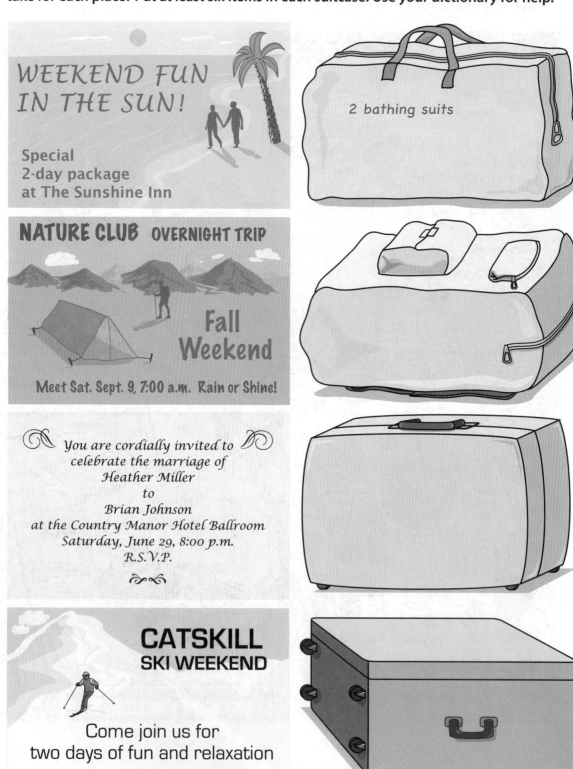

WEEKEND FUN IN THE SUN!

Special
2-day package
at The Sunshine Inn

2 bathing suits

NATURE CLUB OVERNIGHT TRIP

Fall Weekend

Meet Sat. Sept. 9, 7:00 a.m. Rain or Shine!

You are cordially invited to celebrate the marriage of
Heather Miller
to
Brian Johnson
at the Country Manor Hotel Ballroom
Saturday, June 29, 8:00 p.m.
R.S.V.P.

CATSKILL SKI WEEKEND

Come join us for two days of fun and relaxation

For information visit us at www.ski.us

Crossword Puzzle

Complete the crossword puzzle.

1 I	2 D		3		4	5		6	7	8

(grid numbers: 1 I, 2 D, 3, 4, 5, 6, 7, 8, 9, 10, 11, 12, 13, 14, 15, 16, 17, 18, 19, 20, 21, 22, 23, 24, 25, 26, 27, 28, 29, 30, 31, 32, 33, 34, 35)

ACROSS

1. Identification (short form)
3. _____ your teeth
6. A hole in a tooth
9. It holds your hair in place
10. She's _____ the hospital
13. Women wear it to smell good
14. Take with milk _____ food
15. _____ smoking!
17. Your brain is inside it
19. Your throat is inside it
20. It helps you walk
23. They operate on patients
26. Throw up
28. It's part of the foot
29. It's another part of the foot
32. _____-the-counter medication
34. High temperature
35. Your eye_____ covers your eye

DOWN

2. A serious disease
4. An eye specialist
5. You do this with your eyes
6. Cardiopulmonary resuscitation (short form)
7. Opposite of *arteries*
8. Listen _____ your heart
11. _____ not operate heavy machinery
12. One of the five senses
16. You put a bandage on this
18. Part of your face
21. *Break* (past form)
22. The dentist _____ a cavity yesterday
24. You shave with this
25. You do this with your nose
27. A doctor can look _____ your throat
30. Put _____ sunscreen
31. Intravenous (short form)
33. Registered nurse (short form)

247

Things Change

Look at the maps of Middletown 50 years ago and Middletown today. What's different? What's the same? Write sentences. Use your own paper.

Example: *There was a bakery on the southeast corner of Elm and Grove. Now there's a coffee shop. There's still a...*

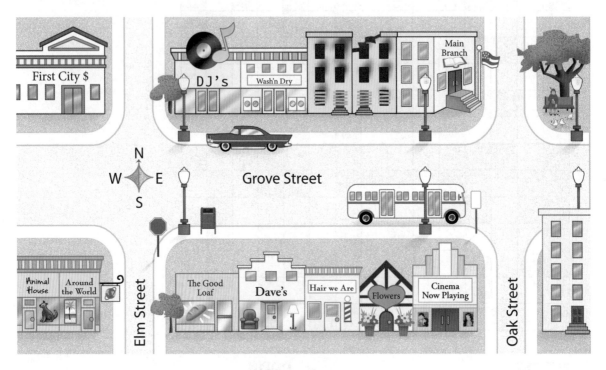

50 Years Ago

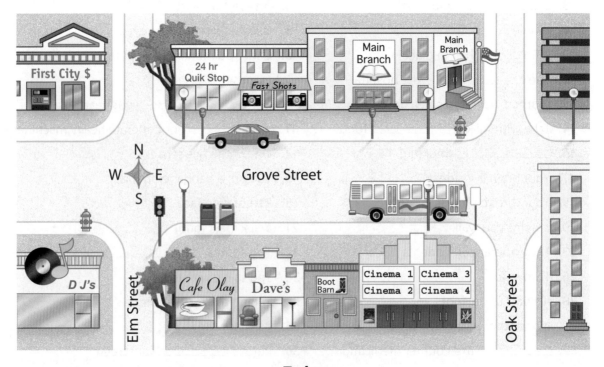

Today

What's Wrong With This Picture?

Look at the picture. Describe ten more problems.

Example: *A subway car is going over the bridge.*

On the Job

Look at the pictures. Describe each photograph and answer the questions for each picture. Use your own paper.

1.

2.

3.

4.

a. Where are the people?

b. What are they doing?

c. What type of equipment are the people using?

d. Are they using safety equipment? If *yes*, what type?

e. What types of job skills do the people need to do these jobs?

f. How do you think the workers feel?

g. Compare the four jobs. How are they the same? How are they different?

h. Would you like to work in any of these places? Why or why not?

Word Map

Complete the diagram. Use the words in the box.

~~add~~	astronaut	chemistry	comma	computers
desert	~~DVD drive~~	English composition	~~essay~~	exploration
geography	~~high school~~	~~invention~~	light bulb	magnet
~~math~~	mountain peak	mountain range	multiply	ocean
paragraph	~~physics~~	product	~~sand dune~~	science
sentence	~~sum~~	test tube	~~tower~~	world history

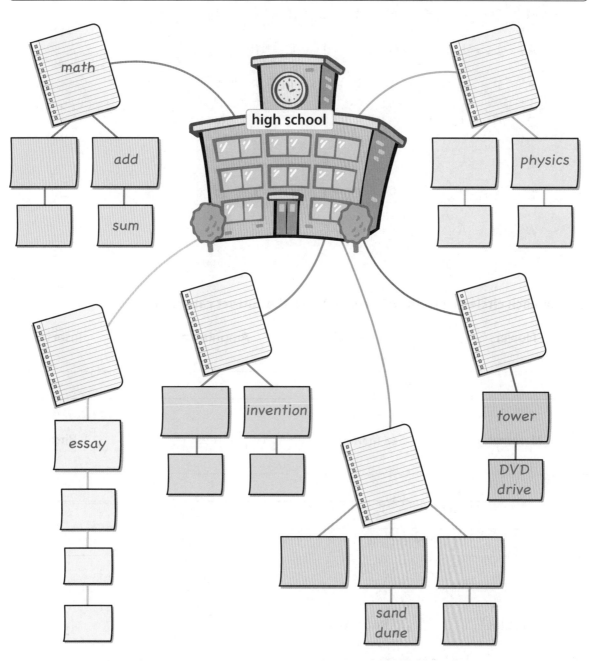

Word Search

1. There are 25 plant and animal words in the box. The words go → and ↓.
   Find and circle them.

L	I	O	N	P	A	R	O	S	E
L	C	A	T	I	R	O	O	E	L
A	D	K	O	N	A	O	C	A	E
M	O	N	K	E	Y	S	T	L	P
A	L	L	I	G	A	T	O	R	H
P	P	L	L	G	N	E	P	R	A
O	H	I	F	O	E	R	U	A	N
W	I	L	L	O	W	A	S	P	T
L	N	Y	Y	S	T	T	O	A	D
W	H	A	L	E	A	G	L	E	Y

2. Put each circled word from Exercise 1 into the correct category.

Flowers	Sea Animals	Amphibians	Insects
_____	_____	_____	_____
_____	_____	_____	_____

Mammals	Sea Mammals	Trees	Birds
llama	_____	_____	_____
lion	_____	_____	_____
_____	_____	_____	_____
_____			_____
_____			

Reptiles	Rodents
_____	_____

Complete the puzzle.

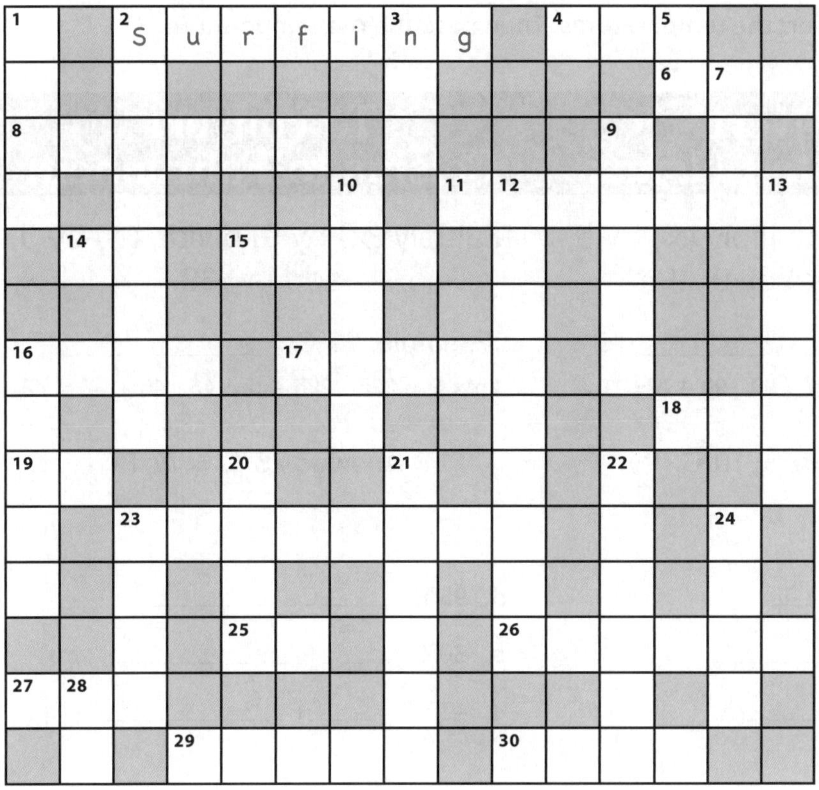

The crossword grid with 2 Across filled in: s u r f i n g

ACROSS

2. A water sport
4. Type of player for movies
6. Type of paint
8. It goes up and down
11. You can use them to light a campfire
14. Compact disc (short form)
15. Bucket
16. _____ and touch your toes
17. You see them in a theater
18. Type of block for your skin
19. Opposite of *Yes*
23. A bike with three wheels
25. 35 _____ camera
26. It has three legs; you put your camera on it
27. _____ the ball with the bat
29. You can swim in it
30. String instrument

DOWN

1. _____ a swing
2. A winter snow sport
3. _____ Year's Day
5. _____ crafts
7. _____ skating
9. New York 5, Los Angeles 3
10. Track and _____
12. Type of park
13. Downhill _____
16. You can sit on it in the park
20. Type of camera
21. You can look at pictures and charts on it
22. You can see them in a theater
23. You can sleep in it
24. Billiards
28. This _____ the end of the Down clues!

Challenge Exercises

Challenge for page 13

Use the formulas to convert the temperatures. Then describe the temperature.

To convert Fahrenheit to Celsius:	To convert Celsius to Fahrenheit:
Subtract (−) 32, multiply (×) by 5, divide (÷) by 9	Multiply (×) by 9, divide (÷) by 5, add (+) 32
Example: 50°F = _____?_____ °C	Example: 25°C = _____?_____ °F
50 − 32 = 18 18 × 5 = 90 90 ÷ 9 = 10	25 × 9 = 225 225 ÷ 5 = 45 45 + 32 = 77
Answer: 50°F = 10°C	Answer: 25°C = 77°F

a. 25°C = _77°_ F ____warm____

b. 41° F = ____ C _____

c. 68°F = ____ C _____

d. 95°F = ____ C _____

e. 30°C = ____ F _____

f. −20°C = ____ F _____

Challenge for page 15

Look up the information in a phone book or online.

a. What are the area codes for these cities?

Dallas, TX _____

Boston, MA _____

San Francisco, CA _____

Milwaukee, WI _____

b. What are the city and country codes for these locations?

	Country code	City code
Mexico City, Mexico		
Montreal, Canada		
Beijing, China		
Moscow, Russia		

Write six sentences comparing times in different cities. Use words, not numbers.

Example: *When it's five in the afternoon in Athens, it's eleven at night in Hong Kong.*

When it's noon Eastern Standard Time, it's ... in ... .

Athens	**7** P.M.	Hong Kong	**1** A.M.*	Riyadh	**8** P.M.
Baghdad	**8** P.M.	Mecca	**8** P.M.	St. Petersburg	**8** P.M.
Bangkok	**12** MIDNIGHT	Mexico City	**11** A.M.	San Juan	**12** NOON
Buenos Aires	**2** P.M.	Paris	**6** P.M.	Seoul	**2** A.M.*
Halifax	**1** P.M.	Rio de Janeiro	**2** P.M.	Tokyo	**2** A.M.*

* = morning of the next day

**Add to the chart. Look up the information online.
Continue on your own paper if you need more space.**

International Holidays		
Date	**Holiday**	**Country**
January 26	Republic Day	India
February 5	Constitution Day	Mexico
May 5	Children's Day	South Korea
June 20	Flag Day	Argentina
July 14	Bastille Day	France
December 26	Boxing Day	Canada

Challenge for pages 34 and 35

Look at the pie chart. *True* **or** *False*?

Children living with two parents and . . .

- ■ one or more brothers and sisters
- ■ one or more stepbrothers or stepsisters
- ▨ one or more half brothers or half sisters
- ▨ no brothers or sisters
- ▨ other

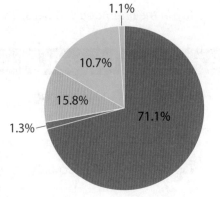

1.1%

10.7%

15.8%

1.3%

71.1%

Based on information from: The U.S. Census Bureau, (2001).

a. Most children living with a mother and father also live with one or more brothers or sisters.   *true*

b. Only 10.7% of children living with two parents don't live with brothers or sisters.   _____

c. More than 10% of children living with two parents live with stepbrothers or stepsisters.   _____

d. More children living with two parents live with half-brothers and half-sisters than with stepbrothers and stepsisters.   _____

Challenge for pages 42 and 43

Imagine that you are the person in the far left of this picture. Complete the story.

When I went into the room, I felt

_____.
　　　　a.
Everyone looked _____.
　　　　　　　　b.
One person seemed _____.
　　　　　　　　　c.
The first thing I did was _____.
　　　　　　　　　　d.
That made me feel _____.
　　　　　　　　　e.
Then I . . .

Challenge for page 59

What's your opinion? Write appropriate toys for each group. Use your dictionary for help.

Age group	Activities	Toys
Babies (under 2)	looking and listening holding things	*rattle*
Toddlers (age 2-3)	throwing, rolling, and pushing objects listening to stories and songs	
Children over age 3	learning stories and songs drawing	

Challenge for pages 72 and 73

Look at the receipts. Compare prices. Write six sentences.

Example: *Black beans are cheaper at Dave's.*

```
           DAVE'S
       54 CHURCH STREET
         CHICAGO, IL

1 CAN BLACK BEANS      $0.60
1 GAL APPLE JUICE      $4.99
2 LB FLOUR             $1.69
6 FROZEN BAGELS        $1.09
1 PINT ICE CREAM       $3.99
1 6-OZ FAT FREE
  BANANA YOGURT        $0.80


        THANK YOU FOR
       SHOPPING WITH US
```

```
        SHOPWELL

1 6-OZ FAT FREE
  BANANA YOGURT        $0.90
6 FROZEN BAGELS        $1.19
1 PINT ICE CREAM       $3.99
1 GAL APPLE JUICE      $4.39
2 LB FLOUR             $1.39
1 CAN BLACK BEANS      $0.80


        THANK YOU FOR
       SHOPPING WITH US
```

Challenge for page 75

**Check the labels on the containers of four of your favorite foods.
Make a chart like the one below.**

Food	Serving Size	Calories	Calories from fat	Protein	Carbohydrate
ice cream	*1/2 cup*	*170*	*90*	*3g*	*17g*

What type of punishment should crimes get? What do you think?
Check (✓) the columns to complete the chart.

Crimes	Prison	Hospitalization	Community service*	Fines**
assault				
burglary				
drunk driving				
identity theft				
murder				
illegal drugs				
shoplifting				
vandalism				

* *Community service* is work that a person does without pay. An example is cleaning up the sidewalks.
**A *fine* is an amount of money a person has to pay for doing something wrong.

Look at the pairs of jobs. Compare them. What is the same for both jobs?
Use your own paper.

Example: *A childcare worker and a babysitter both work with children.*

a. a childcare worker and a babysitter

b. an accountant and a cashier

c. a butcher and a baker

d. an auto mechanic and an appliance repair person

e. a businessperson and an administrative assistant.

List three job skills. Check (✓) the ones you and a classmate have.

Job Skills	Your Name	Classmate's Name
_____	☐	☐
_____	☐	☐
_____	☐	☐

Challenge for page 173

What do you think are the best ways to find a job? Rank the ways.
(Number 1 = the best). Add to the list. Explain your choices to your classmates.

Ways to find a job

_____ network

_____ classified ads

_____ employment service offices

_____ Other: _____

_____ school/college placement services

_____ employment agencies

_____ the Internet

_____ Other: _____

Challenge for page 179

Look at the worker. Write about the safety hazards. What should the worker do
to protect herself?

Example: _She's wearing sandals. She should wear safety boots._

Complete the quiz. Look up the information online.

Name: _____   Class: U.S. History 101

Circle the letter of the correct answer.

1. The slaves became free after _____.

   a. the Civil War   **b.** Progressivism   **c.** World War I

2. Armstrong walked on the moon during the _____ Age.

   a. Global   **b.** Space   **c.** Jazz

3. Millions of people died during the few years of _____.

   a. the Cold War   **b.** the Industrial Revolution   **c.** World War II

4. Many people moved to California in search of gold during _____.

   a. Western Expansion   **b.** Reconstruction   **c.** the Information Age

5. More than 25% of all workers couldn't find jobs during the _____.

   a. Global Age   **b.** Great Depression   **c.** Industrial Revolution

Challenge for page 213

Find out more information about at least two animals in Exercise 4. Look online, in an encyclopedia, or a science book to make a chart like the one below. Use your own paper.

Name	Type	What it eats	How it protects itself
salamander	amphibian	insects and worms	produces poison

Challenge for page 229

Interview five or more people. Which sports do they like to play? Which sports do they like to watch? Complete the chart.

Number of people who like to ...							
	Basketball	Baseball	Softball	Football	Soccer	Ice hockey	Volleyball	Water polo
Play								
Watch								

Listening Exercises

Meeting and Greeting pages 2 and 3, CD 1, Track 2

Listen. *True* or *False*? Check (✓) the answers.

	True	False
1. Laila and Anita met last week.	☐	✓
2. The man is introducing Kim and Laila.	☐	☐
3. The teacher is greeting his students.	☐	☐
4. Anita and Laila are shaking hands.	☐	☐
5. Fred isn't smiling now.	☐	☐
6. Fred is leaving.	☐	☐

Personal Information page 4, CD 1, Track 3

Listen. Circle the mistakes in the form. Then listen again and correct the mistakes.

IBS INTERNATIONAL BUSINESS SCHOOL

SCHOOL REGISTRATION FORM

FIRST NAME	MIDDLE INITIAL	LAST NAME
Ana	M Ⓝ.	Rivera

ADDRESS	APARTMENT NUMBER	CITY	STATE	ZIP CODE
2515 Orange St.	4-D	Los Angeles	California	90015

AREA CODE	PHONE NUMBER	CELL PHONE NUMBER
(310)	555-3133	(310) 555-0275

DATE OF BIRTH (DOB)	PLACE OF BIRTH	SOCIAL SECURITY NUMBER
5-1-85	Mexico	146-98-9426

SEX: MALE ☐ FEMALE ✓

SIGNATURE *Ana M. Rivera*

School page 5, CD 1, Track 4

Listen. Where are they? Check (✓) the answers.

1.	✓ a. classroom		☐ b. field
2.	☐ a. cafeteria		☐ b. library
3.	☐ a. quad		☐ b. hallway
4.	☐ a. bleachers		☐ b. computer lab
5.	☐ a. main office		☐ b. track
6.	☐ a. gym		☐ b. library
7.	☐ a. auditorium		☐ b. lockers

A Classroom pages 6 and 7, CD 1, Track 5

Look at the top picture on pages 6 and 7 in your dictionary. Listen. *True* or *False*? Check (✓) the answers.

	True	False
1.	☐	✓
2.	☐	☐
3.	☐	☐
4.	☐	☐
5.	☐	☐
6.	☐	☐
7.	☐	☐

Studying pages 8 and 9, CD 1, Track 6

Listen. Circle the words to complete the sentences.

1. Karl is <u>discussing a problem</u> / <u>(reading a definition)</u>.

2. Mei-ling is <u>asking a question</u> / <u>answering a question</u>.

3. Ms. Johnson is <u>dictating a sentence</u> / <u>discussing a problem</u>.

4. Antonio is <u>translating a word</u> / <u>checking pronunciation</u>.

5. Erika is <u>copying a word</u> / <u>helping a classmate</u>.

6. The students are <u>filling in the blanks</u> / <u>working in a group</u>.

7. The students are <u>drawing a picture</u> / <u>sharing a book</u>.

Succeeding in School page 10, CD 1, Track 7

Listen. Check (✓) the things the student does.

STUDENT PROGRESS REPORT

- ✓ sets goals
- ☐ participates in class
- ☐ takes notes
- ☐ studies at home
- ☐ asks for help
- ☐ passes tests
- ☐ gets good grades
- ☐ makes progress

A Day at School page 11, CD 1, Track 8

Listen. Circle the words to complete the sentences.

1. The students are ~~entering~~ / leaving the room.
2. The students are walking / running to class.
3. He is going to turn on / off the lights.
4. He is going to buy / deliver the books.
5. The students are eating / drinking.
6. The students are buying a snack / having a conversation.
7. The students need to go back to class / take a break.

Everyday Conversation page 12, CD 1, Track 9

Listen. Check (✓) the correct reply.

1. ✓ **a.** That's OK.　　　　　　☐ **b.** Thank you.
2. ☐ **a.** Yes, it is.　　　　　　☐ **b.** Yes, thanks. Coffee, please.
3. ☐ **a.** Oh, thanks. I'll be there.　☐ **b.** No! It's great!
4. ☐ **a.** Make small talk about the weather.　☐ **b.** Disagree with her.
5. ☐ **a.** Yes, it is.　　　　　　☐ **b.** No, it isn't.
6. ☐ **a.** Sorry, I can't.　　　　☐ **b.** Yes, that's right.
7. ☐ **a.** Great. I'm glad you can come.　☐ **b.** Oh. Sorry you can't come.

Weather page 13, CD 1, Track 10

Look at the pictures from a weather map. Listen. *True* or *False*? Check (✓) the answers.

LOS ANGELES 78°F　VANCOUVER 60°F　CHICAGO 30°F　NEW YORK 40°F　MIAMI 80°F　BOSTON 50°F

	True	False
1.	✓	☐
2.	☐	☐
3.	☐	☐
4.	☐	☐
5.	☐	☐
6.	☐	☐

The Telephone   pages 14 and 15, CD 1, Track 11

Listen. Number the items.

Numbers   page 16, CD 1, Track 12

Listen. Complete the sentences.

1. Ana is _____25_____ years old.

2. She has _____ brothers.

3. Tomas is _____, and Miguel is _____.

4. Her mother is _____ years old, and her father is _____.

5. They live at 600 _____ Avenue.

6. Their apartment is on the _____ floor.

7. It has _____ rooms, and the rent is $ _____ a month.

Measurements page 17, CD 1, Track 13

Listen. *True* or *False*? Check (✓) the answers.

		True	False
1.	She's going to use a calculator.	☐	✓
2.	They're dividing.	☐	☐
3.	She's converting Fahrenheit to Celsius.	☐	☐
4.	He's calculating the answer.	☐	☐
5.	She needs a ruler.	☐	☐
6.	The width is one foot.	☐	☐
7.	Juan had two wrong answers on the test.	☐	☐

Time pages 18 and 19, CD 1, Track 14

Listen. Complete the schedule.

1. **Leave home:** _7:30_
2. **Arrive at school:** _____
3. **English:** _____ to _____
4. **Lunch:** _____ to _____

5. **Computer lab:** _____ to _____
6. **Math:** _____ to _____
7. **Library:** _____ to _____

The Calendar pages 20 and 21, CD 1, Track 15

Listen. Complete the calendar. Use the words in the box. You will use some words more than once.

English	gym	computer lab	movie	math

JANUARY

SUN	MON	TUE	WED	THUR	FRI	SAT
1	2	3 *English*	4	5	6	7
8	9	10	⑪ TODAY	12	13	14

Calendar Events   page 22, CD 1, Track 16

Listen. When did they say . . . ? Write the number of the conversation.

____ **a.** New Year's Day

____ **b.** wedding

____ **c.** vacation

____ **d.** birthday

____ **e.** parent-teacher conference

_1_ **f.** anniversary

____ **g.** Columbus Day

Describing Things   page 23, CD 1, Track 17

Listen. Check (✓) the correct words.

The Little Inn Restaurant

Customer Satisfaction Survey

1. QUALITY OF FOOD	GOOD	BAD
2. PORTION SIZE	BIG	LITTLE
3. SERVICE	FAST	SLOW
4. VIEW	BEAUTIFUL	UGLY
5. CHAIRS	SOFT	HARD
6. NUMBER OF CUSTOMERS	EMPTY	FULL
7. NOISE LEVEL	QUIET	NOISY
8. DIRECTIONS TO RESTAURANT	EASY	HARD
9. PRICE OF MEAL	CHEAP	EXPENSIVE

Colors page 24, CD 1, Track 18

Listen. Check (✓) the colors Ana orders.

✓ white	☐ beige	☐ brown	☐ light blue
☐ black	☐ pink	☐ purple	☐ dark blue
☐ gray	☐ orange	☐ yellow	☐ bright blue
☐ cream	☐ green	☐ red	☐ turquoise

Prepositions page 25, CD 1, Track 19

Look at the picture. Listen. *True* or *False*? Check (✓) the answers.

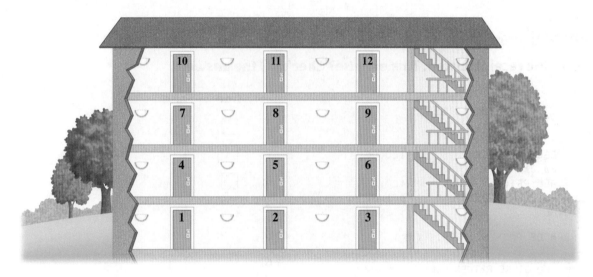

	True	False
1.	✓	☐
2.	☐	☐
3.	☐	☐
4.	☐	☐
5.	☐	☐
6.	☐	☐
7.	☐	☐
8.	☐	☐
9.	☐	☐
10.	☐	☐

Money   page 26, CD 1, Track 20

Listen. Check (✓) the amount.

1. ☐ **a.** $15.00   ✓ **b.** $50.00

2. ☐ **a.** 25¢   ☐ **b.** 50¢

3. ☐ **a.** two quarters and ten nickels   ☐ **b.** two quarters and four dimes

4. ☐ **a.** $6.00   ☐ **b.** $5.00

5. ☐ **a.** $70.00   ☐ **b.** $90.00

6. ☐ **a.** four half dollars   ☐ **b.** two quarters and two half dollars

7. ☐ **a.** 30¢   ☐ **b.** 75¢

Shopping   page 27, CD 1, Track 21

Look at the receipt. Listen. *True* or *False*? Check (✓) the answers.

```
        H & B CLOTHES

 1 SWEATER
   REGULAR PRICE          $30.00
   -33.3%
   SALE PRICE             $20.00
 SALES TAX (8.25%)        $ 1.65
 TOTAL                    $21.65

 FORM OF PAYMENT: DEBIT CARD


::::::::::::: STORE RETURN POLICY :::::::::::::
 YOU CAN RETURN OR EXCHANGE MERCHANDISE
 IN 2 WEEKS. YOU MUST HAVE THE RECEIPT
 AND THE PRICE TAG MUST STILL BE ON THE
 CLOTHES.

     THANK YOU FOR SHOPPING AT H & B
```

	True	False
1.	☐	✓
2.	☐	☐
3.	☐	☐
4.	☐	☐
5.	☐	☐
6.	☐	☐

Same and Different   pages 28 and 29, CD 1, Track 22

Listen. *True* or *False*? Check (✓) the answers.

		True	False
1.	Paula and Rena are twins.	✓	☐
2.	The twins wear matching clothes.	☐	☐
3.	The clothes at Palmers are on sale.	☐	☐
4.	She bought sweaters in different colors.	☐	☐
5.	Nalina is disappointed.	☐	☐
6.	Nalina will exchange the pants.	☐	☐

Adults and Children   pages 30 and 31, CD 1, Track 23

Look in your dictionary. Listen. Circle the words to complete the sentences.

1. A boy / (man) is asking about an infant.

2. A teen / toddler is talking about her chair.

3. Two women / girls are talking about some food.

4. A man / teenager is thinking about his friends.

5. A girl / senior citizen and a man / woman are talking about some food.

6. A ten-year-old girl / boy is angry at a boy / toddler.

Describing People   page 32, CD 1, Track 24

Listen. *True* or *False*? Check (✓) the answers.

	True	False
1. Katya is pregnant.	✓	☐
2. Some of the woman's students are hearing impaired.	☐	☐
3. The woman wants pierced ears.	☐	☐
4. Mr. Santucci is middle-aged.	☐	☐
5. Tanya's mother is attractive.	☐	☐
6. Harry is short.	☐	☐

Describing Hair   page 33, CD 1, Track 25

Listen. Who is talking? Write the number of the conversation.

___ a.

___ b.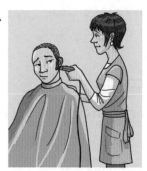

___ c.

___ d.

_1_ e.

___ f.

Families pages 34 and 35, CD 1, Track 26

Look at Ana Garcia's family at the bottom of page 34 of your dictionary. Listen. Who is talking? Write the number.

The speaker is Ana's . . .

____ **a.** mother-in-law

____ **b.** daughter

____ **c.** sister-in-law

____ **d.** father-in-law

_1_ **e.** husband

____ **f.** niece

Childcare and Parenting pages 36 and 37, CD 1, Track 27

Listen. Write the number of each conversation next to the schedule.

Conversation

____ **a.**

____ **b.**

____ **c.**

____ **d.**

____ **e.**

_1_ **f.**

____ **g.**

____ **h.**

SUNNY CHILDCARE CENTER

YOUR CHILD'S DAY: Child _Eloy_

Date _Tuesday, October 13_

TIME	ACTIVITY	COMMENTS
10:00	Eloy arrived with Mr. Salas.	Teething ring is in baby bag.
11:00	Feeding: 2 ounces of formula	Gave him his pacifier.
12:00	Changed diaper Sleeping: 1/2 hour	Rocked him and sang a lullaby.
1:00	Feeding: 6 ounces of formula 1/2 jar of baby food	Walked in the stroller after lunch.
2:00	Changed diaper, then floor play	Asked Mrs. Salas to bring diapers.
3:00	Reading: *The Foot Book*	Eloy pointed to his foot!
4:00	Feeding: 1/2 jar of baby food	He wants to use his spoon now.
5:00	Left with Mrs. Salas.	She forgot the baby bag.

Daily Routines pages 38 and 39, CD 1, Track 28

Look at page 38 in your dictionary. Listen. *True* or *False*? Check (✓) the answers.

	True	False
1. Mom is eating breakfast with Dad and the kids.	☐	✓
2. The kids are taking the bus to school.	☐	☐
3. Dad is at the gym.	☐	☐
4. Mom is at the grocery store.	☐	☐

Now look at page 39 in your dictionary.

	True	False
5. Mom and the kids are cleaning the house.	☐	☐
6. The kids are playing computer games.	☐	☐
7. Dad is watching TV.	☐	☐

Life Events and Documents pages 40 and 41, CD 1, Track 29

Listen. Number the life events for each group in the correct order (1–4).

A   ___   **a.** He immigrated to the United States.

      _1_   **b.** Jerry was born in Taiwan.

      ___   **c.** He graduated from high school.

      ___   **d.** His father died.

B   ___   **a.** He traveled to Japan.

      ___   **b.** He fell in love with Akiko.

      ___   **c.** Jerry graduated from college.

      ___   **d.** Jerry and Akiko went back to the United States.

C   ___   **a.** Jerry and Akiko got married.

      ___   **b.** Yahoo! was a big success.

      ___   **c.** Jerry and Akiko volunteer in San Francisco.

      ___   **d.** Jerry and David started a business.

Jerry Yang

Feelings pages 42 and 43, CD 1, Track 30

Listen. Circle the words to complete the sentences.

1. Steve is afraid /(homesick).

2. Cara and Brendan are sad / worried.

3. Cara and Brendan are relieved / proud.

4. Cara and Brendan are tired / hungry.

5. Cara and Brendan are confused / bored.

6. Brendan is angry / embarrassed.

7. Cara is calm / excited.

8. Cara is sick / tired.

9. Steve is sad / proud.

A Family Reunion pages 44 and 45, CD 1, Track 31

Look in your dictionary. Listen. Circle the words to complete the sentences.

1. They're talking about the banner /(balloons).

2. They're talking about a family reunion / baseball game.

3. They're talking about the banner / food.

4. Leo is laughing / misbehaving.

5. Ben is happy to see all his friends / relatives.

6. The teenagers are misbehaving / laughing.

7. Ben agrees / doesn't agree with his aunt's opinion.

The Home pages 46 and 47, CD 1, Track 32

Listen. Circle the words to complete the sentences.

1. They're in the (kitchen) / attic.

2. They're in the <u>living room / basement</u>.

3. They're worried about the <u>roof / floor</u>.

4. He's going to the <u>garage / basement</u>.

5. He's going to the <u>living room / baby's room</u>.

6. They're going to clean the <u>floor / ceiling</u>.

7. They're in the <u>living room / attic</u>.

Finding a Home pages 48 and 49, CD 1, Track 33

Listen. What are they doing? Write the number of the conversation.

_____ **a.** looking at houses

_____ **b.** meeting with a realtor

_____ **c.** arranging the furniture

_____ **d.** painting

_1_ **e.** taking ownership

_____ **f.** packing

_____ **g.** making an offer

Apartments pages 50 and 51, CD 1, Track 34

Listen. Circle the words to complete the sentences.

1. The man is the (manager) / tenant.

2. They are in the <u>recreation room / hallway</u>.

3. The woman likes the <u>courtyard / roof garden</u>.

4. The manager is showing her the <u>garage / laundry room</u>.

5. They're talking through the <u>intercom / security gate</u>.

6. He wants her to look through the <u>peephole / window</u>.

7. The woman is signing a <u>lease / mortgage</u> for the apartment.

Different Places to Live page 52, CD 1, Track 35

Listen. Write the number of the conversation.

_1_ a.

___ b.

___ c.

___ d.

A House and Yard page 53, CD 1, Track 36

Listen. Check (✓) the answer to complete the replies.

1. We need to fix it ____.

   ✓ **a.** before it rains

   ☐ **b.** or the dog will get out

2. Good. ____

   ☐ **a.** It's getting cold.

   ☐ **b.** It's getting hot.

3. That's why ____.

   ☐ **a.** these tomatoes taste so good

   ☐ **b.** these hamburgers taste so good

4. I think so. ____

   ☐ **a.** There's no water coming out of it.

   ☐ **b.** We're only getting three channels.

5. It's great. ____

   ☐ **a.** We grill on it all the time.

   ☐ **b.** We sit on it all the time.

6. It's dangerous. We might ____.

   ☐ **a.** hit your bike with the car

   ☐ **b.** fall over your bike

A Kitchen page 54, CD 1, Track 37

Listen. Circle the words to complete the sentences.

1. Ali's going to break the eggs into a ⟨mixing bowl⟩ / blender.

2. Ali wants to use the can opener / electric mixer.

3. The blender / garbage disposal is broken.

4. They're going to put the butter in the pan / microwave.

5. Ali's turning on the broiler / burner.

6. He's going to slice the bread on the counter / cutting board.

A Dining Area page 55, CD 1, Track 38

Listen. Write the number of the conversation.

___ a. 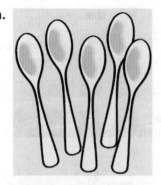   ___ b.    _1_ c.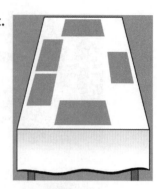

___ d.    ___ e. 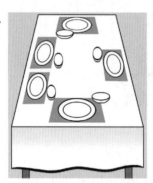   ___ f.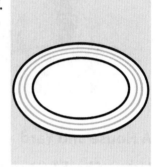

A Living Room page 56, CD 1, Track 39

Look in your dictionary. Listen. Circle the letter to complete the replies.

1. Let's move it. It's too ___ the window.

   a. close to

   (b.) far from

2. It looks nice on ___.

   a. the mantle

   b. the end table

3. Yes. I put them on the ___.

   a. love seat

   b. easy chair

4. He loves playing on the ___.

   a. floor

   b. sofa

5. Please don't. I'm ___.

   a. still watching this show

   b. reading and I need the light

6. No, I'm not. It's ___.

   a. in the magazine holder

   b. on the coffee table

A Bathroom page 57, CD 1, Track 40

Listen. What are they using? Write the number of the conversation.

___ a. toothbrush holder

___ b. bathtub

_1_ c. scale

___ d. mirror

___ e. hamper

___ f. wastebasket

A Bedroom   page 58, CD 1, Track 41

Look in your dictionary. Listen. Circle the words to complete the replies.

1. Yes, I do. It's on my (nightstand) / headboard.

2. Oh, I see it. It's on your dresser / mattress.

3. No, the bed frame is OK. I'm trying to fix this pillowcase / dust ruffle.

4. Sure. It's on the door / lamp.

5. I like this carpet next to / under my bed.

6. Yes, I put one out for you. It's on the bed / in the drawer.

7. It's on the wall next to the window / lamp.

The Kids' Bedroom   page 59, CD 1, Track 42

Listen. *True* or *False*? Check (✓) the answers.

	True	False
1. They put together a toy chest.	☐	✓
2. His grandfather made a dollhouse for his mother.	☐	☐
3. The bunk bed probably has a safety rail.	☐	☐
4. She loves her stuffed animal.	☐	☐
5. The baby is on the changing table.	☐	☐
6. The doll is in the cradle.	☐	☐

Housework   page 60, CD 1, Track 43

Listen. What are they doing? Write the number of the conversation.

____ a.

____ b.

____ c.

____ d.

_1_ e.

____ f.

____ g.

____ h.

____ i.

Cleaning Supplies page 61, CD 1, Track 44

Listen. Write the number of the aisle.

	Item	Aisle		Item	Aisle
1.		_3_	2.		___
3.		___	4.		___
5.		___	6.		___

Household Problems and Repairs pages 62 and 63, CD 1, Track 45

Listen. Write the number of the conversation.

___ **a.** plumber

___ **b.** exterminator

___ **c.** repair person

_1_ **d.** locksmith

___ **e.** roofer

___ **f.** electrician

___ **g.** carpenter

The Tenant Meeting pages 64 and 65, CD 1, Track 46

Listen. Circle the words to complete the sentences.

1. Tina found a new <u>apartment</u> / <u>roommate</u>.

2. They can't go to <u>the rec room</u> / <u>Tom's apartment</u>.

3. Tina is <u>sorry</u> / <u>irritated</u>.

4. The people don't like the <u>mess</u> / <u>noise</u> from the party.

5. Sally invited Mr. Clark to a <u>meeting</u> / <u>party</u>.

6. Alicia is a new <u>DJ</u> / <u>neighbor</u>.

Back from the Market pages 66 and 67, CD 1, Track 47

Look in your dictionary. Listen. Circle the words to complete the sentences.

1. The woman is going to look at the coupon /(shopping list.)

2. The woman is asking about the vegetables / fruit.

3. They're talking about fish / a coupon.

4. They're in the refrigerator / grocery bag.

5. They're talking about the rice / pasta.

6. The man is putting some tomatoes / eggs in the refrigerator.

Fruit page 68, CD 1, Track 48

Listen. Check (✓) the fruits the customers bought.

☐ apricots	☐ tangerines	☐ bananas	☐ cherries
☐ figs	☐ mangoes	☐ papayas	☐ pears
☐ plums	☐ raspberries	☐ strawberries	✓ watermelon

Vegetables page 69, CD 1, Track 49

Listen. Which recipes can they cook? Check (✓) the recipe.

1. ✓ a.
   Eggplant Parmesan
   1 eggplant
   2 ripe tomatoes
   3 cloves of garlic
   1 onion

   ☐ b.
   Eggplant Loaf
   1 eggplant
   1 sweet pepper
   1 small onion

2. ☐ a.
   Stuffed Zucchini
   6 zucchini
   1 potato
   2 cups of peas

   ☐ b.
   Baked Zucchini
   5 zucchini
   2 carrots
   1/2 onion

3. ☐ a.
   Artichoke Soup
   8 artichokes
   1 large potato
   2 cloves of garlic

   ☐ b.
   Artichoke with Broccoli
   10 artichokes
   2 cups of broccoli
   1/2 cup of onion

4. ☐ a.
   Potato Delight
   4 potatoes
   1 cup of carrots
   1/2 cup of string beans
   1/2 onion

   ☐ b.
   Carrot Soup
   2 large carrots
   2 cups of potatoes
   1/4 cup of onion

Meat and Poultry page 70, CD 1, Track 50

Listen. What are they cooking? Check (✓) the kinds of meat.

Country	What's Cooking							
	bacon	beef ribs	chicken	lamb	liver	pork	sausages	tripe
1. Anguilla			✓					
2. Korea								
3. South Africa								
4. Serbia								

Seafood and Deli page 71, CD 1, Track 51

Listen. Check (✓) the food the people order.

1.
BELLA'S DELI SANDWICHES

Meats	Cheese	Bread
☑ Roast beef	☐ American	☐ White
☐ Pastrami	☐ Swiss	☐ Wheat
☐ Salami	☐ Cheddar	☐ Rye
☐ Smoked turkey	☐ Mozzarella	

2.
BELLA'S DELI SANDWICHES

Meats	Cheese	Bread
☐ Roast beef	☐ American	☐ White
☐ Pastrami	☐ Swiss	☐ Wheat
☐ Salami	☐ Cheddar	☐ Rye
☐ Smoked turkey	☐ Mozzarella	

3.
BELLA'S DELI SANDWICHES

Meats	Cheese	Bread
☐ Roast beef	☐ American	☐ White
☐ Pastrami	☐ Swiss	☐ Wheat
☐ Salami	☐ Cheddar	☐ Rye
☐ Smoked turkey	☐ Mozzarella	

4.
BELLA'S DELI SANDWICHES

Meats	Cheese	Bread
☐ Roast beef	☐ American	☐ White
☐ Pastrami	☐ Swiss	☐ Wheat
☐ Salami	☐ Cheddar	☐ Rye
☐ Smoked turkey	☐ Mozzarella	

5.
BELLA'S DELI SANDWICHES

Meats	Cheese	Bread
☐ Roast beef	☐ American	☐ White
☐ Pastrami	☐ Swiss	☐ Wheat
☐ Salami	☐ Cheddar	☐ Rye
☐ Smoked turkey	☐ Mozzarella	

6.
BELLA'S DELI SANDWICHES

Meats	Cheese	Bread
☐ Roast beef	☐ American	☐ White
☐ Pastrami	☐ Swiss	☐ Wheat
☐ Salami	☐ Cheddar	☐ Rye
☐ Smoked turkey	☐ Mozzarella	

A Grocery Store pages 72 and 73, CD 2, Track 2

Listen. Where are they? Write the number of the conversation.

____ **a.** baking products

____ **b.** self-checkout

____ **c.** baked goods

_1_ **d.** bottle return

____ **e.** aisle

____ **f.** dairy

____ **g.** frozen foods

Containers and Packaging page 74, CD 2, Track 3

Listen. Complete the shopping list.

> ### SHOPPING LIST
>
> 1. 4 _____rolls_____ of paper towels
>
> 2. 2 _____ of orange juice
>
> 3. 1 _____ of eggs
>
> 4. 5 _____ of tuna fish
>
> 5. 2 _____ of soda
>
> 6. 2 _____ of chips

Weights and Measurements page 75, CD 2, Track 4

Listen. Circle the words to complete the recipe.

1. (1/2)/ 1/4 cup of margarine

2. 1 cup / pound of sugar

3. 1/2 / 1 cup of bananas

4. 1 1/2 cups / tablespoons of flour

5. 1/2 tablespoon / teaspoon of baking powder

6. 3 tablespoons / teaspoons of milk

7. 1/2 cup / a cup of raisins

Food Preparation and Safety pages 76 and 77, CD 2, Track 5

Listen. Number the steps in the correct order (1–4).

A   ___ **a.** Boil the pasta.

     _1_ **b.** Preheat the oven.

     ___ **c.** Grate the cheese.

     ___ **d.** Grease a baking pan.

B   ___ **a.** Add the cheese.

     ___ **b.** Bake for 30 minutes.

     ___ **c.** Put the pasta in the baking pan.

     ___ **d.** Spoon the sauce on top.

Kitchen Utensils page 78, CD 2, Track 6

Listen. Circle the words to complete the sentences.

1. He needs a (vegetable peeler) / grater.
2. He needs a double boiler / roasting pan.
3. He needs a colander / kitchen timer.
4. He needs a can opener / garlic press.
5. He needs some tongs / pot holders.
6. He needs a carving knife / rolling pin.

Fast Food Restaurant page 79, CD 2, Track 7

Listen. Write the number of the conversation.

____ a.

```
ANDY'S

1 MUFFIN      1.99
1 ICED TEA    0.99
TAX           0.10

TOTAL         3.08
```

____ b.

```
ANDY'S

2 HOT DOGS    3.98
1 CHICKEN
  SANDWICH    3.98
1 SALAD BAR   4.95
TAX           0.45

TOTAL        13.36
```

____ c.

```
ANDY'S

1 SALAD BAR   4.95
1 PIZZA       1.99
1 SODA        1.39
TAX           0.29

TOTAL         8.62
```

_1_ d.

```
ANDY'S

1 CHEESEBURGER
              3.99
1 FRENCH
  FRIES       0.99
1 MILKSHAKE   1.99
TAX           0.24

TOTAL         7.21
```

____ e.

```
ANDY'S

1 ICE CREAM
  CONE        1.99
1 DONUT       0.99
TAX           0.10

TOTAL         3.08
```

____ f.

```
ANDY'S

2 TACOS       5.96
1 SODA        1.39
1 ICED TEA    0.99
TAX           0.29

TOTAL         8.63
```

A Coffee Shop Menu pages 80 and 81, CD 2, Track 8

Look in your dictionary. Listen. *True* or *False*? Check (✓) the answers.

	True	False
1. It's after 11:00 a.m.	☐	✓
2. The woman is using a lot of sweet syrup on her pancakes.	☐	☐
3. The man ordered ranch dressing for his salad.	☐	☐
4. The man is going to have a grilled cheese sandwich.	☐	☐
5. The man will pay extra for coleslaw.	☐	☐
6. The woman is ordering lunch.	☐	☐
7. The server was using the coffee pot with the orange handle.	☐	☐

A Restaurant   pages 82 and 83, CD 2, Track 9

Listen. Who's talking? Check (✓) the columns for each conversation.

	Busser	Chef	Dishwasher	Hostess	Patron	Waiter	Waitress
1.					✓	✓	
2.							
3.							
4.							
5.							
6.							
7.							

The Farmers' Market   pages 84 and 85, CD 2, Track 10

Look in your dictionary. Listen. Circle the words to complete the sentences.

1. The children are eating samples of (fruit) / cookies.

2. The children are going to listen to <u>a vendor / live music</u>.

3. Mrs. Novak needs <u>limes / avocados</u>.

4. Eva is <u>buying / counting</u> avocados.

5. The lemonade is too <u>sweet / sour</u>.

6. They're talking about <u>herbs / vegetables</u>.

Everyday Clothes   pages 86 and 87, CD 2, Track 11

Listen. Write the number of the conversation.

____ a.

____ b.

_1_ c.

____ d.

____ e.

____ f.

Casual, Work, and Formal Clothes   pages 88 and 89, CD 2, Track 12

Listen. Circle the words to complete the sentences.

1. She's going to wear <u>an evening</u> / <u>(a cocktail)</u> dress to the wedding.

2. He's going to wear a <u>tuxedo</u> / <u>sports jacket</u> to the wedding.

3. He'll pack some <u>overalls</u> / <u>shorts</u>.

4. She's going to carry a <u>briefcase</u> / <u>clutch bag</u>.

5. He wore a <u>pullover</u> / <u>business suit</u>.

6. They see a man in a <u>tuxedo</u> / <u>uniform</u>.

Seasonal Clothing   page 90, CD 2, Track 13

Listen. Write the number of the conversation.

_____ a.

_1_ b.

_____ c.

_____ d.

_____ e.

_____ f.

Underwear and Sleepwear   page 91, CD 2, Track 14

Listen. How many did they order? Write the number next to the pictures.

1. _5_ a.    _____ b.    _____ c.

2. _____ a.   _____ b.   _____ c.

3. _____ a.   _____ b.    _____ c.

4. _____ a.    _____ b.   _____ c.

Workplace Clothing pages 92 and 93, CD 2, Track 15

Look in your dictionary. Listen. Write the number of the person talking.

___ **a.** emergency worker

___ **b.** construction worker

___ **c.** chef

___ **d.** salesperson

_1_ **e.** road worker

___ **f.** nurse

___ **g.** automotive painter

Shoes and Accessories pages 94 and 95, CD 2, Track 16

Listen. Circle the words to complete the sentences.

1. The woman is (assisting a customer) / purchasing a wallet.

2. The two women are waiting in line / assisting a customer.

3. The boy is trying on belts / shoes.

4. The man is going to buy some beads / earrings.

5. The man is going to buy a cell phone holder / belt buckle.

6. The woman is talking to a customer / salesclerk.

Describing Clothes pages 96 and 97, CD 2, Track 17

Listen. Write the number of the conversation.

___ a.

___ b.

___ c.

___ d.

___ e.

___ f.

_1_ g.

___ h.

Making Clothes pages 98 and 99, CD 2, Track 18

Listen. Check (✓) the column for each kind of clothing.

Type of Clothing	Type of Material					
	cashmere	corduroy	denim	leather	linen	wool
1. skirt					✓	
2. jacket						
3. overalls						
4. pants						
5. sweater						
6. scarf						

Making Alterations page 100, CD 2, Track 19

Listen. Match. Write the letter.

1. My mother is _c_.

2. He can ___ your clothes for you.

3. Why don't you use ___?

4. I can show you how to ___ the seams.

5. I had to ___ all her skirts.

6. Do you want ___?

7. I have ___ in my desk.

a. a thimble

b. a needle and thread

c. a dressmaker

d. lengthen

e. a hem or a cuff

f. take in

g. let out

Doing the Laundry page 101, CD 2, Track 20

Listen. Write the number of the conversation.

    a. Unload the dryer.

    b. Load the washer.

  1 **c.** Sort the Laundry.

    d. Clean the lint trap.

    e. Fold the Laundry.

    f. Load the dryer.

    g. Add the detergent.

A Garage Sale pages 102 and 103, CD 2, Track 21

Look in your dictionary. Listen. Circle the words to complete the replies.

1. **Mom:** Put it on the tree /(folding card table).

2. **Lisa:** They should look at the flyer / stickers.

3. **Customer:** I see some nice used clothing / accessories.

4. **Lisa:** It's $10.00 / $1.00.

5. **Chris:** Yes, we have a few things. There's a VCR / box of books in front of the garage.

6. **Lisa:** Well, the woman bargained / paid full price for it.

7. **Chris:** I don't see a sticker. I'll ask my Mom. Mom, is the kitchen / folding chair for sale?

The Body pages 104 and 105, CD 2, Track 22

Listen. Write the number of the instructions.

    a.

    b.

  1 **c.**

    d.

    e.

    f.

Inside and Outside the Body   pages 106 and 107, CD 2, Track 23

**Look at the bottom of page 107 of your dictionary. Listen. *Right* or *Wrong*?
Check (✓) the answers.**

	Right	Wrong		Right	Wrong
1.	✓	☐	5.	☐	☐
2.	☐	☐	6.	☐	☐
3.	☐	☐	7.	☐	☐
4.	☐	☐			

Personal Hygiene   pages 108 and 109, CD 2, Track 24

Listen. Write the number of the advertisement.

____ a.   ____ b.   ____ c.

____ d.   _1_ e.   ____ f.

Symptoms and Injuries   page 110, CD 2, Track 25

Listen. Circle the words to complete the sentences.

1. He has a rash /(backache.)

2. She probably has a fever / bruise.

3. He has a stomachache / sunburn.

4. She's coughing / throwing up because of the cigarette.

5. The little girl feels dizzy / nauseous.

6. The man has an insect bite / nasal congestion.

Illnesses and Medical Conditions page 111, CD 2, Track 26

Look in your dictionary. Listen. *True* or *False*? Check (✓) the answers.

		True	False
1.	The baby has an ear infection.	✓	☐
2.	The woman has the flu.	☐	☐
3.	The man has allergies.	☐	☐
4.	The woman has mumps.	☐	☐
5.	The woman has strep throat.	☐	☐
6.	The man has chicken pox.	☐	☐

A Pharmacy pages 112 and 113, CD 2, Track 27

Listen. Write the number of the conversation.

___ a.

___ b.

___ c.

_1_ d.

___ e.

___ f.

Taking Care of Your Health pages 114 and 115, CD 2, Track 28

Listen. Write the number of the conversation.

Ways to Get Well

___ a. Seek medical attention.

___ b. Take medicine.

___ c. Drink fluids.

___ d. Get bed rest.

Ways to Stay Well

___ e. Stay fit.

___ f. Have a regular checkup.

_1_ g. Don't smoke.

___ h. Get immunized.

Medical Emergencies page 116, CD 2, Track 29

Listen. Circle the words to complete the sentences.

1. The man (fell) / drowned.

2. Taylor is having a heart attack / an allergic reaction.

3. Anita broke a bone / is bleeding.

4. Mr. Gonzales got frostbite / swallowed poison.

5. The man burned himself / was hurt.

6. The woman choked / got an electric shock.

First Aid page 117, CD 2, Track 30

Listen. Number the items.

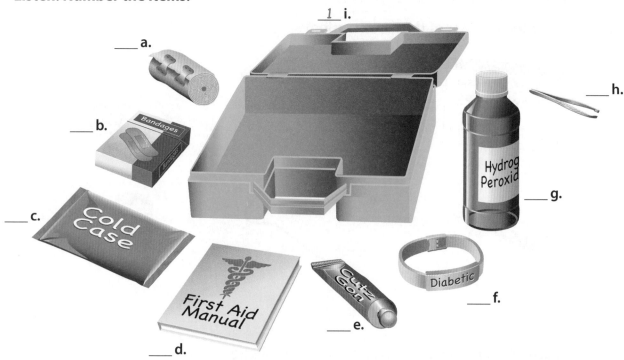

_1_ i.

___ a.

___ b.

___ c.

___ d.

___ e.

___ f.

___ g.

___ h.

Medical Care page 118, CD 2, Track 35, CD 2, Track 31

Listen. Circle the words to complete the sentences.

1. The woman is talking to a doctor / (receptionist).

2. She's talking to a nurse / doctor.

3. She used a stethoscope / thermometer.

4. She used a blood pressure gauge / syringe.

5. Mrs. Wang is talking to the doctor / receptionist.

6. They'll use a thermometer / syringe in the lab.

Dental Care page 119, CD 2, Track 32

Listen. *True* or *False*? Check (✓) the answers.

		True	False
1.	An orthodontist is talking to Ryan.	✓	☐
2.	The dental assistant is talking to Mr. Parker.	☐	☐
3.	The woman is drilling a tooth.	☐	☐
4.	The dentist is going to pull a tooth.	☐	☐
5.	The dentist filled a cavity.	☐	☐
6.	The woman just had her teeth cleaned today.	☐	☐

Hospital pages 120 and 121, CD 2, Track 33

Listen. Circle the words to complete the sentences.

1. The woman is talking to an LPN / ⬭admissions clerk⬭.

2. A volunteer / doctor delivered the flowers.

3. They're using the bed control / call button.

4. The patient is talking to an anesthesiologist / a dietician.

5. The nurse is bringing her medical charts / medication.

6. The patient is talking to a phlebotomist / radiologist.

7. The administrator / orderly will take her downstairs.

A Health Fair pages 122 and 123, CD 2, Track 34

Listen. Circle the words to complete the sentences.

1. The woman is giving a lecture about ⬭nutrition labels⬭ / vitamins.

2. The man is doing yoga / aerobic exercise.

3. The man is having a low-cost exam / an acupuncture treatment.

4. The man is going to have an acupuncture treatment / eye exam.

5. The woman has a booth / clinic at a Saturday health fair.

6. The man is giving a lecture / demonstration.

Downtown pages 124 and 125, CD 2, Track 35

Listen. Where are they? Write the number of the conversation.

___ **a.** gas station

___ **b.** police station

___ **c.** hotel

_1_ **d.** Department of Motor Vehicles

___ **e.** bank

___ **f.** restaurant

___ **g.** library

City Streets pages 126 and 127, CD 2, Track 36

Listen. Where are the people? Number the six places on the map.

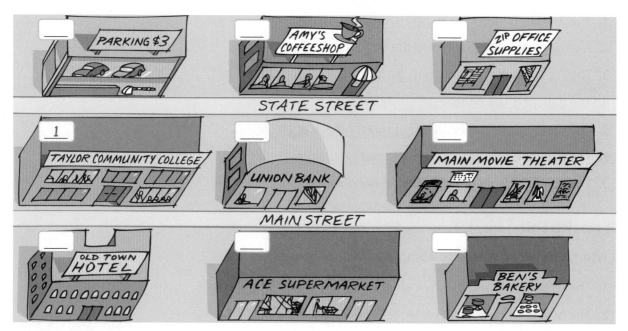

An Intersection pages 128 and 129, CD 2, Track 37

Listen. Circle the words to complete the sentences.

1. He's going to <u>cross the street</u> / (<u>park the car</u>.)

2. He wants to <u>wait for the light</u> / <u>jaywalk</u>.

3. He's <u>riding a bike</u> / <u>walking a dog</u>.

4. He <u>rides his bike</u> / <u>parks his car</u> every day.

5. She's going to meet him in the <u>convenience store</u> / <u>laundromat</u>.

6. She doesn't want to <u>wait for the bus</u> / <u>jaywalk</u>.

7. She wants to use the <u>drive-thru window</u> / <u>crosswalk</u>.

A Mall pages 130 and 131, CD 2, Track 38

Listen. Where are they? Write the number of the conversation.

____ **a.** pet store

_1_ **b.** directory

____ **c.** electronics store

____ **d.** escalator

____ **e.** food court

____ **f.** hair salon

____ **g.** elevator

The Bank page 132, CD 2, Track 39

Listen. Circle the words to complete the sentences.

1. They're going to the ATM /(vault).

2. She's making a deposit / cashing a check.

3. He's talking to the security guard / account manager.

4. She's going to withdraw cash / bank online.

5. She forgot her savings account number / personal identification number.

6. She's banking online / going to the bank.

The Library page 133, CD 2, Track 40

Listen. Write the number of the conversation.

____ **a.**

____ **b.**

_1_ **c.**

____ **d.**

____ **e.**

____ **f.**

The Post Office pages 134 and 135, CD 2, Track 41

Listen. Number the pictures.

____ a.

__1__ b.

____ c.

____ d.

____ e.

____ f.

Department of Motor Vehicles (DMV) pages 136 and 137, CD 2, Track 42

Listen. Circle the words to complete the sentences.

1. He gave her a (DMV handbook) / learner's permit.

2. He's taking a written test / vision exam.

3. Anita is taking a driver's training course / driving test.

4. He just got his license plate / driver's license.

5. He's showing his identification / learner's permit.

6. He didn't pass his vision test / driving test.

Government and Military Service pages 138 and 139, CD 3, Track 2

Listen. *True* or *False*? Check (✓) the answers.

	True	False
1. This year, Marie Valbrun is running for city council.	☐	✓
2. After high school, she served in the military.	☐	☐
3. After she left the Coast Guard, she moved to the state capital.	☐	☐
4. She worked for a senator in the U.S. Congress.	☐	☐
5. She ran for office in River City.	☐	☐
6. She was elected by more than 10,000 votes.	☐	☐
7. She served on the city council for ten years.	☐	☐
8. Now she's running for governor.	☐	☐
9. The election is next month.	☐	☐

Civic Rights and Responsibilities page 140, CD 3, Track 3

Listen. What rights and responsibilities are they talking about? Check (✓) the columns.

	Vote	Fair trial	Pay taxes	Be informed	Free speech	Peaceful assembly	Serve on a jury	Freedom of the press
1.	✓			✓				
2.								
3.								
4.								

The Legal System page 141, CD 3, Track 4

Listen. *True* or *False*? Check (✓) the answers.

		True	False
1.	Beth is still in prison.	☐	✓
2.	She was arrested in November 2001.	☐	☐
3.	Her lawyer was worried.	☐	☐
4.	The judge didn't set any bail.	☐	☐
5.	The witnesses at the trial had sad stories.	☐	☐
6.	Beth was convicted.	☐	☐
7.	The judge sentenced Beth to seven years.	☐	☐
8.	Beth learned to cook in prison.	☐	☐
9.	She found a job before she was released.	☐	☐
10.	She wrote a book before she was released.	☐	☐

Crime page 142, CD 3, Track 5

Listen. Write the number of the news story.

____ **a.** identity theft

_1_ **b.** assault

____ **c.** burglary

____ **d.** arson

____ **e.** mugging

____ **f.** shoplifting

Public Safety page 143, CD 3, Track 6

Listen. Number the pictures.

____ a.

____ b.

____ c.

_1_ d.

____ e.

____ f.

Emergencies and Natural Disasters pages 144 and 145, CD 3, Track 7

Listen. What are they talking about? Write the number of the conversation or report.

____ **a.** tsunami

____ **b.** blizzard

____ **c.** car accident

_1_ **d.** flood

____ **e.** earthquake

____ **f.** forest fire

____ **g.** drought

____ **h.** fire

Emergency Procedures pages 146 and 147, CD 3, Track 8

Listen. What are they talking about? Circle the words to complete the sentences.

1. They're learning about batteries / (the gas shut-off valve).

2. They're checking their first aid / disaster kit.

3. They're planning their escape / evacuation route.

4. They're evacuating / taking cover.

5. They agreed on their meeting place / important papers.

6. The woman's mother is their out-of-state contact / hurricane warning.

7. He told his son to watch the weather / stay away from the window.

Community Cleanup pages 148 and 149, CD 3, Track 9

Look in your dictionary. Listen. Circle the words to complete the sentences.

1. Marta is talking about paint /(graffiti).

2. Marta wants to <u>change things / move her store</u>.

3. The woman is going to sign a <u>petition / letter</u> to the city council.

4. Marta <u>applauded / gave a speech</u> at the city council meeting.

5. Mike <u>donated / sold</u> some paint for cleaning up the block.

6. Steve is a <u>volunteer / store owner</u>.

Basic Transportation pages 150 and 151, CD 3, Track 10

Listen. *True* or *False*? Check (✓) the answers.

	True	False
1. Todd drove his car to the subway station.		✓
2. He took the subway to a bus stop.		
3. He tried to take the bus to the airport.		
4. The bus went fast because there wasn't much traffic.		
5. He took a taxi to his friend's house.		
6. He drove a motorcycle in Denver.		

Public Transportation page 152, CD 3, Track 11

Listen. Check (✓) the answers.

1. The women are standing ___.
   a. ✓ on a subway platform
   b. ☐ at a taxi stand

2. The man bought a ___.
   a. ☐ one-way ticket
   b. ☐ round-trip ticket

3. A ___ is speaking to a passenger.
   a. ☐ conductor
   b. ☐ taxi driver

4. The driver is giving the woman a ___.
   a. ☐ transfer
   b. ☐ token

5. The man learned how to use a ___.
   a. ☐ fare card
   b. ☐ schedule

6. The woman is looking for a ___.
   a. ☐ vending machine
   b. ☐ shuttle

Prepositions of Motion page 153, CD 3, Track 12

Listen. Circle the words to complete the sentences.

1. John got <u>off</u> / <u>(on)</u> the bus.

2. Sue is going to get <u>into</u> / <u>out of</u> the taxi.

3. Marcos needs to go <u>across the street</u> / <u>around the corner</u> to get milk.

4. Judi is going <u>under</u> / <u>over</u> the bridge.

5. Donna wants to walk <u>up</u> / <u>down</u> the steps.

6. Ed and Lee are trying to get <u>on</u> / <u>off</u> the highway.

Traffic Signs page 154, CD 3, Track 13

Listen. Check (✓) the traffic signs they see.

1. ☐ a. YIELD   ✓ b. STOP   2. ☐ a. SPEED LIMIT 45   ☐ b. 5

3. ☐ a.   ☐ b. ONE WAY   4. ☐ a. (No Parking)   ☐ b. PARKING

5. ☐ a.   ☐ b. DO NOT ENTER   6. ☐ a.   ☐ b.

Directions and Maps page 155, CD 3, Track 14

Look at the map. Find the arrow at Clinton Street. Listen. Where did they go? Trace their route. Number the places.

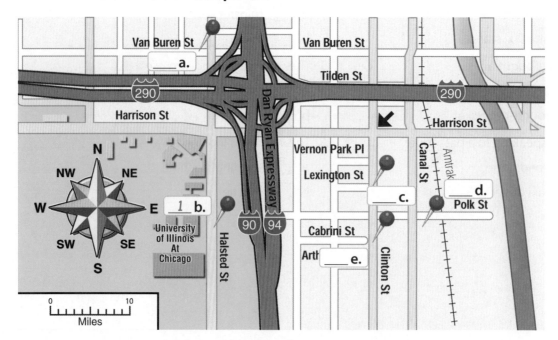

Cars and Trucks page 156, CD 3, Track 15

Listen. Match. Write the letter.

1. Sheryl's car is a _d_.
2. The man needs a ___.
3. The family is in their ___.
4. Sue's friends often borrow her ___.
5. Marcos doesn't want a ___.
6. The woman drives a ___.

a. school bus
b. pickup truck
c. tow truck
d. hybrid
e. RV
f. minivan

Buying and Maintaining a Car page 157, CD 3, Track 16

Listen. Write the number of the conversation.

___ a. Look at car ads. Check the ads in your local newspaper and on the Internet.

_1_ b. Ask the seller about the car. How many miles does it have?

___ c. Take the car to a mechanic. Are there any big problems?

___ d. Negotiate a price. It's OK to bargain.

___ e. Get the title from the seller. This certificate shows that you are the new owner.

___ f. Register the car. Go to the DMV. Bring the title with you.

Parts of a Car pages 158 and 159, CD 3, Track 17

Listen. Check (✓) the items the mechanic finished.

MR. FIX-IT MECHANICS	Date: NOVEMBER 3 Work Number: #4567-01 Owner: LISA FUENTES Car: 4-DOOR SEDAN Mechanic: JOSH GLOVER	**2. PARTS—NEW**	
		REPLACED THE HUBCAPS	☐
		REPLACED THE FENDER	☐
		REPLACED THE TAIL LIGHTS	☐
1. SERVICES		REPLACED THE MUFFLER	☐
CHECKED THE RADIATOR	☐	REPLACED THE REARVIEW MIRROR	☐
CHECKED THE TURN SIGNALS	✓	**3. PARTS—REPAIRED**	
CHECKED THE HEADLIGHTS	☐	FIXED THE HEATER	☐
CHECKED THE BATTERY	☐	FIXED THE BRAKE LIGHT	☐
CHECKED THE HAZARD LIGHTS	☐	FIXED THE CD PLAYER	☐
CHECKED THE TEMPERATURE GAUGE	☐	FIXED THE HORN	☐
CHECKED THE HEATER	☐	FIXED THE DOOR LOCK	☐

An Airport   pages 160 and 161, CD 3, Track 18

Listen. *True* or *False*? Check (✓) the answers.

	True	False
1. The woman already has her boarding pass.	☐	✓
2. Flight 205 is delayed.	☐	☐
3. The flight attendant will put the bag in an overhead compartment.	☐	☐
4. The bag is still on the plane.	☐	☐
5. The flight is taking off.	☐	☐
6. The man is a passenger.	☐	☐

Taking a Trip   pages 162 and 163, CD 3, Track 19

Listen. Circle the words to complete the sentences.

1. Chicago was their (starting point)/ destination.

2. On the second day of their trip, they ran out of gas / got lost.

3. They asked a police officer / gas station attendant for directions.

4. Pam got a speeding ticket / ran out of gas on the third day.

5. They paid for the repairs with cash / their auto club card.

6. For their next trip, they plan to drive / take the train to California.

The Workplace   pages 164 and 165, CD 3, Track 20

Look in your dictionary. Listen. *True* or *False*? Check (✓) the answers.

	True	False
1. The woman is the supervisor.	☐	✓
2. Kate is asking about a deduction.	☐	☐
3. Bill is the supervisor.	☐	☐
4. The woman is the owner.	☐	☐
5. Marcos is an employee.	☐	☐
6. He's putting the computer in Irina's office.	☐	☐

Jobs and Occupations A–C   page 166, CD 3, Track 21

Listen. Circle the words to complete the sentences.

1. Sue is a <u>cashier</u> / <u>(business owner)</u>.

2. Pat is an <u>administrative assistant</u> / <u>auto mechanic</u>.

3. The man is an <u>appliance repair person</u> / <u>assembler</u>.

4. Vera is a <u>baker</u> / <u>butcher</u>.

5. They're <u>artists</u> / <u>carpenters</u>.

6. Lynn is <u>an artist</u> / <u>a childcare worker</u>.

7. The man is an <u>accountant</u> / <u>architect</u>.

Jobs and Occupations C–H   page 167, CD 3, Track 22

Listen. What's the occupation? Write the number of the job description.

a. ____ electronics repair person

b. ____ gardener

c. ____ firefighter

d. _1_ computer technician

e. ____ commercial fisher

f. ____ graphic designer

Jobs and Occupations H–P   page 168, CD 3, Track 23

Listen. Number the pictures.

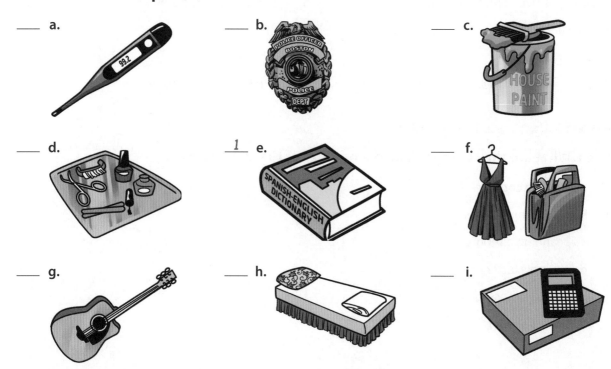

____ a.

____ b.

____ c.

____ d.

_1_ e.

____ f.

____ g.

____ h.

____ i.

Jobs and Occupations P–W page 169, CD 3, Track 24

Listen. Circle the words to complete the sentences.

1. The man is a (postal worker)/ stock clerk.
2. The woman is a <u>welder / security guard</u>.
3. The man is a <u>social worker / veterinarian</u>.
4. The woman is a <u>writer / reporter</u>.

5. The woman is a <u>server / social worker</u>.
6. The woman is a <u>truck driver / receptionist</u>.
7. The man is a <u>stock clerk / retail clerk</u>.

Job Skills page 170, CD 3, Track 25

Listen to the interviews. What can they do? Check (✓) two skills for each person.

1. The man can ____.
   - a. ☐ sell cars
   - b. ✓ operate heavy machinery
   - c. ✓ supervise people
   - d. ☐ sew clothes

2. The woman can ____.
   - a. ☐ wait on customers
   - b. ☐ program computers
   - c. ☐ speak another language
   - d. ☐ teach English

3. The man can ____.
   - a. ☐ assist medical patients
   - b. ☐ assemble components
   - c. ☐ program computers
   - d. ☐ fly a plane

4. The man can ____.
   - a. ☐ make furniture
   - b. ☐ solve math problems
   - c. ☐ cook
   - d. ☐ use a cash register

5. Ted can ____.
   - a. ☐ type
   - b. ☐ drive a truck
   - c. ☐ sell cars
   - d. ☐ take care of children

Office Skills page 171, CD 3, Track 26

Listen. What are they doing? Write the number of the conversation.

____ **a.** making copies

_1_ **b.** transcribing notes

____ **c.** scanning a report

____ **d.** typing a letter

____ **e.** taking a message

____ **f.** faxing a report

Career Planning page 172, CD 3, Track 27

Listen. Number the steps in the man's career.

___ **a.** found a new job as an assistant designer

___ **b.** went to a job fair and talked to recruiters

_1_ **c.** worked as a retail sales clerk

___ **d.** got a promotion

___ **e.** talked to a career counselor

___ **f.** got vocational training

Job Search page 173, CD 3, Track 28

Listen. Write the number of the conversation.

___ **a.**

___ **b.**

___ **c.**
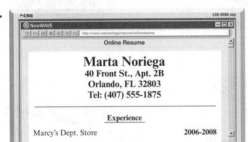

___ **d.**

___ **e.**

_1_ **f.**

Interview Skills page 174, CD 3, Track 29

Listen. Write the number of the conversation.

Tips for a Successful Interview

___ **a.** Prepare for the interview: Learn about the company. Visit their website.

___ **b.** Greet your interviewer: Say your name clearly. Shake hands.

___ **c.** Listen carefully: What's important to your interviewer?

___ **d.** Ask questions: How many people work here?

_1_ **e.** Talk about your experience: What have you done? What do you enjoy?

___ **f.** Thank the interviewer: Say, "Thank you."

A Factory page 175, CD 3, Track 30

Look in your dictionary. Listen. Circle the words to complete the sentences.

1. Mr. Chung is the line supervisor / ~~owner~~.
2. Fred is the shipping clerk / designer.
3. The boxes are on the pallet / hand truck.
4. The woman is training another order puller / factory worker to assemble lamps.
5. The man is training another packer / line supervisor.
6. Marcy assembles / designs lamps.

Landscaping and Gardening page 176, CD 3, Track 31

Listen. What equipment are they using? Write the number of the conversation.

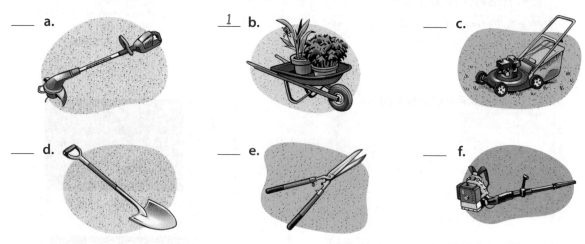

____ a.　　　_1_ b.　　　____ c.

____ d.　　　____ e.　　　____ f.

Farming and Ranching page 177, CD 3, Track 32

Listen. Circle the words to complete the sentences.

1. They're in the ~~barn~~ / corral.
2. The machine is feeding / milking the cows.
3. They're looking at the vegetable garden / wheat field.
4. They're looking at the vineyard / fields.
5. They hire a few farm workers / growers.
6. They're talking about a tractor / rancher.
7. They're in the vineyard / orchard.

Construction page 178, CD 3, Track 33

Listen. Check (✓) the answers.

1. Carlos will use a(n) ___.
   a. ✓ backhoe   b. ☐ I beam

2. The workers will use a ___.
   a. ☐ cherry picker   b. ☐ jackhammer

3. Marcia used a ___.
   a. ☐ trowel   b. ☐ shovel

4. To get the girders up, they use a ___.
   a. ☐ crane   b. ☐ pickaxe

5. He's going to use a ___.
   a. ☐ ladder   b. ☐ girder

6. They're putting up some ___.
   a. ☐ shingles   b. ☐ scaffolding

Job Safety page 179, CD 3, Track 34

Listen. Number the safety equipment.

Tools and Building Supplies pages 180 and 181, CD 3, Track 35

Listen. What do they need? Circle the words to complete the sentences.

1. He needs a (level) / plane.

2. She needs a paint pan / drop cloth.

3. He needs a pipe wrench / wire stripper.

4. They need a tape measure / some duct tape.

5. He needs a hammer and some screws / nails.

6. They need some electrical tape / an extension cord.

An Office   pages 182 and 183, CD 3, Track 36

Listen. Match. Write the letter.

1. Ted is the _f_.   a. file cabinet

2. The woman is the ___.   b. janitor

3. Mark is a ___.   c. presentation

4. Mr. Verdi is asking about a ___.   d. receptionist

5. The woman wants Paul to go to the ___.   e. clerk

6. The woman is talking to the ___.   f. office manager

A Hotel   page 184, CD 3, Track 37

Listen. Circle the words to complete the sentences.

1. He's calling (maintenance) / the bell captain.

2. The woman is the housekeeper / concierge.

3. They're going to call the front desk / room service.

4. The guest is talking to the desk clerk / doorman.

5. They're in the meeting room / gift shop.

6. The couple is in a suite / ballroom.

7. She's going to send a housekeeper / bellhop.

Food Service   page 185, CD 3, Track 38

Look in your dictionary. Listen. Circle the words to complete the sentences.

1. The man is the (executive chef) / food preparer.

2. Lee is the sous chef / short-order cook.

3. Brenda wants Tomas to go to the storeroom / walk-in freezer.

4. They're at the buffet / in the banquet room.

5. The man is the headwaiter / maitre d'.

6. The woman is a caterer / runner.

7. The man is the server / headwaiter.

A Bad Day at Work pages 186 and 187, CD 3, Track 39

Listen. *True* or *False*? Check (✓) the answers.

		True	False
1.	Benny is going to the clinic.	✓	☐
2.	Sam wants to change the floor plan.	☐	☐
3.	Jack is a contractor.	☐	☐
4.	Something dangerous happened.	☐	☐
5.	They're talking about the budget.	☐	☐
6.	There's a problem with the schedule.	☐	☐

Schools and Subjects pages 188 and 189, CD 4, Track 2

Listen. Where do they work or go to school? Check (✓) the school.

	Preschool	Elementary school	Middle school	Vocational school	Community college	University
1.		✓				
2.						
3.						
4.						
5.						
6.						

English Composition pages 190 and 191, CD 4, Track 3

Listen. Check (✓) the things that Paula did.

✓ **a.** She wrote a first draft.

☐ **b.** She wrote an introduction.

☐ **c.** She wrote a conclusion.

☐ **d.** She wrote a title.

☐ **e.** She organized her ideas.

☐ **f.** She used footnotes.

☐ **g.** She proofread her essay.

☐ **h.** She used quotations.

☐ **i.** She revised her paper.

☐ **j.** She wrote a final draft.

Mathematics   pages 192 and 193, CD 4, Track 4

Listen. Check (✓) the answers.

1. Katia is counting ___ numbers.

   a. ☐ odd   b. ✓ even

2. Dan needs to figure out the ___.

   a. ☐ sum   b. ☐ product

3. Five is the ___.

   a. ☐ quotient   b. ☐ sum

4. Susan is going to draw a ___.

   a. ☐ variable   b. ☐ graph

5. Marcos is going to draw a(n) ___ angle.

   a. ☐ acute   b. ☐ right

6. Lisa forgot how to add ___.

   a. ☐ fractions   b. ☐ integers

7. The ___ of her garden is forty feet.

   a. ☐ perimeter   b. ☐ circumference

Science   pages 194 and 195, CD 4, Track 5

Listen. What do they need? Number the items.

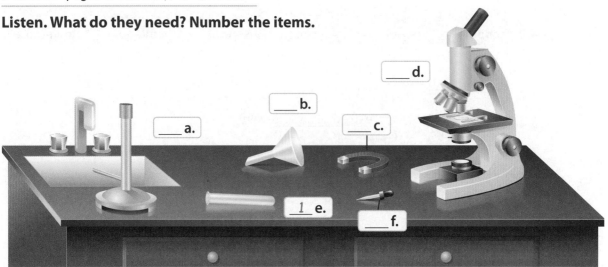

___ d.

___ b.

___ a.

___ c.

_1_ e.

___ f.

Computers   page 196, CD 4, Track 6

Listen. *True* or *False*? Check (✓) the answers.

	True	False
1. The printer isn't working.	✓	☐
2. The man has a webcam.	☐	☐
3. The woman is going to put the DVD in the DVD drive.	☐	☐
4. The boy's mouse connects to the computer with a cable.	☐	☐
5. The girl's computer has a tower.	☐	☐
6. The man used software to fix the photograph.	☐	☐

The Internet page 197, CD 4, Track 7

Listen. What did Mindy do? Number the steps (1–6).

___ **a.** She closed a pop-up ad.

___ **b.** She followed a link.

___ **c.** She looked at the drop-down menu.

___ **d.** She used the back button.

_1_ **e.** Mindy typed the website address.

___ **f.** She used the website's search box.

U.S. History page 198, CD 4, Track 8

Look in your dictionary. Listen. Circle the words to complete the replies.

1. **Woman:** Yes, our family was part of Reconstruction / the Western Expansion.

2. **Girl:** I guess that's why it's called the Information Age / Jazz Age.

3. **Woman:** Because the Civil Rights Movement / Reconstruction really changed things.

4. **Boy:** The Great Depression / Cold War sounds terrible.

5. **Boy:** Those were both important events during the Space Age / Civil War.

6. **Girl:** Were there jobs like that before the Industrial Revolution / Global Age?

World History page 199, CD 4, Track 9

Listen. Check (✓) the columns.

	Dictator	President	Prime minister	Composer	Explorer	Inventor
1. Erik the Red					✓	
2. Fine						
3. Sulla						
4. Mori						
5. Bachelet						
6. Cochrane						

North America and Central America   pages 200 and 201, CD 4, Track 10

Listen. Match. Write the letter.

1. Meg wants to explore __d__ .

2. Denise is working in ___ .

3. Brian and Ted are from ___ .

4. Nancy's mother lives in ___ .

5. Tim just got back from ___ .

6. Leo studied in ___ .

a. Ontario

b. Nebraska

c. the Midwest

d. Northern Canada

e. the Chiapas Highlands

f. Nicaragua

World Map   pages 202 and 203, CD 4, Track 11

Look in your dictionary. Listen. Where are they from? Write the number.

___ **a.** Australia

___ **b.** France

___ **c.** India

_1_ **d.** Madagascar

___ **e.** Norway

___ **f.** Portugal

___ **g.** Russia

Geography and Habitats   page 204, CD 4, Track 12

Listen. Circle the words to complete the sentences.

1. Don and Jim's boat is on an ocean / a lake.

2. Kate and Will are hiking in a rain forest / meadow.

3. Caiman live on sand dunes / in rivers.

4. The hotel was near the beach / an island.

5. Josh and Paul are hiking to the top / bottom of the mountain.

The Universe page 205, CD 4, Track 13

Listen. Check (✓) the planets.

	Earth	Mars	Mercury	Jupiter	Neptune	Saturn	Uranus	Venus
1. ice and water	✓							
2. only ice								
3. the most moons								
4. the hottest								
5. the coldest								
6. the windiest								

A Graduation pages 206 and 207, CD 4, Track 14

Listen. *True* or *False*? Check (✓) the answers.

	True	False
1. Keisha graduated two years ago.	☐	✓
2. Keisha's Dad took photos.	☐	☐
3. Keisha's Mom cried at the ceremony.	☐	☐
4. The mayor gave a funny speech.	☐	☐
5. Keisha's family celebrated with her after the ceremony.	☐	☐
6. Keisha took off her cap and gown at the restaurant.	☐	☐

Nature Center pages 208 and 209, CD 4, Track 15

Listen. Check (✓) the answers.

1. The guide is pointing to _____.

   a. ✓ a tree **b.** ☐ a mammal

2. The people are looking at _____.

   a. ☐ a nest **b.** ☐ birds

3. The guide thinks the _____ will make a nice picture.

   a. ☐ path **b.** ☐ flowers

4. The fish sometimes eat _____ on the top of the water.

   a. ☐ other fish **b.** ☐ insects

5. The man wants to take a _____.

   a. ☐ flower **b.** ☐ plant

6. The insects are under _____.

   a. ☐ a rock **b.** ☐ the soil

Trees and Plants page 210, CD 4, Track 16

Listen. Circle the words to complete the sentences.

1. Carla is going to use a <u>leaf /pinecone</u> for her art project.

2. Jerry wants to live near a lot of <u>palm / redwood</u> trees.

3. Ted touched <u>poison sumac / poison ivy</u> in his backyard.

4. They're going to climb an <u>oak / elm</u> tree.

5. The dad is going to show his daughter some <u>poison oak / pine trees</u>.

6. Jane doesn't believe it's a <u>dogwood / cactus</u>.

Flowers page 211, CD 4, Track 17

Listen. Check (✓) the items Luisa completed.

SUN GREENHOUSE

Volunteer's Name: _Luisa_

Date: _May 15_

NEW GARDENER'S CHECKLIST

- ☑ planted marigold seeds
- ☐ planted tulip bulbs
- ☐ watered violets
- ☐ watered lilies
- ☐ cut roses
- ☐ removed thorns
- ☐ arranged flowers
- ☐ moved houseplants

Marine Life, Amphibians, and Reptiles pages 212 and 213, CD 4, Track 18

Listen. Check (✓) the columns.

	Gills	Fins	Scales
1. cobra			✓
2. lizard			
3. whale			
4. alligator			
5. jellyfish			
6. seahorse			

Birds, Insects, and Arachnids page 214, CD 4, Track 19

Listen. Match. Write the letters.

1. Hummingbirds move their _e_.
2. Eagles use their ____.
3. Male peacocks open the ____.
4. Butterflies have ____.
5. Geese have ____.
6. Woodpeckers use their ____.

a. bills to get food out of tree bark
b. beaks to tear meat
c. colorful wings that protect them
d. feathers that are sometimes used in pillows
e. wings up to eighty times per second
f. feathers on their tails so females will notice them

Domestic Animals and Rodents page 215, CD 4, Track 20

Listen. Circle the words to complete the sentences.

1. Doug has a (dog) / cat.
2. A rooster / cat woke Mindy up last night.
3. Nel has a puppy / parrot.
4. The children saw a gopher / chipmunk.
5. Guinea pigs / pigs are pets in the girl's country and wild in the boy's country.

Mammals pages 216 and 217, CD 4, Track 21

Look at page 217 in your dictionary. Listen. Write the number of the conversation.

____ a. koala

____ b. camel

____ c. anteater

____ d. kangaroo

_1_ e. leopard

____ f. elephant

Energy and Conservation pages 218 and 219, CD 4, Track 22

Listen. Write the number.

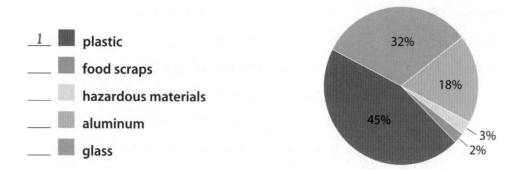

_1_ ☐ plastic

___ ☐ food scraps

___ ☐ hazardous materials

___ ☐ aluminum

___ ☐ glass

32%

18%

45%

3%

2%

U.S. National Parks pages 220 and 221, CD 4, Track 23

Listen. _True_ or _False_? Check (✓) the answers.

	True	False
1. Deb didn't see any wildlife in Bryce Canyon.	☐	✓
2. Mark and Dean took a tour at Acadia National Park.	☐	☐
3. Pauline liked going into the caves.	☐	☐
4. There's a lot of coral in Capitol Reef National Park.	☐	☐
5. The man can't take a ferry to Round Island.	☐	☐

Places to Go pages 222 and 223, CD 4, Track 24

Look in your dictionary. Listen. Circle the words to complete the sentences.

1. They're at (an art museum) / a rock concert.

2. They're at the opera / a play.

3. They're at the county fair / zoo.

4. They're at an amusement park / a flea market.

5. They're at an aquarium / a bowling alley.

6. They're at a classical concert / botanical garden.

The Park and Playground page 224, CD 4, Track 25

Listen. What are the people doing? Write the number of the conversation.

____ **a.** looking for a drinking fountain

_1_ **b.** pushing the swing

____ **c.** playing with a jump rope

____ **d.** having a picnic

____ **e.** climbing the bars on the climbing apparatus

____ **f.** playing baseball in the ball field

The Beach page 225, CD 4, Track 26

Listen. *True* or *False*? Check (✓) the answers.

	True	False
1. The woman is going to go in the water.	✓	☐
2. They're talking about the cooler.	☐	☐
3. The little boy found a seashell.	☐	☐
4. The woman is carrying a lifesaving device.	☐	☐
5. The lifeguard wants everyone to get out of the water.	☐	☐
6. The man is in a sailboat.	☐	☐

Outdoor Recreation page 226, CD 4, Track 27

Listen. What did they bring? Check (✓) the items.

✓ **a.**

☐ **b.**

☐ **c.**

☐ **d.**

☐ **e.**

☐ **f.**

☐ **g.**

☐ **h.**

☐ **i.**

☐ **j.**

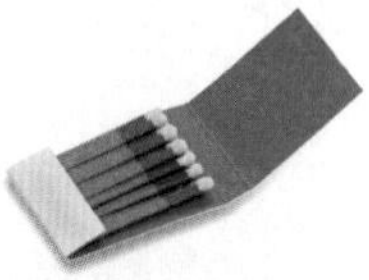

Winter and Water Sports page 227, CD 4, Track 28

Listen. Circle the words to complete the sentences.

1. The people are downhill skiing / (waterskiing).

2. Tara is sailing / windsurfing.

3. The woman is learning snorkeling / scuba diving.

4. The man is surfing / snowboarding for the first time.

5. The people are sledding / cross-country skiing.

6. The people are cross-country skiing / ice skating.

Individual Sports page 228, CD 4, Track 29

Listen. Is Tom right? Check (✓) *Right* or *Wrong* for each answer.

	Right	Wrong
1.	✓	☐
2.	☐	☐
3.	☐	☐
4.	☐	☐
5.	☐	☐
6.	☐	☐

Team Sports page 229, CD 4, Track 30

Listen. Match. Write the letter.

1. The woman is a _b_ .
2. The man is a ___.
3. The kids are playing ___.
4. The man plays ___.
5. Marsha is going to play ___.
6. The woman plays ___.

a. soccer
b. fan
c. water polo
d. softball
e. ice hockey
f. coach

Sports Verbs page 230, CD 4, Track 31

Listen. What did they do? Circle the words to complete the sentences.

1. Emerson (pitched) / dropped the ball, and Taylor hit / caught it.
2. Selig served / passed the ball to Chavez, and Chavez shot / swung.
3. Thompson is racing / skating, and she might start / finish today.
4. She wants to dribble / dive, but her friend only wants to swim / swing.
5. Martino passed / served, and Kournikov returned the ball.
6. The woman stretches / pitches after she hits / works out.

Sports Equipment page 231, CD 4, Track 32

Listen. Match the price with the sports equipment.

_c_ 1. $299

____ 2. $120

____ 3. $22

____ 4. $9

____ 5. $12

____ 6. $15

a.

b.

c.

d.

e.

f.

Hobbies and Games pages 232 and 233, CD 4, Track 33

Listen. What's the hobby or game? Write the number of the conversation.

____ a.

_1_ b.

____ c.

____ d.

____ e.

____ f.

Electronics and Photography pages 234 and 235, CD 4, Track 34

Listen. What are they talking about? Write the number of the conversation.

____ a.

____ b.

_1_ c.

____ d.

____ e.

____ f.

Entertainment pages 236 and 237, CD 4, Track 35

Look in your dictionary. Listen. What type of TV program or movie is it? Write the number.

a. ____ drama

b. _1_ mystery

c. ____ soap opera

d. ____ nature program

e. ____ game show

f. ____ action story

g. ____ science fiction story

Music page 238, CD 4, Track 36

Listen. Circle the name of the instrument.

1. (tuba) / tambourine

2. violin / flute

3. accordion / guitar

4. piano / trombone

5. saxophone / drums

6. harmonica / accordion

Holidays page 239, CD 4, Track 37

Listen. What holiday are they talking about? Write the number of the conversation.

___ a.

___ b.

_1_ c.

___ d.

___ e.

___ f.

A Birthday Party pages 240 and 241, CD 4, Track 38

Listen. Circle the words to complete the sentences.

1. The woman is <u>making a wish</u> / <u>wrapping a present</u>.

2. Chen <u>brought / hid</u> the cake.

3. Tito is almost finished with the <u>presents / decorations</u>.

4. The people are <u>hiding / videotaping</u>.

5. Tito is <u>on the deck / in the kitchen</u>.

6. Chen is <u>blowing out candles / videotaping the party</u>.